# DECIPHERING RACE

# DECIPHERING RACE

*White Anxiety, Racial Conflict,*
*and the Turn to Fiction in Mid-Victorian*
*English Prose*

## LAURA CALLANAN

THE OHIO STATE UNIVERSITY PRESS
*Columbus*

Library of Congress Cataloging-in-Publication Data
Callanan, Laura
Deciphering race : white anxiety, racial conflict, and the turn to fiction in mid-Victorian English prose / Laura Callanan.
    p. cm.
Includes bibliographical references (p.  ) and index.
ISBN 0–8142–1011–2 (alk. paper)—ISBN 0–8142–9089–2 (CD-ROM) 1. English fiction—19th century—History and criticism. 2. Race in literature. 3. Literature and society—Great Britain—History—19th century. 4. Race relations in literature. 5. Imperialism in literature. 6. Racism in literature. I. Title.
PR878.R34C35 2005
823.'8093552—dc22
                    2005018917

Paper (ISBN: 978-0-8142-5146-1)
Cover design by Janna Thompson-Chordas.
Text design and typesetting by Jennifer Shoffey Forsythe.
Type set in Adobe Minion.

# CONTENTS

~

# ACKNOWLEDGMENTS

~

C ompleting this project would have been impossible without the help and support of many individuals and institutions. An Emory University Graduate Arts and Sciences Fellowship and a Dean's Teaching Fellowship provided me the time and support to get the project off the ground. A Mount Holyoke College Faculty Grant allowed me to complete my research. A Philip H. and Betty L. Wimmer Family Foundation grant and a National Endowment for the Humanities summer fellowship at Duquesne University allowed me to complete final revisions. The excellent staff of the Emory University Woodruff Library Interlibrary Loan Office, the Mount Holyoke College Library, and the Duquesne University Gumberg Library helped me find and obtain numerous documents and materials. The wonderful staff at The Ohio State University Press made the entire publication process from initial submission to final printing efficient and enlightening. In particular I want to thank Heather Lee Miller, Maggie Diehl, and Sandy Crooms, who each walked me through a stage in the process with grace and professionalism. I am very grateful to my research assistant, Ms. Heather Shippen, who worked tirelessly on the project during the final stages of manuscript preparation.

I have been the grateful recipient of support and advice from many fine scholars. Martine Brownley, John Sitter, and Michael Elliot all encouraged me during the project's initial gestation. Kate Nickerson's enthusiasm about the topic in its planning stages helped me to see the larger ramifications. Linda Dittmar helped shape my future research interests and continues to be a mentor and friend. Jerome Beaty guided the project through its early stages and provided valuable advice on its development. Margot Finn provided crucial feedback and suggestions, as well as a model for responsible and ethical mentoring. My debt to Walter Reed is incalculable.

He provided pedagogical, intellectual, and professional guidance. I am particularly indebted to Christopher Lane, who generously shared with me his insights, vast knowledge, and intellectual discipline. The feedback provided by my colleagues in the British Studies Workshop at Emory University helped clarify my argument. My colleagues at Duquesne University—in particular, Linda Kinnahan, Daniel Watkins, and Magali Michael—have welcomed me into a dynamic intellectual community that has inspired and supported me over the past two years. The extraordinary graduate students in my seminar on Victorian racial representation at Duquesne University helped clarify my perspective on the materials discussed here.

I owe personal as well as professional debts of gratitude to Karen Poremski, Gale Elizabeth Pearce, Peter Logan, and Anne Brannen. Jennifer Nesbitt tirelessly read drafts, engaged with my conceptual and rhetorical struggles, and provided key insights throughout the revision process. Karen Cardozo-Kane's intellectual fearlessness continually pushes me to look deeper and more complexly. Danielle Mitchell supports and inspires me with her critical acuity and personal strength each day.

Finally, I am grateful to my parents, Harold Callanan and Isabella Callanan, for introducing me at an early age to the joys and rewards of intellectual exploration.

༒

# Aestheticizing Mid-Victorian
# Racial Tropism

*I*n the final pages of Frances Anne Kemble's *Journal of a Residence on a Georgian Plantation in 1838–1839*, in a chapter entitled "The Wreck of the *Pulaski*," the author recounts the story of a shipwreck told to her by her neighbor, Mr. Couper. The steamship *Pulaski* sank June 14, 1838, about 150 miles off the coast of South Carolina. Very briefly, Kemble writes that at the first sound of the boiler exploding, Couper moved the two women and small boy for whom he was responsible into one of the lifeboats and then took charge of the boat, encouraging the men to continue rowing even when they were exhausted. As they began the difficult task of turning the lifeboat toward the coast and making their way to shore, Couper assigned each of the women, including a black woman, to an individual man who would be responsible for her safety. The boat then capsized as it made its way through the rough waters near shore, and everyone was thrown into the water. Kemble narrates that the man responsible for the safety of the black woman made it to shore having left her in the water. Couper, Kemble admiringly notes, even with the burden of saving Mrs. Nightingale, "had power of command enough left to drive the fellow back to seek her, which he did, and brought her safe to land" (Kemble, 340).

In John A. Scott's edition of the *Journal*, Scott notes that Kemble's account in general agrees with Couper's, as documented in a letter Couper wrote to his father immediately after the incident, in all but a few minor details.[1] However, it is in the most significant of the minor changes, I would argue, that we see evidence of Kemble's frustration and sense of futility with her ability to effect any change in the slave system: the events leading to the rescue of the unnamed black woman. In a footnote, we learn not only that the incident had not occurred as rendered in Kemble's *Journal*, but also that in fact the slave woman had not even been in that particular lifeboat. Scott writes, "There is no mention, in Couper's original version, of this interesting detail about the Negro woman; as a matter of fact she had been transferred to the other lifeboat earlier in the day" (340, fn 5). There are two possible explanations for this change: either Couper told Kemble a different version of the events, or Kemble rewrote the incident to create a narrative in which a brave white man pressures another to honor his responsibility to a black woman.

Thus, Kemble either latched onto the story because of its reflection of a state of benevolent masculine paternalism she hoped to, but ultimately did not, find in Georgia, or she herself revised the tale to reflect that vision. In either case, the version of the shipwreck found in the *Journal* brings into reality a social dynamic she saw infrequently at best in her daily experience and that she hoped, as she expressed early in the *Journal*, to find more prevalent: "Nevertheless, I go prepared to find many mitigations in the practice to the general injustice and cruelty of the system" (11). These "mitigations" she never found. Instead, she creates or recreates a scene in which a brave white man turns a cowardly white man back into the water to save a black woman from death. This narrative adjustment allows Kemble to render the kinds of relationships between races and individuals that she is unable to achieve or discern in her daily confrontation with the slave system. Kemble uses the tale to compensate for her frustration and horror with the slave system and, increasingly over the narrative, with her husband's role in propagating that system, to create the racial dynamic that she hoped to be able to bring into being.

Kemble's rendering of this rescue occurs at the end of a narrative in which she is increasingly aware of the suffering of the slaves on the Butler properties, her husband's complicity with this exploitative system, and her own powerlessness to effect any real change for these people. At the beginning of the journal, in anticipation of her trip south, she famously declares her abhorrence for the system of slavery: "[a]ssuredly I *am* going prejudiced against slavery, for I am an Englishwoman, in whom the absence of such a prejudice would be disgraceful" (11, original italics). By the end of the text, after endless entreaties by slaves for food, clothing, relief from work, and extended rest after childbirth, to name just a few of the issues she hears about on a regular basis, Kemble finds herself angry, frustrated, and powerless. She is critically aware enough to be able to connect her own powerless position as a married woman in a situation of moral chaos with the slaves' inability to effect their own emancipation. And throughout the journal, she repeatedly attempts to effect change in the material conditions of the slaves on the property. By the end of her visit, however, Kemble appears to become overwhelmed with the vast amount of suffering with which she is confronted on an hourly basis and with her inability to alleviate any of it.

As her sense of hopelessness grows, the narrative takes on an increasingly dreamlike quality. She takes more trips away from the grounds with her slave companion, Jack, and increasingly describes the environment as a blend of fictional and nonfictional elements:

> I stopped for some time before a thicket of glittering evergreens, over which hung, in every direction, streaming garlands of these fragrant golden cups, fit for Oberon's banqueting service. These beautiful shrubberies were resounding with the songs of mocking-birds. I sat there on my horse in a sort of dream of enchantment, looking, listening, and inhaling the delicious atmosphere of those flowers; and suddenly my eyes opened, as if I had been asleep, on some bright red bunches of spring leaves on one of the winter-stripped trees, and I as suddenly thought of the cold Northern skies and earth, where the winter was still inflexibly tyrannizing over you all, and, in spite of the loveliness of all that was present, and the harshness of all that I seemed to see at that moment, no first tokens of the spring's return were ever more welcome to me than those bright leaves that reminded me how soon I should leave this scene of material beauty and moral degradation, where the beauty itself is of an appropriate character to the human existence it surrounds: above all, loveliness, brightness, and fragrance; but below! it gives one a sort of Melusina feeling of horror—all swamp and poisonous stagnation, which the heat will presently make alive with venomous reptiles. (226)

This fascinating passage vividly displays the ways in which Kemble's confrontation with the realities of slavery, and with her failure to carry out the changes she planned on the trip down to Georgia, precipitate a turn to fiction. Kemble, one of the foremost actresses of her time, blends Shakespearian allusions, with which she was so intimately familiar, with descriptions of the lush natural environment of Georgia and thoughts of the harsher Northeastern countryside in which resides Elizabeth Dwight Sedgewick, the addressee of the letters that constitute the journal. The performative rhetoric, evident throughout Kemble's writings, begins to break down as she yokes together a range of images to try to describe her state of mind. Kemble finds herself in a sentimentalized moment of "enchantment," reminiscent of her famous description of her first ride on the new railway so frequently anthologized. However, here the momentary static state of "enchantment" leads to Kemble's expression of being caught between conflicting experiences of horror and beauty, even as she lives in a moment in which different geographies of north and south, representative of her horror and repulsion at the slave system, blend in her mind. Her thoughts drift to a time when she will leave the plantation and the moral, familial, and emotional chaos it has produced.

In other words, as Kemble becomes increasingly aware of the complexity of slave psychology, and of her position within the hierarchy as the mistress of the plantation and thus the target of incessant pleading, she begins to aestheticize her reality, both as an escape from the horrors of the plantation and as a palette with which to express her ideals. As Kemble's faith in her ability to effect change on the plantation falters, she turns to the aesthetic in order to assuage a sense of anxiety produced by a confrontation with racial otherness and systemic oppression. This narrative method reveals a state of white bourgeois anxiety—where Kemble confronts her inability to bring into reality her goals for social transformation and, at the same time, becomes aware of and overwhelmed by the interlacing of gender, class, sexual, and racial oppressions. Her naïve belief that she would be able to use her position as benevolent slave mistress to dismantle the structures of oppression erodes even as she becomes the target of pleadings and requests throughout each day. Thus she finds herself slowly extricating herself from the realities of oppression and suffering on the plantation as she more frequently rambles about the estate with Jack.

This book explores five texts in which a white English author or character turns to the aesthetic in order to assuage a sense of anxiety produced by a confrontation with racial otherness. These moments reveal an anxiety of indeterminacy—where white characters or narrators confront the limitations of preconceived ideologies or the interlacing of oppressions, and subsequently falter. This is not a psychoanalytic study, but instead a narrative exploration—looking at the ways white anxiety, when confronted with racial otherness, manifests itself in narrative. Although I do refer to psychoanalytic concepts, especially in my discussion of fetishism, in general I agree with Judith Halberstam that "[w]ithin modern Western culture, we are disciplined through a variety of social and political mechanisms into psychoanalytic relations and then psychoanalytic explanations are deployed to totalize our submission" (Halberstam, 9). Rather than follow this route, I am more interested in unpacking the ways in which the narrative turn to the aesthetic in writings by white English individuals reveals instability in the cultural understanding of race at mid-century. I am interested in continuing the project pointed to by Toni Morrison in *Playing in the Dark:* "But equally valuable is a serious intellectual effort to see what racial ideology does to the mind, imagination, and behavior of masters" (Morrison, 12). In the texts I discuss, white writers confront the complexity, indeterminacy, and irrationality of both racial difference and the systems put in place to understand that difference.

When I say that white authors and characters turn to the aesthetic, I use that term in a broader sense than is perhaps common. The term, in my study, refers to standards of form and genre, systems of social evaluation that contribute to producing the beautiful, and issues of desire and compatibility. The interrelationship between aesthetic ideologies and racial categories runs deep in the Enlightenment philosophies that underpin the Victorian social plan. Emmanual Chukwudi Eze argues, in the introduction to *Race and the Enlightenment: A Reader,* that the concept of aesthetics was central to the creation of a racial hierarchy in Enlightenment thought (Eze, 98). There is a sense of prescriptiveness as well as judgment implied in the aesthetic that speaks to the relationship between aesthetic issues and structures of social stratification. So, for example, when Matthew Lewis describes the slave woman Mary Wiggins in *Journal of a West India Proprietor* (1834), he creates an explicit connection between race, objectification, and the realm of art: "I really think that her form and features were the most *statue-like* that I ever met with [. . .] Mary Wiggins and an old Cotton-tree are the most picturesque objects that I have seen for these twenty years" (Lewis, 46–47). Later, we will see Robert Knox, the notorious racial scientist, make the same connections while sitting in the British Museum gazing upon the Elgin marbles and musing upon his recollections of the *Venus Génitrix* viewed in the Jardin des Plantes.

In *The Ideology of the Aesthetic,* Terry Eagleton argues that the sense of flexibility in aesthetic criteria enhances its ability to function in relationship with social conflicts and structures of power:

> But if the aesthetic returns with such persistence, it is partly because of a certain indeterminacy of definition which allows it to figure in a varied span of preoccupations: freedom and legality, spontaneity and necessity, self-determination, autonomy, particularity and universality, along with several others. My argument, broadly speaking, is that the category of the aesthetic assumes the importance it does in modern Europe because in speaking of art it speaks of these other matters too, which are at the heart of the middle class's struggle for political hegemony. The construction of

the modern notion of the aesthetic artifact is thus inseparable from the construction of the dominant ideological forms of modern class-society, and indeed from a whole new form of human subjectivity appropriate to that social order. (Eagleton, 3)

Looking more specifically at the issue of race, Nancy Stepan argues that the evaluative criteria for beauty changed in relation to blackness as English culture became more invested in exploiting Africans for material gain: "Slowly blackness itself, which in the ancient world had often been associated with positive qualities such as physical or moral beauty, came to be associated negatively with the degraded condition of slavery. Eventually, a black skin was taken as a 'natural', outward sign of inward mental and moral inferiority. The association between blackness and inferiority produced by racial slavery was grafted onto an earlier, primarily literary tradition, in which blackness and whiteness comprised the terms of a binary opposition" (Stepan, xii).

Stepan outlines the ways in which the evaluative criteria contributing to a definition of the beautiful changed in order to suggest an inferiority that justified exploitation. *Deciphering Race* is concerned with the structural, political, and thematic dynamics evident in moments in which racial discourse comes into direct confrontation with aesthetic issues. Connections between the body, the beautiful, the political, and racial categorization are central to my analysis.

My study works from the premise that mid-Victorian racial discourse was often tropological. By this statement, I mean that a series of rhetorical figures developed, with which writers conveyed shorthand allusions to complex social negotiations taking place within the culture. These figures took a variety of forms, including symbols, narrative patterns, historical events, and geographical locations. In *Rule of Darkness* (1988), Patrick Brantlinger notes how the figure of Nana Sahib became synecdochical for the 1857 Indian Rebellion (202–3). I argue that this linguistic phenomenon was more widespread, and that its prevalence reveals how the term "race" became imbued with a constellation of meanings and controversies during the period. These tropes themselves became what Mary Louise Pratt terms "'contact zones,' social spaces where disparate cultures meet, clash, and grapple with each other, often in highly asymmetrical relations of domination and subordination" (4). Informing my argument is Hayden White's work on the tropological nature of historical narratives, especially in *Metahistory: The Historical Imagination in Nineteenth-Century Europe* (1975) and *Tropics of Discourse: Essays in Cultural Criticism* (1978).

I contend that it is from within these structures that we can begin to understand the social transformation of racial attitudes that took place in Victorian culture. And it is anxieties about these changes that reveal themselves in the broader turn to the aesthetic that brings these tropes into relief. For, as Paul Gilroy argues, "[r]acism does not, of course, move tidily and unchanged through time and history. It assumes new forms and articulates new antagonisms in different situations" (11). Many scholars argue that English attitudes about race underwent a radical transformation during this period. Eric Hobsbawm observes that "racism pervades the thought" of this time "to an extent hard to appreciate today, and not always easy to understand" (267). Catherine Hall asserts that "[b]y the 1850s [. . .] thinking about race was shifting away from ideas of black men and women as brothers and sisters, to a racial vocabulary of biological difference" (Hall, *Civilising Subjects*, 21). Late eighteenth- and early nineteenth-century humanitarian arguments, which led to the abolition of the slave trade and, later, of slavery itself, lost influence in midcentury England, only to be replaced by violently derogatory racial representations fueling an increasingly zealous imperial project.

Early in Book IV of George Eliot's *Daniel Deronda,* we find a particularly vivid example of the aestheticizing of this tropological structure. In this scene, dinner conversation takes an abrupt turn towards Governor Edward Eyre's recent actions to suppress the Morant Bay Rebellion in Jamaica. Participants in the discussion express a variety of opinions about the event, revealing a range of attitudes and stereotypes about Africans, Jamaica, colonialism, and racial representation circulating in mid-Victorian English culture:

> Grandcourt held that the Jamaican negro was a beastly sort of baptist Caliban; Deronda said he had always felt a little with Caliban, who naturally had his own point of view and could sing a good song; Mrs Davilow observed that her father had an estate in Barbadoes, but that she herself had never been in the West Indies; Mrs Torrington was sure she should never sleep in her bed if she lived among blacks; her husband corrected her by saying that the blacks would be manageable enough if it were not for the half-breeds; and Deronda remarked that the whites had to thank themselves for the half-breeds. (Eliot, 331)

This passage condenses into a brief moment a startlingly diverse set of perspectives on racial issues in one easily deployed conversational exchange.[2] Equally curious is its abrupt emergence and disappearance in the course of the novel's plot. Eliot uses the historical moment of cultural conflict spurred by the Governor Eyre controversy as a complex racial trope that provides a vehicle for communicating identifying information about characters. It also speaks to Eliot's understanding that her readers would be familiar with the context of events and would recognize the representative positions taken by each of the characters. The author is thus able to use the controversial event to suggest personality characteristics for each of the dinner guests. Grandcourt, the cold, brutal future husband of Gwendolen, has little sympathy for the blacks. Sensitive Deronda sympathizes with Caliban in his outcast status, and at the same time employs conventional stereotypes of the African as, for instance, musical. The superficial women express ties with the West Indian planter society and fears of black savagery, including reference to the geographical displacement between the economic benefits reaped in the imperial center and the exploitation upon which those benefits are predicated. The passage ends with a thinly veiled, yet nonetheless startling, reference to miscegenation and interracial rape. The movement between these positions is essentially metonymic, with one leading to the other in an unstable ricochet between positionalities. By unpacking the implied arguments embedded within tropes such as the Governor Eyre controversy, we can view the array of views and points of contention that fueled and transformed the ideological climate of English culture during the mid-Victorian period. Moments such as the one in Eliot's novel signal the power of representations of racial conflict to figuratively spark and contain a collection of ideas, positions, and attitudes about race in Victorian culture. It is the purpose of this study to model a reading strategy for explicating the complex systems of meanings evident in such moments.

Contemporary scholars have given significant attention to the question of race as a tropological phenomenon. Douglas Lorimer's study of the overlap of class and race in mid-Victorian England, *Colour, Class and the Victorians* (1978), points out the interconnectedness of these factors within the figure of the "Negro." In a discussion of the significance of the Governor Eyre controversy, for example, Lorimer argues that, by the 1860s, "disputes about the Negro became a jousting ground for rival social and political philosophies. The transformation in English racial attitudes was not simply a response to the demands of imperial rule, but an extension into the Empire of social and political attitudes moulded within the changing environment of mid-Victorian England" (200).

The figure of the "Negro" became a symbol for an array of social issues connected with race in Victorian culture, including labor relations, immigration, class definitions, and emancipation. In addition, public reaction to the Governor Eyre controversy precipitated a breakdown in the social and legal distinctions between the metropolis and the colony. Often during the first half of the nineteenth century, these social, legal, and geographical distinctions dynamically interacted within metaphors of racial and biological determinism.

Henry Louis Gates, Jr. suggests that race itself is a trope that brings together a virtually limitless collection of characteristics under its umbrella: "Race has become a trope of ultimate, irreducible difference between cultures, linguistic groups, or adherents of specific belief systems which—more often than not—also have fundamentally opposed economic interests. Race is the ultimate trope of difference because it is so very arbitrary in its application" (Gates, *"Race," Writing, and Difference,* 5). My study builds on Lorimer's and Gates's observations to suggest that a range of individual tropes emerged rooted in historical, cultural, and philosophical conflicts about race in Victorian England. To decipher these tropes is to gain a window into the complexity of Victorian racial attitudes, social ideologies, and strategies of representation.

I am not suggesting that writers simply reduced a limitless collection of factors to an all-encompassing ideology of race. Quite the opposite: social controversies exist in active dialogue within a range of tropes with which authors engaged on these issues. The aestheticizing of these factors helped produce texts in which racial themes intersect within fractured and disjointed narratives, thus illustrating Christopher Lane's point that racial representations are not limited by a need for logic (2). Racial texts are often conflicted and irrational, and those very conflicts give us the opportunity to examine the complex array of elements within each figure. I do not argue that by providing a careful, formal analysis of texts engaged with race, we can find the inconsistencies and therefore undermine their ability to hold social and discursive power. I am suggesting, instead, that the irrational, conflicted nature of these texts was part of their representation, that the power of racial rhetoric lies in its ability to outlast the formal exigencies of reason. Race is an irrational, yet powerful, ubiquitous, and persistent concept.

This study adds to current scholarship on nineteenth-century racial tropes by identifying and further explicating a range of tropes that have received varying degrees of critical attention, within the context of uses of and references to issues of the aesthetic. It is this combination of factors that this study seeks to explore as a way into the ideological complex in which race was produced. Chapter 1 examines how Haiti and Toussaint

L'Ouverture became complicated and multivalent signifiers in early nineteenth-century writing. This analysis then fuels a close explication of the way both tropes function in Harriet Martineau's abolitionist novel *The Hour and the Man* (1841), and, more particularly, in her overt dramatic staging of the various issues at work in the St. Domingo Revolution. Martineau's novel is a fictional biography of Toussaint, leader of the slave rebellion that resulted in Haiti's independence. Two issues become centrally important in my examination of this little-discussed work: Martineau's paradoxical emphasis on historical accuracy, despite her decision to eradicate the British presence in the fight to quell the rebellion; and an intriguing scene near the end of the novel, in which interpretation itself is represented as a metafictional key to understanding her text. In my discussion of both issues, I argue that Martineau's abolitionist political stance fuels her desire to turn Toussaint into a symbol of African potential, to make him as European as possible, and to delete any information that could possibly alienate readers. Martineau uses Haiti as a standard for black self-determinacy and potential. Additionally, my discussion of Martineau's use of interpretive indeterminacy suggests that this abolitionist text ironically relies on the very irrationality that often glues together racist texts. This binding force is often more comfortably attributed to texts with radically racist agendas, because it indicates their unreasonableness. However, no such easy distinction exists in mid-Victorian representations of race.

*Deciphering Race* then elaborates on Gates's observation that race itself functions as the ultimate trope of difference by looking at the term in the most notorious of anthropological and scientific studies, Robert Knox's *The Races of Men* (1850). Often considered to be one of the most extreme of the "scientific" racists, Knox declares that race should be understood as the determining factor of all human history. In this way, "race" became a term containing virtually unlimited explanatory power. Knox's text ends with a consideration of the importance of art in understanding race. "Race" functions throughout the text as both an empty and an overloaded signifier. The paradox of Knox's text is that it insists on the biological inability of particular races to coexist within the same political system, thus offering, through its segregationist rhetoric, a compelling critique of the imperialist project. This paradox explains why Knox views the St. Domingo Revolution as a failure; Africans, he suggests, are not able to live within European social systems, and so should be left alone. Contradictions in his presentation, however, become resolved and obfuscated by the concluding recourse to issues of aesthetics and beauty.

Chapter 3 examines the fetish as a particular type of racial trope in Charles Dickens and Wilkie Collins's 1857 Christmas story, "The Perils of Certain English Prisoners." Dickens consciously allegorized the events of the 1857 Indian Rebellion in this pirate tale set in South America. Within the fetish, the figures of metaphor and metonymy work together to produce a dialectic of identification and disavowal that speaks to the issues at work in discourses about events in India. Homi K. Bhabha argues that "the fetish represents the simultaneous play between metaphor as substitution (marking absence and difference) and metonymy (which contiguously registers the perceived lack)" (98). Race, at this time, was often seen as an ever-increasing collection of boundary crises about social, structural, and generic criteria. Dickens and Collins depict colonials transgressing traditional expectations of behavior in order to maintain the alleged integrity of their national identity. The conflict in a colonial outpost gives both authors' characters the opportunity to move beyond social norms, but only in the service of eradicating or outwitting the pirate demon bent on destroying both the colonials and the British way of life. "Perils" concludes with a catharsis that attempts to resolve the cultural rage triggered by the Indian Rebellion. The colonials humiliate a treacherous pirate demon, and a heroic British officer kills a traitorous black servant. I argue that these two figures function in the story as racialized fetishes, the eradication of which suggests an attempt at narrative closure. Ultimately, however, the two scenes fail to provide a sense of fictional resolution.

Turning then to governmental discourse, chapter 4 addresses the way the term "truth" functions as an implicit trope in the transcript of the Royal Commission's inquiry into the events of the Morant Bay Rebellion in Jamaica. Perhaps more than any other event over the course of the century, the Governor Eyre controversy polarized the British public, thus explaining the lack of contextual grounding needed by Eliot when she deploys the event in her novel. The transcript of the British government's inquiry into Eyre's actions is an exceedingly detailed set of documents, including hundreds of pages of interview sessions conducted with innumerable persons from the island's different communities. In my discussion of this text, I use the term aesthetic to speak to the rigid generic parameters governing the structure of the inquiry and its resulting text. Owing to a particularly acute Victorian belief in the ability to obtain the truth, the Royal Commission's transcript superimposes the hyperrational format of governmental inquiry with testimonies from a wide range of witnesses. The various social and economic positions of the witnesses partly determined individual testimony and the ability of the Royal Commission to establish what they considered the real facts of the situation. An examination of this text, therefore, gives us an opportunity to address the figurative construction of "truth" and its place in the development of racial and social ideologies. When the British government tried to be most rational, the entire enterprise paradoxically collapsed into virtual meaninglessness.

My final chapter examines the trope of the ruin site in James Grant's *First Love and Last Love* (1868). Written in the midst of the Governor Eyre controversy, Grant's novel is a fiercely jingoist portrayal of the 1857 Indian Rebellion. Like Martineau's novel, this text conveys the violent repercussions of racial rebellion from the perspective of its fighting participants. Both texts also engage more broadly with violence, as well as with nationalism and the centrality of women in colonial conflict. The main protagonist, Jack Harrower, carries with him a drawing of his home in England, and he turns to it for comfort in the midst of the chaos, as represented by the ruin sites in which he and the heroine of the novel take shelter. Grant's use of the ruin scene—an image common to racial narratives during the period, and one I trace throughout this project—suggests a conflation of the domestic and colonial environments and functions as the spatialized racial other to Harrower's drawing of home. Central to this dynamic is the figure of the Englishwoman and the trope of rape as articulated by Sara Suleri, Jenny Sharpe, and Nancy Paxton. Through his use of the raped and terrorized white female, Grant exploits exaggerated reports of widespread rape of white women by Indian men as a way to trigger rage against the Indian population. The conflation in his novel of violence, female exploitation, foreign danger, the domestic, and ruin structures creates a mood similar to one recurring in Gothic novels of the late-eighteenth and early-nineteenth century, suggesting an earlier manifestation of what Brantlinger has called the "imperial Gothic."

In the conclusion, I look at the recent return of the remains of Sara(h) Ba(a)rtman(n) and explore this event as a possible way in which we can begin to remove the image of the racial other from the realm of the aesthetic and return to it the dignity and respect accorded to all human beings. Throughout this study, I have chosen to illustrate the fractured identities of this woman by rendering her name Sara(h) Ba(a)rtman(n). This strategy keeps before me the multiple identities and constructions of this woman's life as well as the anatomized and divided way her body was treated, both as a public spectacle and as an object for scientific dissection. Elements of her name are separated off in much the same way that parts of her body were isolated to prove her inferiority, aberrant nature, and radical difference from those who examined her. Ultimately, I argue that

Ba(a)rtman(n)'s life stands as a powerful example of the failure of Enlightenment scientific rationalism's aestheticizing and anatomizing project to produce any real, ethical, or useful knowledge about racial difference.

My interest in the aesthetics of Victorian racial tropism stems from a fascination with both the content and the underlying structure and dynamics of these resilient figures. We can understand a trope as a particularly complex sign, in which the space between the signifier and the signified works within the logic of a range of relationships, depending on the trope employed. In a simple metaphor, for example, a relationship of equivalence is set up between a sign and a signifier, based on an uncommon similarity embedded in their respective meanings. The space where the transaction occurs, and the bodies of information that intersect to create the equivalence, is of particular interest to me. Critics describe this tropic transaction between signifier and signified in a variety of ways. In Hayden White's analysis, tropes are "linguistic containers" holding a collection of complex, contested, and often irrational ideas about social distinction. Thus, for White, the space of tropic transaction is demarcated as a closed and finite one that contains a variety of linguistic negotiations. In his discussion of poetic figures, Gérard Genette suggests that what is important is not so much the container, to use White's term, but the gap, or space, implied by the boundaries of that container: "We see that here, between the letter and the meaning, between what the poet has *written* and what he *thought,* there is a gap, a space, and like all space, it possesses a form" (47).

What is intriguing about the example from Eliot's *Daniel Deronda* is that the moment, in essence, is a rendering of the world of the gap or the container. The figure, the Eyre crisis, is aestheticized in order to create firmer characterizations of the primary personages in the novel. Within the text, the trope is used as a way to delineate the ethical and moral differences between characters. But the event is not named specifically, and the resulting conclusions are not stated baldly. What we get is the dynamics of the gap—the various conflicting ideas, attitudes, and beliefs brought into interaction in cultural understandings of Eyre's decisions in Jamaica. The complex linguistic negotiations contained in the gap between signifier and signified, evident in tropic structure, parallels the service racial tropes provide to the cultures in question. Central to each of the texts I examine is the problem of racial conflict or unrest. The appearance of tropes speaks to the attempt to bridge the gap between the two cultures. As White argues, "Metaphors are crucially necessary when a culture or social group encounters phenomena that either elude or run afoul of normal expectations or quotidian experiences" (*Tropics,* 184). Metaphors, in other words, provide a space where the characteristics of the two conflicting systems are brought together in the service of finding commonality or producing momentary dialogue. The contained nature of the moment in Eliot's novel also harkens back to Edward Said's famous reading of *Mansfield Park* in *Culture and Imperialism.* Said powerfully illustrates the importance of these moments for understanding the crucial ways the colonial environment underpins the cultural representations put forth in the nineteenth-century realist novel. I suggest that these moments, these discrete references to racial unrest and colonial economic structures, function tropically in Victorian writing. They provide a bridge between cultures in conflict. All of the texts I examine have at their root the problem of racial conflict in places such as Haiti, India, and Jamaica. The appearance of tropic structures as a way to represent conflicting cultural and value systems is to be expected.

I argue that the dramatic enactment of racial tropes also implies a simultaneous call to interpretation. Eliot's reference to competing perspectives on the Governor Eyre crisis provides a trope that allows Eliot to bridge the differences between her characters, to bring together a wide variety of viewpoints on the crisis itself, and to create a momentary link between England and Jamaica. The moment also has built within itself the process of interpretive reflection. By having this moment abruptly appear and disappear, the text draws attention to the contructedness of the trope as a vehicle in itself; the trope encourages the reader both to understand the discussion as representative of the cultural crisis and to see the discussion itself as, in a sense, modeling the type of reflection that such events should precipitate. Certainly, the discussion of the event is not complex— positions would appear to align with the social and economic positions of the particular characters in question. But the encapsulation of these diverse viewpoints into this moment suggests the nature of social conflict and the ways in which rather simplistically formed attitudes have global ramifications. This reality in itself suggests, in chilling starkness, the connection between dinner table and colonial outpost.

In Victorian racial tropism, a complex array of controversies about categories of social stratification became reduced to one succinct reference. Race was a flash point for many social questions in mid-Victorian England: the rise of scientific racism; the expansion of the colonial project; the increasing instability of the conventional social hierarchy; anxieties about miscegenation; changing ideas about what constitutes "Englishness"; and increasing colonial unrest. As the public became impatient with repeated outbreaks of violence in the colonies, domestic controversies dovetailed with accounts of these rebellions, greatly increasing racial animosity in the 1850s and 1860s. Abolitionist rhetoric, which held so much moral authority and popular support during the early part of the century, came under harsh attack as the economic problems of the newly emancipated West Indies and the conflict over slavery in the American context reached critical levels. The movement toward more democratic social relations weakened traditional social boundaries. Agitation by working-class populations, especially in the late 1840s and early 1850s, widening opportunities for women, and deteriorating distinctions among social classes—all these factors contributed to a growing concern about the security of social position, a concern that revealed itself in the tropes Victorian writers used to represent these issues.

The types of information boiled down within these tropes can be divided into three general categories: reports of the events of particular uprisings in the colonial context, such as the St. Domingo Revolution of the 1790s and the Indian Rebellion of 1857; accounts of the erosion of traditional boundaries, such as class and gender, in the metropolitan context; and studies of race and colonialism in historical, scientific, and travel writing. Often, especially in overtly political discourse, we find the same tropes used by speakers from different ideological positions. However, the complexity of ideological dynamics at work in the trope's structure allows for the manipulation of positions, so that the images or signs can take on very different valences. For example, during Parliamentary debates about the abolition of slavery, a Member of Parliament invoking Haiti could suggest one of two very different responses: Britons' fear of native attack in the colonial territories, or humanistic belief in the ability of the African people to rise to a level of self-determination equivalent to that of the Britons. Either belief, depending on context, could be suggested simply by mentioning the event. This procedure—transforming historical events into tropes condensing a wide array of cultural fears and concerns—occurred not only with the establishment of Haiti, but also with Emancipation, the 1857 Indian Rebellion, and, to a lesser extent, the 1865 Governor Eyre Controversy.

The significance of racial tropism extends beyond formal issues of representation to the ethical dynamics involved in critical examinations of these structures. In other words, the structure of the trope presents us with an ethical quandary: on the one hand, it allows for the communication of a range of viewpoints in one terse reference. When Lorimer refers to the figure of the "Negro," or Brantlinger to "Nana Sahib," they allude to a con-stellation of issues, drives, and complexities surrounding these figures vividly illustrated in the passage from Eliot's novel. On the other hand, alluding to a trope also allows for a certain critical distance, permitting both critic and reader to remain outside the ethically fraught situation of confronting the complexity of racist rhetoric. It is easy, in other words, to remain outside the complex convergences illustrated in the range of per-spectives embedded in these structures. To engage with a racial text, such as Robert Knox's *The Races of Men,* can produce anxiety in critics whose main ideological agenda is to dismantle the structures of racial oppression that still exist in Western society today. Fueled by the need to maintain a posture of judgment against the text's offensive racial typology, critics gen-erally veer away from such issues as Knox's critique of imperialism because of the bizarre and faulty logic at the heart of the argument. However, I argue that conflicting ideological and ethical positions are part and parcel of racial tropism, whether in a liberal, abolitionist novel, or in an offen-sively racist, anthropological treatise. This interpretive crisis ties more gen-erally into the process of formalist analysis. British Cultural Studies critics such as Stuart Hall often criticize American cultural critics for their emphasis on deconstruction, arguing that structural analyses do not take into consideration questions of ethics, given their ahistoricist focus on lin-guistic play. By adding to this opinion the problem of racist rhetoric, which seems to require an emphatic declaration of abhorrence, the process of structurally analyzing racist rhetoric quickly becomes suspect. This study suggests the overlap of the two—the marriage of close textual analysis and an overtly ethically focused project requires the articulation of an ideal of community toward which the work moves. Progressive methodologies have often given up the question of ethics to more conservative and tradi-tional critics—this concept needs to be reclaimed.

Ethical positioning results from the speaker's, narrator's, or author's control over a particular instance of deployment. Daniel R. Schwarz argues that "[r]epresentation of the relationship between author and reader is rep-resentation of an ethical relationship" (188). He continues: "If selfawareness of oneself and one's relationship to family and community—including one's responsibilities, commitments, and values—is part of the ethical life, then reading contributes to greater self-understanding. Reading comple-ments one's experience by enabling us to live lives beyond those we live and experience emotions that are not ours; it heightens one's perspicacity by enabling us to watch *figures*—tropes, that is, personifications of our fellow humans—who are not ourselves, but like ourselves" (Schwarz, 195).

Eliot, for example, activates and stages a representative set of argu-ments about the Morant Bay Rebellion and presents them to the reader. It is, therefore, in the interaction among the author, narrator, trope, text, reader, and cultural context that we can discern a particular interpretation of a trope. It was when examining this transaction that I began to think about the ethical problems posed by the use of this structure to convey social controversies. Influenced by the critique of leftist liberalism carried out by many in the Critical Race Theory movement, my study looks at the ways in which the seeds of overtly racist ideas are to be found in liberal abolitionist rhetoric. I focus on white writers in order to understand bet-ter the dynamics of imperial discourse on race and, more specifically, to understand what led an overwhelmingly white culture, fueled by liberal ideologies and abolitionist rhetoric, to move in the direction of vehement scientific racism. I set out to understand the essential irrationality at the heart of white racial discourse. What I found was that when these writers employ a tropic structure to convey ideas about race, they implicitly con-vey a wide range of ideologies, as illustrated in the passage from Eliot's novel. The ultimate meaning to be derived from a particular usage relies on narrative emphasis to bring out one or another of the viewpoints implied in the trope. What is fascinating about Eliot's passage is that she uses the range in the service of character elucidation, and she implies her own ethical position regarding the events by means of the varying levels of ethical validity implied in her characters. Although Deronda, the character with the most ethical legitimacy, feels sympathy for the African residents, his sympathy is filtered through one of the most fraught racial touchstones in literature—Caliban. Thus there are no clear supporters for the rebellion, and the text's concern without clear support is balanced by the novel's treatment of Jewish identity. Although individuals (Mirah, the Jamaican Rebel, and Caliban) may have admirable qualities, the groups (Jewish and African) as a whole gain little support in the presentation. In fact, Eliot's revisionist understanding of Jewish identity in the metropolis points more clearly to an argument about class and cultural assimilation than about ethnicity and religion. The "good" Jewish characters, in other words, have identities and manners in keeping with conventional, middle-class cultur-al values.

This study is not intended to be an exhaustive examination of racial representation in the period. Rather, each chapter presents a detailed analysis of one work in which authors attend to issues of form in such a way as to stage the deployment of racial tropes. I then place this discursive moment within its cultural context. This contextual work provides an understanding of the central debates about race at the time of the text's production and circulation; it also provides a broader model for reading representations of difference in Victorian writing. These central debates are often revealed in moments when the issue of the aesthetic becomes explicit, thus revealing the system of tropes at work, tropes which reduced to linguistic shorthand different and conflicting elements of the development of cultural attitudes and beliefs about race. Thomas McLaughlin argues that our basic cognitive procedures are interwoven with these tropes, which become so prevalent as to seem critically undetectable: "We come to think by means of figures worn smooth, made invisible" (86). McLaughlin suggests that "[f]igures convince . . . not by a strictly logical presentation but by an appeal to the irrational, the part of the mind that delights in their multiple meanings and deep reassurances" (88). In textual analyses, we study these tropes in order to unravel how cultural issues are reduced to succinct references, signifying such complex and conflicted categories as racial difference. This contextual work helps illuminate the particular tropological structures underpinning much racial rhetoric in mid-Victorian England—structures that continue to haunt British and American racial discourse today.

My goal in conducting this type of analysis is threefold: to explore issues of race and aesthetics; to understand how they are built out of the structural complexity of racial tropism and the conditions and ramifications of figurative deployment; and to comprehend the ways in which these controversies have a stranglehold on our way of understanding cross-racial conflict and communication. Increasingly, postcolonial and nineteenth-century scholars are focusing on alternative paradigms of knowledge and consciousness at work in the colonial environment. A critical shift from understanding these alternative epistemologies as outside of the Western master narrative, to understanding them as part of the construction of the narrative, may perhaps produce tools to help dismantle Western discursive authority structures. Collections such as *After Colonialism* (1995), edited by Gyan Prakash, and *Colonialism and its Forms of Knowledge* (1996), by Bernard Cohn, engage with the epistemological paradigms and historical specificities of the colonial environment so as to disempower the discursive authority of conventional Western histories. *Deciphering Race* aims to contribute to this dialogue by unpacking the tropological structures in which English Victorians—and many contemporary critics—talk about race. The local analyses in my study model a reading strategy that encourages students and critics alike not simply to identify tropes of race, but also to look fearlessly at the ambiguous internal structures and arguments in the tropes' mechanisms. The methodology is in keeping with what Stuart Hall argues is the turn towards "'ethnicity'" which "acknowledges the place of history, language, and culture in the construction of subjectivity and identity, as well as the fact that all discourse is placed, positioned, situated, and all knowledge is contextual" (168). "Ethnicity" brings postmodern emphases on heterogeneity to bear on what is at times a monolithic concept of "race." Whereas Hall's work looks at contemporary British cultures and calls for the need "to *decouple* ethnicity, as it functions in the dominant discourse, from its equivalence with nationalism, imperialism, racism and the state" (169, original italics), my goal is to suggest one way that this coupling took place, and to show that the use of tropes to discuss race helped, in a sense, to solidify this link. This crucial textual work allows us to unmask the irrationality of these discursive structures, and to begin to understand how race functions as a battleground for a myriad of social issues at work in the culture in which it is deployed.

Anthony E. Cook, in his article on the development of Martin Luther King's vision of human community, argues that "I believe the postmodern preoccupation with deconstruction is but a precursor to serious reflection on how we should live in community" (101). The project is fueled by what I see as the ethical imperative to help dismantle structures of oppression, specifically in the languages we use to represent those different from ourselves. I use the term "deconstruction" not in any dogmatic way, but instead to suggest the process Gayatri Spivak articulates. She asserts that deconstruction "simply questions the privileging of identity so that someone is believed to have the truth. It is not the exposure of error. It is constantly and persistently looking into how truths are produced" (Spivak, 27). Tropes have the ability to reveal and obscure at the same time. A variety of ideas, perspectives, and ideologies become imbued within these "contact zones," and depending on the viewpoint of the one deploying the trope, and the aesthetic, historical, political, geographical, and discursive context in which it appears, different constellations of meanings become activated. As I stated earlier, unpacking these tropes will not immediately dismantle their power. The strategy of aesthetically rendering racial tropism, the phenomenon of reducing complexity into images and symbols that contain and maintain the controversies, is still at work in contemporary British and American culture. Our political and media machines thrive on the ability to create scapegoats and define geographical entities as Other in order to reduce difficult historical and cultural differences into easy binaries of good and evil. I argue, however, that the dynamics of the original controversies are not lost—rather, they exist to be unpacked within the obscured meanings embedded within the signs.

To recognize the signifier "race" as a "linguistic container" in which battles rage regarding a constellation of social crises is to begin to understand why productive cultural movement away from racial typologies still eludes us. *Deciphering Race* provides reading strategies for moving beyond the identification of the tropes and themes by which Victorian culture conducted discussions about race to examine both the structure and ramifications of the figurative strategy. In this way, my hope is that this series of readings will help us to see how figurative structures, while providing a bridge between different cultures and epistemologies, also reinforce a distance that keeps groups separate. Only by disentangling these structures, by addressing and unpacking our assumptions and narratives about those different from ourselves, and by understanding our deep cultural anxiety and investment in these ways of talking about one another, can we begin to create the conditions for productive, local understanding between different cultures, races, and communities.

# CHAPTER 1

↜

# Toussaint and the Staging of Political Aesthetics in Harriet Martineau's *The Hour and the Man* (1841)

*H*arriet Martineau's 1841 novel, *The Hour and the Man,* presents a fictional biography of Toussaint L'Ouverture, leader of the rebel slaves during the 1790s St. Domingo Revolution. Martineau uses the St. Domingo Revolution, a powerful signifier during the first half of the nineteenth century, as a vehicle to argue her abolitionist views and to rescue Toussaint from what she felt was an unfair damnation of him in most biographies of the man and accounts of the revolution. She attempts to romanticize the figure of Toussaint, echoing Rousseau's Noble Savage and Aphra Behn's Oronooko, transforming him into the harbinger of a new, egalitarian world. To accomplish this revision, Martineau emphasizes Toussaint's dedication to Western learning and superior critical and interpretive skills, traits problematically symbolized by his frequent allusions to classic Western texts. However, interpretation plays a more significant role in the novel than that of distinctive character traits of the African hero. The arrangement of many scenes aestheticizes the process of interpretation for the reader, turning the reader into both an interpreter and an observer of interpretation within an overt staging of critical reflection. This narrative strategy suggests the importance of critical discernment for an understanding of the dynamics of racial representation, because understanding racial categories is a loaded moment of interpretation. Characters in this novel "read" race as skin color, class, and abilities.

In a crucial scene midway through the novel, Martineau employs a variety of narrative strategies to facilitate the textual enactment of racial decipherment. Toussaint's son and his drawing teacher engage in an extended interpretation, parody, and disempowerment of the French colonial power structure through caricatures and performances of the primary colonial authorities on the island, a process reminiscent of the Signifyin(g) practices of the African American literary tradition. This spirited moment is the culmination of a series of discrete dialogues on love, race, politics, architecture, and class, all of which take place at the overtly aestheticized site of a ruined mansion, and all of which contribute to and enrich the parody. By first establishing the context in which the novel appeared, and then explicating the language of this crucial scene, this chapter will argue that the resolution of this scene serves to complicate issues of race, nation, and political allegiance by throwing into question the process of racial interpretation itself.

## Negotiating History

Martineau's decision to write the historical romance, *The Hour and the Man,* speaks as much to her dedication to a particular ethics of storytelling as it does to her commitment to abolitionism. She became interested in writing about Toussaint and the revolution while reading a *Quarterly Review* article on St. Domingo.[1] A friend encouraged her to drop the idea, however, so she put it aside for a time. When she revisited the project, she debated writing about Toussaint or about a crime story she read of in a police report. She decided not to write the criminal story, explaining, "The reason why I never did is that, as I have grown older, I have seen more and more the importance of dwelling on things honest, lovely, hopeful and bright, rather than on the dark and fouler passions and most mournful weaknesses of human nature. Therefore it was that I reverted to Toussaint [*sic*], rather than to the moral victim who was the hero of the police–court story" (*Autobiography,* 112). She chose Toussaint as a heroic figure that would enliven her readers through his admirable nature and actions. In a pointed reflection in her diary on the choice of Toussaint as a valuable topic, Martineau wrote, "it admits of romance, it furnishes me with a story, it will do a world of good to the slave question, it is heroic in its character" (quoted in Thomas, 93), thus tying together the formal, ethical, thematic, and political motivations for her project.

A commitment to historical accuracy underpins the author's determination to have her work contribute to individual and cultural betterment. In her *Autobiography,* she takes the time to note the need for integrity, "especially in historical writing,—in which I could have no comfort but by directing my readers to my authorities, in all matters of any importance"

(*Autobiography*, 414). To that end, Martineau, in the spirit of a generous researcher, presents in an Appendix to *The Hour and the Man* her sources of information on the topic, and her motivations for writing the novel:

> From the time when my attention was first fixed on this hero, I have been struck with the inconsistencies contained in all reports of his character which ascribe to him cruelty and hypocrisy; and, after a long and careful comparison of such views with his words and deeds, with the evidence obtainable from St. Domingo, and with the temper of his times in France, I have arrived at the conclusion that his character was, in sober truth, such as I have endeavoured to represent it in the foregoing work. (248)

Her project could be generally described as historically revisionist, motivated in large part by the ways she felt that Toussaint had been textually misrepresented. Because of her dedication to abolition and to a rigorous and accessible intellectualism, Martineau undertook the project of representing Toussaint, hero of the largest and most successful of the slave rebellions, to British and American audiences in the context of post-Emancipation Britain.

The powerful images that Haiti and the St. Domingo Revolution evoked in the minds of mid-Victorian readers meant that Martineau needed to shape events in order to win and keep her readers' support for her revisionist biography. Seymour Drescher, in *Capitalism and Antislavery*, argues that "[t]he St. Domingue revolution of 1791 was, of course, the greatest and most successful example of slave resistance in history" (97). Functioning as the specter of many white citizens' fears about black uprisings, the revolution was, ironically, also used by abolitionists to argue for racial equality.[2] Looking briefly at the role Haiti played in the debate over Emancipation, and, more broadly, in the management of the West Indian islands, we get a sense of the ways in which Martineau positioned her text as an overwhelmingly positive vision of slave potential and humanitarian ideals that were ultimately thwarted by the machinations of nations more concerned with imperial and economic benefit than with realizing ethical and egalitarian goals. Written at the beginning of the "Hungry Forties," at a time when abolitionists were turning their attention to the project of dismantling American slavery, Martineau celebrates the success of the St. Domingo Revolution, while at the same time noting the destructive and oppressive nature of much imperial policy.

The danger Haitian independence posed for other slave-holding islands, and the power the Haitian example held as an argument for racial equality, were central issues in the British battle over Emancipation that grew in force in the 1820s. In 1823, British abolitionists turned from the issue of the slave trade to their new goal of gradual emancipation:

> The campaign against British colonial slavery was launched in response to the realisation that, contrary to activists' hopes, the abolition of the British slave trade had not led to improvements in the treatment of slaves or to progress towards their emancipation in the British West Indies. A new national society was formed: the Society for the Mitigation and Gradual Abolition of Slavery Throughout the British Dominions, known popularly as the Anti-Slavery Society. It campaigned initially for the amelioration and eventual abolition of slavery, and then from 1830–31, in conjunction with the Agency Committee, for immediate and entire emancipation. (Midgley, 43)

In the resulting Parliamentary debates, as we will see, Haiti served both the pro- and anti-Emancipation causes. Thomas Fowell Buxton, arguing for the necessity of gradual emancipation, identified the significance of a Jamaican slave seeing his or her free neighbors across the water: "He sees another island, on which every labourer is free; in which eight hundred thousand Blacks, men, women, and children, exercise all the rights, and enjoy all the blessings—and they are innumerable and incalculable—which freedom gives. ("Substance," 9)

Buxton used the specter of interference from Haiti as a warning that the government needed to take emancipation seriously in order to avoid conflict with the enslaved Africans on the islands. He argued that although the present rulers of Haiti pledged noninvolvement, the future might not be so safe: "But, who will venture to secure us against the ambition of their successors?" ("Substance," 9).[3]

Conversely, St. Domingo was also invoked as a positive sign of racial equality. Responding to the statements of Mr. C. Ellis on the dangers of insurrection, the commentary by the Society for the Mitigation and Gradual Abolition of Slavery Throughout the British Dominions argued that St. Domingo was a testament to the civilized potential of African people:

> Notwithstanding the atrocities, and the years of sanguinary conflict, not only with the French but with each other, which marked the revolution in that island, and universal desolation which these occasioned; we find, after a lapse of thirty years, that the Haytians have not reverted to the habits of

savages, but, on the contrary, that they are improving in the arts of civilized life; we find them protected by equal laws, engaged in the pursuits of peaceful industry, adhering to the profession at least of Christianity, and competently discharging every duty attaching to them as citizens and members of a well-regulated community. ("Substance," 146)

In his "Appeal," William Wilberforce notes that "testimony as to the progress of the Negro children, in common school learning, has been given by all the masters who have instructed them in the island of Hayti" (48). The ability of Haitians to win, to establish, and to develop their own system of government and administration thus functioned as a vision of the potential equality of the races in a state of freedom. Because black people are equal—and will always work toward a state of freedom—the only way to avoid the bloodshed of rebellion, this argument suggests, is gradual emancipation.

In *Society in America* (1837), Martineau herself uses the example of Haiti when discussing the ignorance of the southern slave owners. Martineau suggests that some knowledge of Haitian emancipation would help these slave owners understand the potential of the black race: "If they would do themselves and their slaves the justice of inquiring with precision what is the state of Hayti; what has taken place in the West Indies; what the emancipation really was there; what its effects actually are; they would obtain a clearer view of their own prospects" (2:119–20). The emergence of Haiti, then, is both instructive and terrifying, an example of what could happen within the unreformed dynamic of the slave owning system, and of the positive potential of emancipation.

However, the pressures of negotiating this complex signifying terrain surrounding St. Domingo seems to have led Martineau to violate her commitment to historical accuracy regarding British involvement in the revolution. The British entered the St. Domingo conflict for two reasons: the danger the rebellion posed for the security of Jamaica, and the news that the French planters wanted to join England to avoid the implementation of full citizenship for the free people of color on the island. France was at war in Europe with the First Coalition (Austria, Prussia, Spain, Holland, and England), and England saw its chance to achieve control of the Caribbean islands (Ott, 76–77). For a significant time, the historical Toussaint fought in a multilayered conflict in which the alliances among those involved in the fighting—mulattos, free blacks, slaves, French, British—frequently shifted.[4] By the time England finally pulled out of the conflict in 1798, the "campaign had cost over ten million pounds and perhaps as many as 100,000 casualties" (Ott, 93). Between 1793 and 1798, the English had been a significant economic and military factor in the conflict. And, as C.L.R. James notes, in the months following the withdrawal of troops, the British constructed themselves "as the authors of 'the happy revolution,' and rejoicing at the freedom of a people, to enslave whom they had just lost 100,000 men" (James, 227).

Martineau, however, reduces the British presence to two brief scenes: the first is in the opening chapter, when the narrator provides a quick overview of the initial conflict between the mulattos and the whites. This event took place on the island after the French National Assembly decree of March 15, 1791 that gave the rights of full citizenship to free people of color. In her description of planters' reactions to this decree, Martineau notes that some "proposed to one another to offer their colony and their allegiance to England" (*Hour*, 1:4). The second significant mention lies in the predictions made by Madame Ogé, mother of the famous mulatto leader killed by whites in the opening conflict. She tells a group of women about Bonaparte's imminent betrayal of the mulattos and blacks on the island:[5] "It will soon be generally known that the preliminaries of peace between France and England are signed: and I happen to know two things more;—that Bonaparte has agreed to maintain negro slavery in Martinique, Guadaloupe, and Cayenne; and that—(pray, listen, young lady)—he declares to the English that he can do what he pleases in St. Domingo" (*Hour*, 2:234). Both of these passages allude to the presence of the English in the conflict, but nowhere in the narrative is there a direct description of Toussaint or his men actually killing British soldiers. Martineau explicitly refers to French soldiers, and white soldiers, but not to identifiably British soldiers.

Additionally, after Martineau dramatizes Toussaint's rescue of General Laveaux (1:chap. 9), a French General captured by the mulattos, the narrative jumps a significant seven years. The lost seven years in the text would seem to fall between 1791 and 1798, the block of years that roughly corresponds to the years of most intense British involvement. That Martineau should obscure the historical record is not a problem in a work of fiction. But in light of her strong belief in historical accuracy, the omission of overt British involvement suggests the author's wish to downplay the British campaign against the slave rebellion on St. Domingo for her 1840s post-Emancipation English readers. This decision perhaps helped garner the sympathy of her readers for her revision of Toussaint as abolitionist hero, and it evaded directly representing England's previous involvement in the West Indian slavery system. Thus she perhaps calmed her readers' anxieties and feelings of responsibility about this complex historical event while assuring them of her account's accuracy. And at least for one reviewer writing for the *Athenaeum*, her negotiation was a success: "Miss Martineau, considering her special purpose, has chosen her subject judiciously, and treated it well, because she has treated it historically" (958). Instead of offering a sentimental portrayal of the evils of slavery, this reviewer argues that, ironically, the effectiveness of her story is in its factual presentation.

## Rhetorical Abolitionism

Although Martineau saw her novel as participating in the project of abolitionist reform to which she dedicated much of her life, and for which she appears to have qualified her promise of historical accuracy, the novel generally veers away from the conventional tone and emphases of female abolitionist writing. The decision to dramatize the events not only of the St. Domingo Revolution, but also of a heroic black male leader, differentiates Martineau from many other female abolitionists writing during the early to mid-nineteenth century. However, Martineau's narrative does not altogether neglect traditional abolitionist themes. As Clare Midgley argues in her discussion of female abolitionist discourse, "Women focused on three main aspects of female suffering: flogging, 'moral degradation' and separation of mothers from children" (97). Of these three concerns, Martineau incorporated most clearly the last one, within the mysterious story of the death of the slave Thérèse's child, a strange moment that is worth examining more closely.

Throughout the novel, moments of indeterminacy productively problematize aesthetic and ideological structures that underpin racist thinking, thus complicating easy binaries and conventional understandings of race. The text actively involves the reader in this process. The subplot of Thérèse's child is a vivid example of this narrative strategy. At the beginning of the rebellion, Toussaint leads a group of people out of the most dangerous area and toward safety. Thérèse—a slave and mistress of a decidedly racist white man named Papalier—carries with her a baby, which is understood to be her master's child. When troops pass nearby the baby cries but someone snatches the baby from her and the crying stops. She never sees the baby again, and she never knows who took it, but the text strongly suggests that it is Papalier (*Hour*, 1:79–82). This strange scene, like several other moments in Martineau's text, is left completely unresolved.

Toward the end of the novel, Thérèse—now Madame Dessalines, wife of the most brutal of the black generals—watches at Papalier's deathbed, and we expect closure in the form of a confession or an unburdening. Toussaint sends her to watch at the bedside for just this reason, but the expected disclosure never occurs (*Hour*, 3:134–44). Although we assume that Thérèse's baby was smothered to death, we never actually see the act of violence. Martineau consistently shies away from portraying violence in both this subplot and the novel as a whole, perhaps suggesting an authorial anxiety about representing the details of war, rape, and miscegenation. The text is closer to an intellectualized military novel describing strategies for battle and for creating a new state. Although the baby's mysterious death suggests a momentary alignment with the emphases of a female abolitionist tradition, connections with these traditional themes remain generally undeveloped. The unresolved ending of the subplot perhaps indicates a moment of ambivalence in the face of both the realities of rape and of miscegenation, an open-endedness that we will see more elaborately in the novel's direct engagement with racial politics.

Martineau most clearly departs from the female abolitionist tradition by allowing her hero and his followers to maintain prominence in the novel's actions and to retain revolutionary agency. Midgley argues that female abolitionists conventionally lessened black agency and portrayed themselves as saviors: "black agency in undermining slavery is devalued and, under the auspices of the Anti-Slavery Society, freedom is granted as the gift of white philanthropists who leave class relations undisturbed" (90). The popularity of this plot, Midgley argues, explains why the later *Uncle Tom's Cabin* (1852) was so successful: "For this role to be maintained, black nobility had to be represented by white abolitionists as characterised by passive suffering rather than active resistance" (148). Martineau seems deliberately to avoid this type of narrative. Although several of Toussaint's generals and advisors are white, white characters are seldom agents for black people's freedom or military success. The novel consistently presents the revolution as an action undertaken by mulattos and black slaves, who are later led by Toussaint, in response to white treachery. The revolution allows the slaves to win the freedom that is due to them as human beings.

Reviews of the novel suggest that the credibility of the black hero was a problem for some readers, thus suggesting that the autonomy granted to the novel's protagonist perhaps challenged preconceived ideas about black agency. The review in the *Athenaeum*, for example, argues that Toussaint is a completely unrealistic figure: "Now, not only is such a man beyond the possibilities of her hero's early condition—for he was a born slave . . . but also he is above nature and humanity—the mere creature of the imagination. Her hero, moreover, has the African's physiognomy, but the European's tongue" (959). In a more culturally self-conscious reading, the *Westminster Review* suggests that Martineau's representation of Toussaint was instructive rather than ridiculous: "Negro heroes, and black statesmen and generals, sound strangely to the ear in this quarter of the world, and fearfully so across the Atlantic. Our realized idea of a negro is a black footman; the Americans,, [sic] that of a corrupted slave. St Domingo has proved that heroism and statesmanship are not confined to one colour; and we are obliged to Miss Martineau for exhibiting this fact" (235). In contrast to the *Athenaeum* reviewer's racist perspective, this anonymous reviewer describes the novel as illuminating of black character. However, both reviews misunderstand Martineau's generic project and its relationship to the rendering of the slave leader. Martineau labels the novel a "historical romance," and the romantic aspect speaks to the issue of idealized characterization. In Northrop Frye's discussion of the genre, he states that "the essential difference between novel and romance lies in the conception of characterization. The romancer does not attempt to create 'real people' so much as stylized figures which expand into psychological archetypes" (304). Although it is true that those slaves who found themselves in the relatively privileged position of house-servants and other non-field-workers, sometimes, as C.L.R James notes, were "able to profit by the cultural advantages of the system they [were] attacking" (19), Martineau's rendering of her hero has all the earmarks of a romanticized and relatively non-realistic ideal. Toussaint is Martineau's version of a romantic hero, an idealized emblem of the potential heroic stature of the black man, and a testament to the striving for freedom made by all members of the human community.

The choice of the romance genre makes possible a characterization potentially more politically efficacious: "Certain elements of character are released in the romance which make it naturally a more revolutionary form than the novel" (Frye, 304–5). Martineau takes the historical events of the revolution—as well as the conventional understanding of Toussaint—and creates her version of the intellectualized black hero as religious, charismatic, manly, rational, and well read as possible for his situation. A devout Catholic who must decide among allegiances to faith, country, or color, Toussaint is a model of strong piety.[6] There are remarkably few physical descriptions of him. He is described as heroic, charismatic, and a great military leader. At one point Afra, a mulatto girl, and

Euphrosyne, a Creole white girl, are attracted to him, blushing as they speak to him in a hall: "He would have passed them with a smile: but he saw that Afra was urging Euphrosyne to speak, and that the blushing Euphrosyne dared not do so" (*Hour*, 2:37). Thus we assume that he is an attractive man as portrayed in the novel, although James identifies the actual man as a relatively unattractive, yet charismatic, figure: "[d]espite his awkwardness of build and ugliness of feature he managed in the end to make a strong impression upon all with whom he came in contact" (251). But his actual features are left remarkably undefined in Martineau's text, and the reader assumes that his skin is a dark color only because he is the leader of the blacks, rather than of the mulattos. It is his faith and education that define him, and the reader must imagine the physical attributes of the man according to his or her reading of Toussaint's admirable actions, intelligence, and religious belief.

Martineau's depiction of Toussaint as Europeanized and attractive positions her against a Western narrative tradition that denigrates African appearance in order to justify a system of slavery. As David Brion Davis argues in *The Problem of Slavery in Western Culture,* distinguishing marks were necessary in the system of Western slavery in order to justify and naturalize a system that, in Classical times, was more socially based and at least somewhat less rigidly deterministic (Stepan, xi). Eric Williams suggests that characterizations of African looks as inferior have everything to do with the need to justify labor exploitation: "The features of the man, his hair, color, and dentifrice, his 'subhuman' characteristics so widely pleaded, were only the later rationalizations to justify a simple economic fact: that the colonies needed labor and resorted to Negro labor because it was cheapest and best" (Williams, 20). For Martineau to create a physically and ethically attractive African hero was to fly in the face of a tradition that consistently denigrated African physiognomy as a way to justify a system of exploitation.

But Martineau's critique goes beyond positively aestheticizing Toussaint's dark skin color. The novel continually interrogates general assumptions about skin color. Rather than simply exchange one term for another (for example, Toussaint is as intelligent as a white man), or one culture for another (for example, Haiti is as sophisticated as France), the text blends and complicates simple binaries, thus revealing the illusion of rationality where none actually exists. This process amounts to a deconstruction of racial aesthetics. Although the subject of skin color appears repeatedly throughout the novel, direct engagement with this issue occurs only in two conversations between the Creole girl, Euphrosyne, and her grandfather, a former slave owner with a reputation for cruelty. Although dismissed by at least one reviewer because the subplot "conduces little to the interest of the story" (*Westminster Review,* 236), the discussions between Euphrosyne and her grandfather are central to the novel's engagement with the issue of skin color. In the first of two conversations about this issue, Euphrosyne and her grandfather discuss her friendship with a mulatto girl, Afra, who is the daughter of a high government official in Toussaint's administration. Her grandfather suggests, "'It is time you made friends of your own complexion, child; and into the convent you go—this very day.'" Euphrosyne objects: "'Oh, grandpapa, you don't mean that those nuns are of my complexion! Poor pale creatures! I would not for the world look like them. . . . How sorry you would be, grandpapa, when you asked for me next winter, to see all those yellow-faced women pass before you.'" Her grandfather appreciates the humor of her argument, but then reflects to himself, "that there was certainly more colour there than was common in the West Indies; but that it must fade, in or out of the convent, by the time she was twenty; and she had better be in a place where she was safe" (2:10–11).

This exchange suggests the novel's deliberate alignment of skin color, social position, violence, and religious life. The grandfather understands social distinctions and wants to use the systems in place to ensure his granddaughter's position and safety. Euphrosyne counters his argument by going outside of the established categories for skin color, and calls the nuns "yellow-skinned," moving beyond the light and dark distinction by expanding the categories. She employs this strategy again in a later exchange with her grandfather, in which he replies,

> "Do not speak of colour, child. What expressions you pick up from Afra, and such people! It is our distinction that we have no colour,—that we are white."
>
> "That is the distinction of the nuns, I know; but I hoped it was not mine yet. I do not forget how you pinch my cheeks sometimes, and talk about roses." (2:117)

When coupled with her attractiveness as a character, Euphrosyne's resistance to incorporating the stifling categories of color disrupts those lines of demarcation within Martineau's text. In these two scenes, the novel surpasses the idea of simply taking the rebel side in a debate about the St. Domingo Revolution. Instead, categories of skin color that are tied to the conflict are themselves attacked and made ridiculous by a simple acknowledgment of the numerous colors evident in skin that is called "white," as well as used as a way to criticize Catholic traditions and institutions. The novel consistently destabilizes hardened categories of racial distinction and thus disrupts the lines along which battlefronts are drawn.

The ability to understand more complex delineations of skin color ties in with the expressed need throughout the novel for individuals to be widely read and critically engaged. Martineau's text overlaps most strongly with traditional abolitionist themes in its emphasis on the importance of education. A component of emancipation continually emphasized by British female abolitionists, in addition to relief and missionary issues, was education (Midgley, 53–55). The issue of education—and reading in particular—is central to an understanding of Martineau's novel. Education does not simply encourage slave self-determination, however. In fact, at the beginning of the novel, Toussaint's reading encourages him to be passive and accepting, as evidenced in this exchange with his young son:

> "What is it? what is it about?" said the boy, who had heard many a story out of books from his father.
>
> "What is it? Let us see. I think you know letters enough to spell it out for yourself. Come and try."
>
> The child knew the letter E, and, with a good deal of help, made out, at last, Epictetus.
>
> "What is that?" asked the boy.
>
> "Epictetus was a negro," said Génifrède, complacently.
>
> "Not a negro," said her father, smiling. "He was a slave; but he was white."
>
> "Is that the reason you read that book so much more than any other?"
>
> "Partly; but partly because I like what is in it."
>
> "What is in it—any stories?" asked Denis.
>
> "It is all about bearing and forbearing. It has taught me many things which you will have to learn byandby." (1:11)

The role of education in Toussaint's life expands as the novel progresses. The daughter's question as to whether the identity of the author as white makes the text more valuable to her father, and his answer of "[p]artly," suggests the novel's problematic alignment of wisdom with Western white culture. Reading is more than the consumption of books to Toussaint; it is the source of valuable instruction as he negotiates his circumstances. In one sense, he uses texts to help him endure his burden as a slave, a state he detaches from color in the above passage. In another instance, reading gives him the ability to critically understand his situation, and to negotiate among his allegiances to master, nation, God, and race. Throughout the novel he interprets events, edicts, proclamations, messages, and actions in order to determine the correct course of action for both himself and the newly emerging Haitian nation.

Martineau manages anxieties in her readers about the revolutionary potential of educated slaves by suggesting that education breeds loyalty and compassion. In a crucial scene, several members of Toussaint's family and the racist Papalier prepare to flee because of the uprising. Toussaint's children retrieve a few volumes from the library of the master's house. Papalier argues in response to the children's actions that the uprisings are a result of teaching slaves how to read. At the same time, Toussaint has just found a way to save his master, Bayou, getting him onto a ship for America. Isaac, Toussaint's son, asks Papalier if his slaves read: "'No, indeed! not one of them,'" he replies. "'Why do they not take care of you, as father did of M. Bayou?'" Isaac asks (1:68). The question remains unanswered, yet another of the novel's open-ended moments that throw discernment of the scene's moral message back on the reader. This exchange suggests that learning to read does not lead slaves to revolt or find ways to betray their enslavers.[7] Rather, the scene argues that reading helps the slaves be merciful toward those who have held them in captivity. Martineau's depiction supports the idea that educating slaves cultivates compassion between slave and master, an idea that flew in the face of traditional ideas on the subject.

Many antislavery texts and slave narratives directly connect learning to read with a slave's ability to gain freedom.[8] Most famously, in Frederick Douglass's *Narrative* (1845), one of his enslavers, Mr. Auld, reacts dramatically to his wife's decision to teach Douglass how to read:

> "If you give a nigger an inch, he will take an ell. A nigger should know nothing but to obey his master—to do as he is told to do. Learning would *spoil* the best nigger in the world. Now," said he, "if you teach that nigger (speaking of myself) how to read, there would be no keeping him. It would forever unfit him to be a slave. He would at once become unmanageable, and of no value to his master. As to himself, it could do him no good, but a great deal of harm. It would make him discontented and unhappy." (Douglass 274–75, original italics)

Education apparently makes the slave more difficult to control, because it helps to generate the critical and imaginative skills necessary for the slave to begin conceiving of another way of being. This critical awareness results in discontentment and the desire to move beyond the limitations of enslavement. Douglass himself realized that the ability to read was necessary for freedom: "I now understood what had been to me a most perplexing difficulty—to wit, the white man's power to enslave the black man. It was a grand achievement, and I prized it highly. From that moment, I understood the pathway from slavery to freedom. It was just what I wanted, and I got it at a time when I the [*sic*] least expected it" (275).

Douglass goes on to devote virtually the entire seventh chapter to describing the specifics of how he learned to read. As Henry Louis Gates, Jr. argues in his introduction to *The Classic Slave Narratives,* "The direct relation between reading and writing on one hand, and legal freedom on the other, was evident to both the slave narrators and to their reviewers" (xii). Thus education, it would seem from these passages, has the power to undermine the entire system of slavery. Education of the planter and the slave will bring both out of a state of ignorance, encouraging the slave to seek freedom and the enslaver to reject the use of slave labor.

Some argue that Martineau supported education in her work as a way to teach submissiveness, especially for the working class. Toussaint's reading of books to find the strength to bear his enslavement would seem to support this idea. Betty Fladeland disagrees with this characterization, however, and suggests that Martineau's goal was to encourage self-reliance:

Education became the cornerstone of Martineau's philosophy. Often her stands on the Poor Laws and factory legislation were downright hard-hearted and antagonistic to unemployed and exploited workers alike, and her insistence on patience, courage and the helpfulness of middle-class leadership strike one as but modified versions of pie-in-the-sky. But one must examine the purpose which underlay her idea of education. It was not to teach submissiveness and resignation. Quite the contrary, her aim was to enlighten the working classes on basic economic and political issues so that they could intelligently discuss and then act to help solve their own problems, and so fulfil their role in the good society while retaining their self-respect. (77–78)

Martineau's belief in the need for an educated working class, however, does not necessarily translate into a belief that education would be beneficial for slaves. And she certainly did not address her anti-slavery writings to slaves, but instead to reform-minded white people. But the continual emphasis on reading throughout *The Hour and the Man* makes it difficult to believe that her philosophy of education—the key to attaining the ability to be socially and economically self-reliant—did not transfer to her vision of the future for African people.[9]

## Aestheticizing Racial Politics

However, in *The Hour and the Man,* the activity of reading surpasses the role of crucial tool in the black struggle for freedom. The dynamics of interpretation become more radically intrinsic to the narrative structure, thus providing a critique of mid-Victorian conceptions of race and slavery at the rhetorical level, to add to the more overtly thematic challenges. We saw this narrative strategy at work in the dialogue between Euphrosyne and her grandfather regarding categories of skin color. Interpretive structures become visible in the novel's presentation of multiple perspectives, as well as in the shifts that take place among those perspectives. As Wolfgang Iser argues in *The Act of Reading* (1978), "Every articulate reading moment entails a switch of perspective, and this constitutes an inseparable combination of differentiated perspectives, foreshortened memories, present modifications, and future expectations" (116). Several times in Martineau's novel, a scene's dramatic structure mimics the activity of interpretation. We are given the narration of events, the narration of partial motivations, the narration of partial results, and—perhaps most dramatically—the narration of indeterminate moments such as the unexplained disappearance of Thérèse's baby. The process of reading these scenes takes place not only in the reader's mind, but also in the action of the novel itself through the manipulation of these multiple perspectives within a patently stylized—what I am calling an aestheticized—setting. The multilayered nature of Martineau's use of interpretive dynamics emphasizes the crucial role they play in racial representation and understanding.

In a particularly compelling example of this narrative strategy, we follow a scene that weaves together an array of dialogues that all take place at the site of a decaying mansion called "L'Etoile." By examining how the chapter builds to the concluding conversation, it is possible to see how the dialogic interaction among multiple perspectives, cultural discourses, and historical facts combine to focus attention on the interpretive process and disrupt simple Manichean understandings of race and color. Following a chapter in which the reader is privy to the dynamics of the new political state put in place by Toussaint during the seven-year jump in the narrative, the L'Ouverture clan travels to L'Etoile on the way to the family estate at

Pongaudin. The first striking aspect of this chapter is the family's apparently easy transition from slavery to governmental leadership. When in the city, Margot, Toussaint's wife, now travels in European carriages; their children have tutors and a Spanish artist named Azua to teach them drawing; and the women travel on horseback with attendants holding umbrellas over them while they proceed along the road.

The ruined mansion functions as a patently aestheticized site that acts as both a location for and a symbol of the decipherment of racial representation in the novel. All the issues intrinsic to the presentation of this revolution come together for one moment in the description of the house. As the family, attendants, and guests arrive at their destination, we receive this description of the scene:

> The courtyard through which they passed was strewed with ruins [. . . .]
> The whole was shaded, almost as with an awning, by the shrubs which
> grew from the cornices, and among the rafters which had remained where
> the roof once was. Ropes of creepers hung down the walls [. . . .] The mar-
> ble steps and entrance hall were kept clear of weeds and dirt, and had a
> strange air of splendour in the midst of the desolation. The gilding of the
> balustrades of the hall was tarnished; and it had no furniture but the tat-
> ters of some portraits, whose frame and substance had been nearly
> devoured by ants; but it was weathertight and clean. (1:275–76)

In this gothic scene of ruin and grandeur, the newly majestic L'Ouverture clan enters for a visit with the caretakers of the place. This ruin site is the first of several we will encounter in the texts under consideration in this study. In my discussion of James Grant's *First Love and Last Love* in the final chapter, I will address the question of the significance of ruins directly. For now, suffice it to say that this scene contributes to the erosion of easy binaries in this novel by making the line between nature and domesticity somewhat permeable. Christopher Woodward argues in his study *In Ruins,* "No ruin can be suggestive to the visitor's imagination, I believe, unless its dialogue with the forces of Nature is visibly alive and dynamic" (73). The energy of this site derives from its permeable boundaries between not only the inside and outside of the original structure, but also between the revolution's differing factions embodied both in the contents of the mansion and in its visitors.

As the description of L'Etoile moves in to discern the details of the house's interior, the representation becomes a point of intersection among the island's different cultures:

The kitchen corner was partitioned off from the sitting room by a splendid folding screen of Oriental workmanship, exhibiting birds-of-paradise, and the blue rivers and gilt pagodas of China. The other partitions were the work of Bellair's own hands, woven of bamboo and long grass, dyed with the vegetable dyes, with whose mysteries he was, like a true African, acquainted. The dinner table was a marble slab, which still remained cramped to the wall, as when it had been covered with plate or with ladies' work boxes. . . . A harp, with its strings broken, and its gilding tarnished, stood in one corner: and musical instruments of Congo origin hung against the wall. It was altogether a curious medley of European and African civilisation, brought together amidst the ruins of a West Indian revolution. (1:277)

As a visual metaphor of the revolution, this house acts as a canvas for the representation of an array of objects suggesting both colonial destruction and potential. All of the social signifiers of the ongoing cultural conflict on the island stand here, in anticipation of an architectural rebirth. Destruction of the original building has taken place, and the markers of the new rising culture are inserted into the scene. The site presents a polyphony of racial and national symbols, framed to encourage the reader to interpret it as a vision of the new hybrid Haitian culture that is Toussaint's goal. But the house still retains a sense of sadness and ruin, representing the continued conflict and unresolved negotiation of cultures taking place on the island.

The visual hybridity of the decaying mansion is mirrored in the ideological proliferation represented by various dialogues that take place in different locations on the grounds. After the opening introduction to the mansion, a series of independent discussions take place over various parts of the estate that evoke major issues involved in Martineau's representation of the revolution. At the meeting between the caretakers of the estate and Madame L'Ouverture, the visual blending of cultural signifiers joins with a linguistic blending of history and naming. The caretakers of the estate, in lieu of the absent white owners, are two friends of Toussaint and his wife. Charles Bellair,[10] described as "a Congo chief, kidnapped in his youth, and brought into St. Domingo slavery" (1:274), has remained at the estate rather than return to Africa or fight with Toussaint. After greeting Margot, he brings her to his wife:

"Minerve!" cried Madame, on seeing her.
　"Deesha is her name," said Bellair, smiling.

"Oh, you call her by her native name! Would we all knew our African
names, as you know hers! Deesha!" (1:275)

In this exchange, the issue of accurate naming becomes central. Over the
course of the novel, Toussaint takes on many names. "L'Ouverture," trans-
lated as "the opening," is a name bestowed on him first by the French com-
missary Polverel, and then by his followers. He is also called "First of the
Blacks," the "Black Spartacus," the "Black Napoleon," and, in a more
derogatory moment, the "Ape." Here, in this scene at L'Etoile, we see the
rejection of the slave names, which for Bellair's wife is a rejection of
Minerva—the preferred daughter of Zeus in mythology—in favor of original African names. The caretakers' rejection of Western culture in the
form of names remains complex, however, because of their decision not to
leave the site of cultural interaction and return to Africa, but to engage
with the process of social reformation and make it their own.

The narrative then branches out to describe several different discussions taking place in various locations on the estate, each of which broad-
ens consideration of the various ideological challenges inherent in the revolution. Taking a walk around the grounds, Génifrède, Toussaint's daughter, and Moyse, her cousin, discuss their relationship and the war between
the races. Génifrède believes in her father's conciliatory attitude toward the
whites, whereas Moyse is an avowed hater of whites. The two young people are in love and blend a discourse of courting with attention to the complexity of political and racial negotiations involved in the revolution.
Denis, Toussaint's youngest son, appears in the midst of their conversation,
revealing that he has been eavesdropping. So here we have a conversation
that takes place regarding three key issues in the text—race, politics, and
romance—and at the same time the conversation is overheard by another
character who models the reader's attempt to interpret the scene's multiple resonances.

The arrival of Denis brings the issue of class position more prominently into the scene. Denis wants to play with a farmer's son, but
Génifrède and Moyse feel Denis is of too high a social standing to be playing with the boy. Denis disagrees: "Denis had never cared for his rank,
except when riding by his father's side on review days; and now he liked it
less than ever" (1:288). Génifrède then sends Denis to retrieve her sketch-
pad. The young boy returns with it and his own drawing of Moyse and
Génifrède "as he had found them, gathering fruits and flowers" (1:291).
Thus, not only has Denis watched and listened to the young lovers unob-
served, but he has also made a sketch of the scene to surprise them.

Watching, listening, recording, and discussing intermingle here as the variety of interpretive and aesthetic practices continues to proliferate, and the issues requiring critical and interpretive skills multiply. At another location, Toussaint and the African caretakers of L'Etoile trade stories of African pasts and connections to African royalty. By the end of their conversation, "they were perpetually falling unconsciously into the use of their negro language" (1:292). Bringing together African pasts and family histories in a blend of the French and African languages, this conversation represents the cultural reality of the first generation slaves on the island. The narrative reminds us of the historical and familial realities from which these people were taken when they were brought to the island to be slaves.

The text then circles back to address the signifying power of architecture for the revolutionary project by returning and more fully elaborating the discussion of the symbolic power of L'Etoile begun in the scene's opening description. Dialogues, participants, and aesthetic media multiply as the scene continues. Vincent—one of Toussaint's generals with loyalties to France and limited trustworthiness—wanders off from the storytelling and begins a discussion with Loisir, who sketches the house. The architect Loisir has been added to the expedition to design the restoration of L'Etoile as General Christophe's new house. Vincent and Loisir discuss architectural integrity. Vincent, who is black, tells the architect, who is white, that he need not be so attentive to accuracy; the blacks will believe anything he says is European and in good taste. Loisir replies, "'[B]ut Christophe's mansion is to stand for an age,—to stand as the first evidence, in the department of the arts, of the elevation of your race'" (1:294). The house will represent the nature of the new government, and thus it must convey the most regal of messages. The architect understands the significance of the house as a text, and the importance of retaining control over its representational power. Loisir further complicates the earlier presentation of L'Etoile by reflecting on the politics of its future architectural design.

All of these issues converge in a longer conversation at the end of the scene, when the participants meet to discuss the reliability of French allegiance. The main focus of the discussion is the attitude of the French and Napoleon toward Toussaint and the people of color on the island. As a result of the earlier dialogues within the chapter, however, the subjects of love, war, race, class, art, politics, and representation also enter the scene, metaphorically signified by each of the participants. Aimée, another of Toussaint's daughters and a French loyalist, believes Napoleon respects them. Génifrède, her sister, distrusts the French and argues for their duplicity. Moyse, their cousin, argues that the whites in Paris are turning

Napoleon against the island by suggesting that Toussaint's ambition is a threat. And Vincent, the untrustworthy soldier, proclaims his loyalty to both Toussaint and Napoleon. In a compelling climax to the discussion, Génifrède and Moyse usher out the list of commissaries sent by France to the colony, and dwell at length on their limitations and foibles. During this discussion, Denis, Toussaint's young son, mimics each of the commissaries as they are described, and Azua, the artist, sits back watching and listening to the discussion, rendering the various interpretations in sketches. Thus, as we read the conversation and synthesize and interpret the characterizations, Denis performs the descriptions and Azua records them in drawings along with us.

The climax of the scene throws attempts to attain synthesis of the dialogues into virtual indeterminacy. During the larger conversation, a monkey in the tree over Aimée's head watches the group during the discussion, thus adding yet another perspective to the scene. Moyse first notices him: "'If they had taken that monkey which is looking down at your drawing, Aimée, and seven of its brethren, and installed them at Cap, they would have done us all the good the commissaries have done, and far less mischief'" (1:298–99). Then the group returns to their discussion of the failed French commissaries, much to the annoyance of Aimée, who remains faithful to what she perceives as French benevolence. After everyone else had seen Azua's caricatures and laughed at the drawings, they are passed to Aimée: "When the paper came back to her, she looked up into the tree under which she sat. The staring monkey was still there. She made a vigorous spring to hand up the caricature, which the creature caught. As it sat demurely on a branch, holding the paper as if reading it, while one of its companions as gravely looked over its shoulder, there was more laughter than ever" (1:302). Aimée then declares that "'this is the only worthy fate of a piece of mockery of people wiser than ourselves, and no less kind. The negroes have hitherto been thought, at least, grateful. It seems that this is a mistake. For my part, however, I leave it to the monkeys to ridicule the French'" (1:302). This moment represents the climax to a gradually intensifying narrative progression in which a backdrop of cultural chaos and partial reformation nurtures the development of a series of dialogues, culminating in a discussion of trustworthiness, and ending in this intriguing scene of mock-reading.

I suggest that this figure of the monkey becomes a site of mock aesthetic appreciation and analysis representing several intersecting ideas about race, nationality, politics, and interpretation, and that ultimately the figure stands for the instability of meaning within each of these categories.

In Western racial discourse, monkeys inhabit a space between human and animal. In a description of the slave quarters at one particular plantation in her travels in America, Martineau herself uses this symbol to convey the most abhorrent conditions in which the slaves live: "We visited the negro quarter; a part of the estate which filled me with disgust, wherever I went. It is something between a haunt of monkeys and a dwelling place of human beings" (*Society in America*, 1:302). The slave lives in a border territory between monkey and human. Without actually calling the slaves monkeys, Martineau uses the racist association to critique the living conditions in which African people are forced to live. Africans are not naturally animals, she suggests, but pushed toward animal identity by horrendous environmental factors.

By passing Azua's caricatures of central French colonial authorities to the monkeys, Aimée metonymically activates this human/animal threshold, suggesting that a reading of French political motivations as antagonistic to the liberation struggle is inaccurate and unworthy of serious consideration by sophisticated readers. Her identity as loyal French African subject functions to separate the monkey from African subjectivity, and align it with a representation of a critically unsophisticated interpreter. This boundary function ties in with what Anne McClintock argues is the threshold defining nature of the monkey figure: "Monkeys, in particular, were deployed to legitimize social boundaries as edicts of nature" (McClintock, 216). Aimée uses the trope of the monkey to reflect back to the group what she perceives as their ignorant and uncivilized "readings" of French political motivations. National and racial identities intersect.

Aimée's position resonates with Toussaint's problematic belief throughout the novel that black people need to embrace Western learning. Toussaint declares that "'the civilisation of the whites is the greatest educational advantage we could enjoy. Yes, [ . . .] and the more we despise it, the more we prove that we need it" (2:85). And in his conversation with Génifrède, Moyse remarks of Toussaint that "he says they are masters of an intellectual kingdom from which we have been shut out, and they alone can let us in" (1:283–84). By handing the picture to the monkeys, Aimée, who believes wholeheartedly in her father's plan and attitudes toward the whites, symbolically suggests the absurdity of an interpretation of French political actions as antagonistic to Africans. Distrusting the French is thus likened to a regressive embrace of ignorance, represented by the monkeys. Progress is the ability to embrace the educational heritage of Western culture, represented here as literacy and the ability to interpret in a complex manner, without turning away from one's own culture. However, the fact that Toussaint will eventually die in a French prison ironically turns Aimée's judgment back on itself, suggesting her inability to correctly assess the political climate and creating a problematic and racist alignment between herself and the monkey that undermines the authority of her interpretation.

But the moment also suggests the interpretive disruption carried out by the Signifyin(g) Monkey figure of the African American literary tradition. Gates argues that this staple trickster figure "dwells at the margins of discourse, ever punning, ever troping, ever embodying the ambiguities of language" (52). It is the "black trope of tropes" (51) that disrupts, revises, and problematizes the signifying properties of language. Although the monkeys in the tree overhead in Martineau's novel do little but mimic the action of reading without seemingly being able to interpret the text, Denis and Azua have both represented and parodied colonial structures of authority, producing the text transferred to the monkeys. Aimée's transfer of the mimicry, interpretation and performance of each of the commissaries, embodied in the drawing, to the monkeys, metonymically and aesthetically connects the monkeys to the process of interpretive disruption. Denis and Azua engage in Signifyin(g), and when Aimée transfers the text up to the animal in the tree, she transfers it to a symbol of the rebellious reading strategy she so desperately wants to disempower, thus inadvertently referencing the actions of linguistic and political revision and parody, and undermining the authority of the interpretation she supports by illustrating the rhetorical nature of interpretation itself.

## Inconclusive Conclusion

The end of the novel is a point of instability in Martineau's valorization of Toussaint's superior interpretive skills, however. Toussaint misreads the intentions of a French general, and invites him to come to the rebel stronghold. He is captured and taken to France, where he is eventually imprisoned and dies. The revolution continues under the leadership of two very different men: Christophe, a follower of Toussaint's belief in the need for constructive relationships between the races; and Dessalines, who with his wife is known throughout the novel as bent on the destruction of the white population. Martineau does not fictionalize these transitions, however. After the French take Toussaint off the island, the plot never returns there, and so we never see the events of the rest of the revolution. A review in the *Westminster Review* expresses dissatisfaction with this decision: "It is no small compliment to the author that we feel dissatisfied by the conclusion of her book. We wish to know what success attended the endeavours of Toussaint's generals in completing his work" (236). We only see Toussaint communicating with his generals in his own mind, asking them to continue following his orders and philosophies.

What we learn by indirect references to Thérèse's future life as "beloved Empress" is that Dessalines becomes the new Emperor, a figure who throughout the novel has questioned the optimistic way in which Toussaint encouraged trust of the white race (*Hour*, 3:179). This historical fact renders suspect Toussaint's philosophy, and suggests that the most successful way to defeat colonial oppression is to encourage racial separatism. True to her rejection of the need to dramatize any of the violence of the revolution, Martineau's novel does not present the bloody events that follow Toussaint's capture. What does it mean that the reader, once fully immersed in the events on St. Domingo, is never returned to them? It suggests that Martineau believed that Toussaint's dedication to the principle of Christian forgiveness enabled the revolution to succeed. Ultimately, however, the treacherous nature of white behavior made true racial dialogue impossible.

In 1855 an optimistic Martineau wrote that "the old practice of Man holding Man as property is nearly exploded among civilised nations; and the analogous barbarism of Man holding the surface of the globe as property cannot long survive. The idea of this being a barbarism is now fairly formed, admitted, and established among some of the best minds of the time; and the result is, as in all such cases, ultimately secure" (*Autobiography*, 456).

Systems of property, imperialism, and slavery overlap for Martineau, and the unmasking of one would lead, she was confident, to the demise of the others. Education, and the resulting ability to engage critically with one's environment and society, can dismantle these destructive structures, this novel seems to suggest. Martineau's fiction illustrates the belief that education can forge bonds among people of different cultures, and this premise shines through in her biographical presentation of Toussaint L'Ouverture. The author's dedication to intellectualism permeates the narrative, from her research on Toussaint and the events of the St. Domingo Revolution, to the activity of interpretation itself functioning as a structural paradigm. Unfortunately, her vision of an ever-broadening egalitarianism would remain unrealized, as future representations of race took on the burden of English dissatisfaction with post-Emancipation colonial realities, and an increasing valorization of radically racist scientific lines of inquiry. It is to this material that we now turn.

# CHAPTER 2

⌁

# "Life Clothed in Forms"

## RADICAL RACISM AS FORMALIST AESTHETIC IN ROBERT KNOX'S *THE RACES OF MEN* (1850)

*T*he 1850 publication of Robert Knox's *The Races of Men* stands at a crisis point in mid-Victorian attitudes about race. Public support for the abolitionist rhetoric evident in Harriet Martineau's *The Hour and the Man* was eroding, and the influence of radical and polemical scientific racism was growing. Race had been of paramount interest to naturalists and anatomists beginning in the late-eighteenth century. However, by the mid-nineteenth century, an overtly racist scientific agenda was fully in place (Stepan, ix). *The Races of Men* blends sociological, biological, environmental, and aesthetic concerns into a treatise arguing for the centrality of race in all human endeavors. Knox seeks to classify and contain what he sees as the crises precipitated by races coming into contact with one another, inappropriately taking on one another's political structures, and attempting to blend or change what he argues are biologically rooted predispositions for particular cultural forms. Knox's notorious descriptive, taxonomic project is suffused with a sense of racial antagonism, most specifically in its engagement with such conflicts as the Haitian Revolution, as well as Knox's experiences in the Kaffir War in South Africa.

Throughout the text, Knox constructs his argument in part by using race as an empty trope, within which he places all of the social conflicts he sees as critical in his time. Functioning as a kind of linguistic scapegoat, the term "race" becomes at once a definitional certainty and a site in which ideological conflicts regarding shifting relationships within the imperialist project are negotiated. Knox situates race as an elastic and central concept in all human endeavors, which leads him to address issues of history, colonialism, nationalism, and progress. Although he generally takes the stance of radical and offensive racialist, contradictions in his presentation suggest a more ambiguous position than this label implies. The primacy of form over content typifies Knox's work. *The Races of Men* culminates in a formalist aesthetic premised on the importance of exteriority in an organic ideal of beauty. This aesthetic philosophy functions as a temporary resolution for the wide-ranging, multifaceted, and often contradictory uses of the term "race" throughout his study. This chapter will explore the contradictions at the heart of Knox's understanding of race and argue that the work's turn to aesthetics in its concluding chapters becomes a resting point for the erratic and complex nature of the narrative.

## Scientific Racism and the Question of Aesthetics

In the final few chapters of Knox's *The Races of Men,* the author turns, rather abruptly, to the role of aesthetics in his racial system. Knox explains this move in the following passage: "The introduction of the disquisition into a theory of the beautiful was forced upon me here by the necessity of connecting the history of race with the perfect; to trace to it the laws of formation, leading to the perfect; and from it the laws of deformation, leading to the imperfect; or, in other words, to explain the origin of race, or at least to connect the history of race with the great laws regulating the living organic world" (*Races,* 419).

Leaving aside the provocative use of passive voice ("was forced upon me," which of course begs the question of "by whom?"), Knox here makes the connection between scientific understandings of racial identity and aesthetic systems of evaluating the beautiful. Delineating a somewhat detailed aesthetic based on racial identity, scientific anatomy, and complex nineteenth-century understandings of the natural world, Knox argues that the most advanced and beautiful of races, the ancient Greeks, resulted from a historical deformation which happened to produce this kind of beauty. This race has vanished from the earth, Knox argues, but has left behind evidence of its aesthetic superiority in the Classic Greek marbles and the figure of Venus.[1] The Classical Venus figure functions as an ironic counterpart to another "Venus," Sara(h) Ba(a)rtman(n), the so-called Hottentot Venus, a Khoi-Khoi woman brutally exploited by early racial scientists. In fact, in *The Life and Times of Sara Baartman, "The Hottentot Venus,"* Yvette Abrams argues that "[s]cientific racism . . . was built on [Sara(h) Ba(a)rtman(n)'s] body." And the French scientists Cuvier, de Blainville, and Saint-Hillaire, the first the dissector of Ba(a)rtman(n)'s body, became the biographical heroes of Knox's 1852 work, *Great Artists and Great Anatomists: A Biographical and Philosophical Study.*

In *Great Artists and Great Anatomists*, Knox asks directly, "What is the relation of Science to Art?" (xii). His answer lies in the relationship of both disciplines to form, and the primacy of structure in the biology of race. Knox argues for a static racial taxonomy as a way to understand the nature of biology and its relationship to aesthetic evaluation. The tangible defined the perfect for Knox, while at the same time, his evaluative criteria betray his obvious cultural and racial biases: "The correct mind rejects everything which is ideal, or what never had an existence. The monstrous creations of the disordered Hindoo, Chinese, and Saxon minds; these are ideal, fictitious, false; the Venus is real" (*Races*, 419). Thus the connection between artistic philosophy, imperial ideologies of racial domination, and scientific violation of the racialized body are enacted within the structure of Knox's work itself: an elaborate taxonomy that he argues is based on "real" empirical data.

The link between science, aesthetics, and race began much earlier than 1850, of course. In *Ape to Apollo: Aesthetics and the Idea of Race in the 18th Century*, David Bindman argues for the development of this link in the work of prominent Enlightenment aestheticians. More specifically, Bindman asserts the importance of connections between artistic instruction and racial theory, such as in the work of Pieter Camper, proponent of the famous "facial angle" theory of racial identification (206), as well as many physiognomists, that certainly had its roots in Classical discussions of art. However, Christine Bolt argues that the bringing together of the realm of art and race in the nineteenth century brought race out of the realm of biology and gave it a broader social role: "Race became far more than a biological concept: race and culture were dangerously linked" (9). Bindman points to George Mosse's study of European racism, *Toward the Final Solution*, as an inspiration for his study, and presents these chilling words from Mosse: the "'continuous transition from science to aesthetics is a cardinal feature of modern racism. Human nature came to be defined in aesthetic terms, with significant stress on the outward physical signs of inner rationality and harmony'" (quoted in Bindman, 14). And as Peter Fryer argues, regarding the influence of pseudo-scientific thought, "Long after the material conditions that originally gave rise to racist ideology had disappeared, these dead ideas went on gripping the minds of the living" (190). Thus, unpacking the rhetoric evident in this material provides us with insight into the development of structures of contemporary racism that still underpin global relations and policies at the current time.

## Robert Knox, Lecturer, and the Problem of Reception

Knox's early professional development nurtured his interest in human form and racial dynamics. He began his career as a medical student in his hometown of Edinburgh. After studying his craft, Knox left Edinburgh in 1815 to serve as a doctor to soldiers wounded in the battle of Waterloo, a position in which he apparently received some of his most important training as an anatomist (Rae, 12; Lonsdale, 9). After finishing his work with these soldiers, he then went to South Africa in 1817, where George Stocking notes that Knox performed dissections on the bodies of fallen black fighters.[2] Henry Lonsdale argues that it was his experiences observing the different populations in South Africa that sparked Knox's ethnological interests. From the beginning, Knox was interested not only in the darker-skinned races, but in the attributes of races across the spectrum of color (Lonsdale, 12).

After returning from the Cape, Knox then went on to Paris to study anatomy under Cuvier and Geoffroy Saint-Hillaire, both of whom had just recently dissected the body of Sara(h) Ba(a)rtman(n) in 1816. Knox then returned to his home in Edinburgh to begin what looked to become an exemplary career (Stocking, *Victorian Anthropology*, 64; Lonsdale, 12, 17). Knox actually nurtured three successful careers simultaneously: he was a talented anatomist, popular lecturer and dedicated teacher, and conservator at a natural history museum (Rae, 37). As a student, and then, by all accounts, as a phenomenally successful lecturer in comparative anatomy, Knox found himself in the heart of the early nineteenth-century study of racial difference.[3] His promising future evaporated, however, when he was implicated in the notorious Burke and Hare scandal.

As an anatomist, Knox constantly confronted the problem of finding subjects for his dissections. Grave-robbing became a lucrative industry in Edinburgh. However, Burke and Hare took it a step further and actually killed their victims and sold them to willing medical and anatomical schools. Knox was implicated in this scandal because one particular woman's body was taken by accident to the wrong location: "On 2 November, the discovery and identification of a woman's body in the cellar of Dr. Knox's anatomical school had revealed the nefarious practices of the murderers Burke and Hare" (Rae, 1). Because there was nothing directly linking Knox to the victims, he was never tried for complicity in the murders. But in the eyes of the public, Knox was guilty, and he was hanged in effigy on February 12, 1829, by an angry mob (Rae, 91; Stocking, *Victorian Anthropology*, 64). Knox's biographer Rae argues that because

"Dr Knox has rarely been considered apart from Burke and Hare" (1), the loss to the scientific community of this promising anatomist and researcher has not been properly acknowledged.

After the events of the Burke and Hare scandal, Knox perhaps was not entirely inaccurate in feeling that every man's hand was against him. Rae argues that the incident changed Knox's personality forever. "Gone was the genial host, the man who made friends so easily: the new and embittered Knox had venom on his tongue, and his wit had a cruel sarcasm that it had not had before" (114), although both Rae and Lonsdale agree that Knox could be impolitic in his statements at times (Lonsdale, 152–53, 233). Rae claims that the events of the scandal combined with perceptions that Knox was "not only politically a 'radical,' a dangerous thing to be in the aftermath of the Reform Bill, when Britain was highly nervous of 'left' opinion; but he was also an unbeliever, a member of no recognised church, an 'atheist' and an 'infidel'" (121). Such a combination turned him into something of a social pariah. Although after the incident Knox attempted for some time to resume his several careers, Stocking argues that "eventually the odium roused by the murders and by his radical political and religious views forced him to leave Edinburgh" (*Victorian Anthropology,* 64). The final blows came in 1841, when his wife died, and in 1842, when he lost his four-year-old son to scarlet fever. According to Rae, Knox accepted by 1842 that he needed to leave his hometown (124–25).

*The Races of Men* began as a series of lectures given in a number of English cities, including Newcastle, Manchester, and Birmingham, as a way to support his children and himself (Stocking, *Victorian Anthropology,* 64; Rae, 127). The choice of race, in light of Knox's pressing financial considerations, implies his knowledge of the potential popularity of the topic with British audiences. Lonsdale characterizes Knox as bitter and disappointed as he took on the responsibilities of this tour. By all accounts, Knox should have been at the top of his profession and in a position of high esteem. However, the arguably unfair judgment of his centrality in the Burke and Hare scandal never allowed him to return to his level of professional success.[4] Although both biographers confirm that Knox's interest in race fully developed in his time in South Africa, one cannot help but wonder at the relationship between his personal disappointments and circumstances and the vituperative and erratic nature of the discourse of the published version of these lectures. In 1850, Knox published his lectures on race in book form as *The Races of Men: A Fragment.* Knox noted that he specifically tailored the form of the written piece in order to ensure wide access to his ideas: "After various trials I have decided on the following; it may not be the best: it is not systematic; it is not methodical; but it seems to me adapted to a very numerous class of readers, who, though highly educated, are yet not scientific" (*Races,* 7). Knox's decision to put readerly interest before system and methodology suggests his desire to appeal to a wide audience, rather than to contribute to the more limited debates of scientific research.

Scholars debate the influence of the more radical racial ideas on the general British population. Nancy Stepan argues that Knox had an immediate if peripheral effect on racial science (41). Bernard Lightman widens the scope of Knox's possible influence by asserting that "British scientists were deeply involved with general culture," and that "Victorian science and culture were inextricably linked in the eyes of the Victorians themselves, scientists and nonscientists alike" (3). At the other end of the spectrum, Lorimer argues against the idea of Knox and his protégé James Hunt having significant influence: "Knox and Hunt may share a fate common among many Victorian authors. The two racial determinists have had far more readers between 1963 and 1995 than between 1863 and 1895" ("Science and the Secularization," 215). Although he also argues that "From the 1830s through to the 1870s, Victorian racial discourse took place within a common context in which scientific papers presented at learned societies were indistinguishable from the books and articles seeking to address an educated public" ("Science and the Secularization," 213). However, as Gillian Beer suggests, the power of particular ideas is perhaps less related to the actual reading of them and more dependent on their general circulation within the culture: "Ideas pass more rapidly into the state of assumptions when they are *unread*. Reading is an essentially question-raising procedure" (6).[5] The question exists as to whether current scholarly interest derives from the benefit of hindsight on the genocidal horrors of the twentieth century and the related hypothesis that explanations for these events can be found, at least in part, in racial ideologies articulated by Knox and others, or if the radical racialists in fact did hold sway over their contemporaries. For the purposes of this study, Knox's strategic deployment of the site of race as a point of engagement with the pressing controversies of his day suggest a paradigm shift and elasticity of meaning in the term that carry over into our current ideas and struggles with race.

Knox's emotional and fragmented presentation contributes to the indeterminacy of "race" in his study. In the transformation from oral presentation to published book, Knox's writing seems haunted by the original form of the lecture. He digresses, for example, bringing himself back on topic with reference to his formal difficulties: "but I again forget that I am busy, or ought to be, with the introduction to my lectures, and not with the lectures themselves" (*Races*, 19). Lonsdale discussed the limitations of content and style in the published version of *The Races of Men*. He saw the work as "exceedingly characteristic of its author, his vices and his virtues. His discursiveness and repetitions are vastly too common; even the pictorial part, the woodcuts, are made to do duty over and over again, and for what purpose the said deponent knoweth not" (328). It is certainly true that some of the illustrations appear several times, sometimes without even a change in the captions. But this repetition points to Knox's formalist emphasis throughout the work. Three times in the text, he uses a picture of an English country house to describe the character of the Saxon and the Anglo-Saxon. The caption reads first, "A Saxon House; standing always apart, if possible, from all others" (*Races*, 40); then "An Anglo-Saxon house; it always, if possible, stands detached" (56); and, finally, "The Anglo-Saxon House" (136). For Knox, the house represents the basic character and temperament of the Saxon and Anglo-Saxon races, and he declines to represent them by the detailed and sometimes derogatory drawings used to describe other races within his study. Architecture representing home, family, social position, and domesticity stands synecdochically for the Anglo-Saxon race, the one most favored by Knox in his work.

If race is, at least in part, a discursively produced concept, then *Races of Men* suggests the anxiety and indeterminacy at the heart of the project within the very form itself. Knox's inability to create a coherent narrative, which only achieves minimal resolution in the turn to aesthetics at the end of the text, creates the open-ended presentation of race in particularly vivid form. This choice of narrative style can also be seen as influenced by the author's most frequent reading material. Both Rae and Lonsdale point out what appear to be Knox's most significant literary influences: "He used to say that two books were always to be found on the table of his dressing-room, the Bible and 'Don Quixote,' whom he used to style the *beau idéal* of an accomplished gentleman; their positions might be incongruous, and to some it would appear profane or immoral to associate them: he could not help it; there they were for his reading and instruction" (Lonsdale, 240). Both texts provide interesting points of structural comparison with the erratic, formal nature of *Races of Men*: one, a satiric reflection on the picaresque and chivalric forms that provides an ironic commentary on perceptions of reality and absurdity; the other, the fragmented and multivoiced text that provided the moral framework upon which Christian Victorian England rested. The tension in these texts between certainty and fragmentation mirror in many ways the formal challenges of *Races of Men.*

The work's fragmented structure reflects its fractured and ambiguous content regarding a variety of social issues. Exploring Knox's work brings us into the most vehement of racist conversations, and understanding the work helps us to understand the social tensions regarding race Victorian culture experienced at midcentury, by illustrating the associations and connections that informed the construction of these ideas. As Lonsdale's critique suggests, Knox's work employs a variety of formal and discursive methods, producing a narrative that is as much a work of historical and racial fiction as it is a work of science. Knox's rambling and imaginative style suggests the perspective of the anatomist, the experience of the colonist, and the creator of images feeding Britain's colonial imagination. The inconsistencies, ambiguities, and contradictions contained within the argument often sound like a madman's rantings, then moderate to a humanitarian plea against colonialism, and finally revert to the clinical tone of a scientist. By tracing a path through his racial theories, we begin to see how Knox came to the conclusion that formal distinctions are of central importance in the study of races and communities. True to Victorian racial discourse, however, this path is often a meandering journey through a variety of topics, bringing together disparate ideas and opinions within the organizing signifier "race."

## Progress, Politics, and Imperial Policy

Knox considered his study a variation of the standard historical text. Rather than offering history as the narrative of nations and great events, Knox saw history as the delineation of the individual capacities and limitations found in each of the static, permanent racial groups of the world. As Knox explains on the first page of the work, he uses the descriptive term "fragment" for this reason: "I disclaim all pretensions of attempting a complete history of mankind, even from the single point of view from which I contemplate Human history. No materials exist for such a history" (1). Thus, the author makes clear from the work's opening page that race and history are interdependent terms, and that the history of race implies the history of humanity. However, by changing the paradigm within which history is framed, Knox finds himself without the data to complete what he calls a "complete" history, thus the term "fragment" in the title. Knox organized his study by racial categories, and he includes two chapters that outline general points about physiological laws and dominance.

Early in the work, Knox tries to answer a number of methodological questions suggested by his shift in historical perspective. According to Knox's new historical paradigm, "Race is everything: literature, science, art—in a word, civilization, depends on it" (*Races*, v). The way that individual distinctions among different racial groups should be explored is by "[p]hysical structure" (1), an understandable methodology for a skilled anatomist. Distinctions among racial groups are absolute, static and permanent: "Men are of various Races; call them Species, if you will; call them permanent Varieties; it matters not. The fact, the simple fact, remains just as it was: men are of different races" (2). And owing to this permanent distinction, racial categories are the fixed lens through which Knox tries to understand the history of civilization. Race is the great driving force behind group activities, structures, and dynamics: "in human history race is everything" (2).

Knox's doctrine leads predictably to some strongly offensive statements about particular races.[6] He specifically identifies differences among the races in a moralistic and defamatory manner, justified by what he believes is an inherent biological determinism. Races can never permanently blend, because the primary races are fixed. Mulatto people will eventually revert to one of the "dominant" racial types in their genetic makeup.[7] According to Knox, racial relations are generally antagonistic. He argues that the Saxon, Celtic, and Sarmatian races are particularly prone to the destruction of races other than themselves: "What a field of extermination lies before the Saxon[,] Celtic[,] and Sarmatian races!" (229). Although in Knox's schema races are fixed by their nature, they are also organic entities with a birth, maturity, and eventual extinction. Many of the darker-skinned races are not undeveloped, he argues, but are actually overdeveloped and moving toward extinction: "Extinction of the race—sure extinction—it is not even denied" (229–30). In discussion of this point, Knox can be particularly crass, as when he focuses on two particular African races: "Have we done with the Hottentots and Bosjeman race? I suppose so: they will soon form merely natural curiosities; already there is the skin of one stuffed in England; another in Paris if I mistake not. . . . They are shrewd, and show powers of mimicry—acquire language readily, but never can be civilized. That I think quite hopeless" (238–39). That he speaks of stuffed people as easily as he would of animals in a natural history exhibit cannot fail to bring up visions of Sara(h) Ba(a)rtman(n)'s dismembered and dissected body.

But within his discussion of African people lies a contradiction between his violent criticism of their nature and hints of residual tenderness in his sense of how Europeans have warped their "childlike" manners. In his discussion of the effect of European contact on the "Caffre," for example, he says that "they had neither ships nor boats, nor any human arts; properly speaking, they were mere savages, but at that time mild and, to a certain extent, trustworthy; now, by coming into contact with Europeans, they have become treacherous, bloody, and thoroughly savage" (240–41).

Although Knox argues that the "Caffre" are certainly inferior to the European races, his belief that the Caffre's childlike innocence has been ruined by the act of domination is curiously, if problematically, sympathetic. In another passage, Knox argues that the British would cheer if American slaves rose up and threw off their chains: "A million of slaveholders cut off in cold blood tomorrow would call forth no tear of sympathy in Europe: 'Bravo!' we should say; 'the slave has risen and burst his chains—he deserves to be free'" (245). This passage suggests that if a race can rise in status within the culture, it would earn Knox's esteem and modify slightly his claims about the race's characteristics. This argument seemingly places his pre-evolutionary claims of racial fixity at odds with an apparent flexibility regarding racial potential. Additionally, the argument conveys a conflicted view of the relationship between colonizers and colonized. Although relationships of domination and submission between races are "natural" in Knox's presentation, a colonized race could earn the respect of the dominating race only by overthrowing the subjugating force.

Feeding the fears outlined in the previous chapter about the ways in which the Haitian Revolution signified in midcentury English culture, Knox argues that the "Negro" could perhaps threaten the European races because of his ability to function and thrive in environments where white races cannot: "If there be a dark race destined to contend with the fair races of men for a portion of the earth, given to man as an inheritance, it is the Negro. The tropical regions of the earth seem peculiarly to belong to him; his energy is considerable: aided by a tropical sun, he repels the white invader. From St. Domingo he drove out the Celt; from Jamaica he will expel the Saxon; and the expulsion of the Lusitanian from Brazil, by the Negro, is merely an affair of time" (456).

It would appear from these examples that, for various environmental reasons, the "Negro" race has at least an opportunity to achieve a superior position among the races of the world. Knox also has a somewhat detached, uninvested view of the dark-skinned races' potential to succeed. He directly states that "the European has, in my opinion, erred in despising the Negro, who seems to me of a race of occasionally great energy"

(286). One could almost argue that a kind of cautious moderation surfaces in the author's extreme views.

In other passages, however, Knox's potential leniency toward other races, especially the "Negro" race, deteriorates into fits of rage and ranting, displaying, I argue, an irrationality and inconsistency evident at the heart of racial paradigms in general. Belittling the sincerity of English people dedicated to humanitarian causes, he says the following: "What an innate hatred the Saxon has for [the 'Negro'], and how I have laughed at the mock philanthropy of England!" (243). Turning then to the victory of the blacks in the Haitian Revolution directly, he rationalizes the outcome of the conflict in ways quite different from Martineau. Knox strongly argues for white superiority: "Already they defeated France; but, after all, was it not the climate? for that any body of dark men in this world will ever fight successfully a French army of twenty thousand men I never shall believe. With one thousand white men all the blacks of St. Domingo could be defeated in a single action. This is my opinion of the dark races" (243–44).

As I have already noted in my discussion of *The Hour and the Man*, the English, along with the French, did in fact play a large part in the Haitian conflict, thus making this argument appear pure posturing on Knox's part. However the issue further complicates the contradiction between this quotation and the assertion discussed earlier, in which he suggests that the "Negro" race could potentially overthrow the white race because of environment. Knox vacillates among varying levels of sympathy for African races. Although he validates the influence of climate on relations among the races, his position also appears guided by his critical attitudes regarding the colonial project, and his own sense of race loyalty.

## Institutionalizing the Science of Race

Although most often summarily dismissed as a fanatical racist, in "The 'Moral Anatomy' of Robert Knox," Evelleen Richards argues that Knox's work needs to be read in light of his complex position as social determinist, political radical, and, after Burke and Hare, institutional outsider. Knox was greatly influenced by the events of the French Revolution in his youth, and, as we have seen, had an open contempt for many of the policies of imperial domination. Nonetheless, Knox remained grounded in his static racial taxonomy: "In spite of the Jacobin origins of his radicalism, Knox did not subscribe to an Enlightenment egalitarianism and environmentalism. He was uncompromisingly a man of the nineteenth century in his insistence on the universality and inevitability of natural law, and a rigid determinist in his views on social organization and the essential inequality of humanity, which from an early period he linked to race and grounded in materialism" (386).

We begin to understand Knox's seemingly contradictory attitudes by placing his study within the context of humanitarian and scientific explorations of race. The study of race over the first half of the nineteenth century moved from a more humanitarian stance, influenced by the anti-slave trade and abolitionist movements, to a split within the scientific population dividing a less influential humanitarian branch from a more flamboyant and derogatory anthropological vein. Knox was a key figure in the break between these two factions, influencing the move away from humanitarianism.

The seeds of early anthropological exploration were embedded within the early humanitarian organizations, however. An early group formed in 1837 to "civilize," Christianize, and, to a certain extent, monitor the treatment of colonized populations was the Aborigines Protection Society (APS) (Stocking, *Victorian Anthropology*, 242–44).[8] Although the main impulse of the organization was humanitarian concern for the welfare of colonized peoples, "some of its central activities were," Stocking suggests, "at least in a broad sense, 'anthropological'" ("'What's in a Name?'" 370). This tension between the humanitarian and anthropological impulses in this early organization became increasingly polarized over the next thirty years, splintering this early organization into several different groups before it was brought back together in the later nineteenth century Anthropological Institute.

Motivated by a desire to pursue the "scientific impulse" rather than "humanitarian" causes, and exacerbated by "the general waxing and waning of the Society's fortunes," a movement of scientifically oriented members began to push the organization toward a more dispassionate analysis of other races (Stocking, "'What's in a Name?'" 371). In 1842 "the printed statement of the object of the Society was changed: rather than 'protecting the defenceless', it would 'record the[ir] history', and a resolution was passed to the effect that the best way to help aboriginals was to study them" (371). The more religiously inspired benevolence of the APS was slowly eclipsed by the drive for scientific research, though the organization still retained the illusion of humanitarian emphasis. Keeping in mind Johannes Fabian's assertion that "there is no knowledge of the Other which is not also a temporal, historical, a political act" (1), we can understand this institutional switch in emphasis as representing a modified attitude towards aboriginals from individuals requiring care (understanding the fraught meanings this term can contain in a colonial relationship) to objects requiring study. This split in the APS was formalized in late 1843 and 1844 with the founding of the Ethnological Society of London (Lorimer, "Race, Science, and Culture," 25; Stocking, "'What's in a Name?'" 372). Stocking argues that although "those who entered the ESL had decided it was a good idea to separate humanitarian purpose and ethnological research" ("'What's in a Name?'", 372), the organization retained the Biblical roots that inspired a belief in monogenesis, or a unitary source for all human peoples on the planet.

Lorimer suggests that monogenesis, represented most prominently by the work of James C. Prichard, first gained authority early in the nineteenth century because it fit well with humanitarian attitudes toward race and racial relations (*Colour, Class and the Victorians,* 134). Rather than challenge the commonality of ancestry, Stocking argues that ethnology's primary goal "was in effect to document that unity, to fill the gap between the dispersion of the tribes of man over the earth and the first historical records of each present nation, and in doing so to tie all men together into a single ethnological family tree" ("'What's in a Name?'" 372). In early scientific explorations of race, the impulse to keep all the planet's peoples organically connected remained intact. The fracturing influence of later anthropological "scientists" was yet to be felt. Here again we see the tension between fragmentation and unity evident in the very structure of Knox's work. The unifying impulse, however, began to lose favor in the mid-nineteenth century, and was replaced by a more widespread, if still by a minority, embracing of the theory of polygenesis (Stepan, 3). Proponents of this theory argued that the different races have different origins, that they remain different even in the face of racial mixing, and that the Biblical genesis story is about the origin of white cultures rather than all the races of the planet. During the early 1850s, a group of young anthropological scholars supporting polygenesis reinvigorated the diminishing popularity of the Ethnological Society. This group included Robert Knox who, Stocking says, "after being blackballed in 1855—was made an honorary fellow in 1858" (*Victorian Anthropology,* 246). The incorporation of Knox into the organization in such a celebratory manner suggests the radically modified trajectory of the organization's attitudes toward their scientific objects. However, Stocking's study of the transition suggests that the "incorporation of these newer trends . . . was not accomplished without friction between the Society's older Quaker humanitarian element and the racialist current represented by several of the younger members" (247).

The most prominent of these young anthropologists was the radical racialist James Hunt, who claimed Knox as a significant influence on his thinking (247). Richards argues that it was James Hunt, founder of the radical and openly racist Anthropological Society, who brought Knox's ideas into institutional relevance (386).

Looking at the ideological trends fueling these movements within the ethnological and anthropological communities, we begin to see the truth of Lorimer's observation that during this period, "racism grew in power, in sophistication and in intensity" ("Race, Science and Culture," 32). By 1850 the protectionist impulse toward indigenous races had waned, and what Lorimer calls a "revived polygenesis," represented in large part by the work of Knox, took its place (Colour, Class and the Victorians, 136–37). Tim Barringer suggests that the idea of the "savage as a natural man" was slowly replaced by "the idea that savagery resulted from a process of degeneration from a state of primal grace" (37). Lorimer's work supports this assertion by arguing that the "sentimental caricature" made popular in abolitionist rhetoric was replaced by "a more derogatory stereotype of the Negro" (Colour, Class and the Victorians, 12). This movement was not limited to English culture, but was a "general phenomenon within Europe" (206). Key to the transition was a move toward biologically rooted explanations of racial difference. Environmental and theological explanations of racial differences were increasingly challenged by static biological paradigms such as that put forth by Knox (Stepan, 4). Knox's lecture series and publication of The Races of Men occurred just before the general proliferation of a belief in polygenesis, and was often invoked as an inspirational text, especially by Hunt (Stocking, "'What's in a Name?'" 374).

The actual break between the two factions of the Ethnological Society occurred over the admission of women to its scientific discussions.[9] In 1863 Hunt broke from the organization to form the Anthropological Society of London (Lorimer, "Race, Science and Culture," 25–26; Stocking, "'What's in a Name?'" 376; Lorimer, Colour, Class and the Victorians, 138). The gender component of this shift usefully brings together scientific research, race, and the question of women's place in mid-Victorian culture. Although they had been prominent members of the abolitionist movement earlier in the century, women were increasingly excluded when changes funneled interest from humanitarian concern for other races toward scientific study. The Anthropological Society excluded women completely; the Ethnological Society excluded women from some discussions but not all; and the Aborigines Protection Society, which retained the humanitarian focus through these changes, had a membership that was roughly 40% female. The participation of women appears to have been confined to organizations that had an ostensibly humanitarian or religious emphasis, whereas science remained the exclusive preserve of men (Stocking, *Victorian Anthropology,* 256; Richards, "Huxley and Woman's Place in Science: The 'Woman Question' and the Control of Victorian Anthropology").

Scholars disagree about how strongly the Anthropological Society influenced the British public's racial attitudes. Lorimer argues that scientific racism was "symptomatic of the changing values within English society," but that the "anthropologicals" "attracted only a limited following, failed to meet the tests of mid-Victorian science, and were not a significant cause of the change in racial attitudes" (*Colour, Class and the Victorians,* 204).[10] He suggests instead that a constellation of issues—including strong ethnocentrism, scientific and philosophical doctrine, and a generally hierarchical view of social structure—paved the way for a view of the races that put English men in a comfortable place of racial and gender superiority (*Colour, Class and the Victorians,* 133).

Eric Hobsbawm addresses the fundamental contradiction existing between hierarchical capitalist social structures and Enlightenment egalitarian ideals that arguably formed the root of inconsistencies in contemporary racial thinking. Racism, Hobsbawm argues,

> [a]part from its convenience as a legitimation of the rule of white over coloured, rich over poor . . . is perhaps best explained as a mechanism by means of which a fundamentally inegalitarian society based upon a fundamentally egalitarian ideology rationalized its inequalities, and attempted to justify and defend those privileges which the democracy implicit in its institutions must inevitably challenge. Liberalism had no logical defense against equality and democracy, so the illogical barrier of race was erected: science itself, liberalism's trump card, could prove that men were *not* equal. (268)

This argument places the rise of scientific racism in the context of a class bound society in which social roles were understood in terms of vertical relationships of economics, lineage, and profession. Anthropology partly served this social stratification by balancing the leveling forces of democracy and capitalism, providing a justification and rationalization for keeping other races in a subservient position.

According to Lorimer, the shift toward a more racist culture was most evident in the way African and West Indian individuals began to lose the opportunity to achieve the status of "gentleman" in British culture. The "racial theorizing" of the "anthropologicals," he argues, "did not have much bearing upon mid-Victorian behaviour. The experience of eminent black abolitionists shows that the mid-Victorians did not treat all blacks alike." In social interactions in mid-Victorian England, it was "still bad manners to object to the colour of a black gentleman" (*Colour, Class and the Victorians*, 53). The change came, Lorimer argues, when the white population began to believe that blacks could only "perform labouring tasks and never approach gentlemanly status" (60). Thus,

> respectable Victorians simply applied to all men with black skins the same judgments, manner, and bearing that they adopted toward their social inferiors within English society. When this association between African descent and lowly social status became more firmly fixed, and was added to the latent suspicions and aversions produced by xenophobia and ethnocentrism, racial attitudes became more rigid and emotive in character, and a new inflexibility and contempt characterized English attitudes to the Negro. (60)

Therefore, according to Lorimer, it was the meanings attached to class, rather than to race, that contributed most significantly to the increase of contemptuous attitudes toward the black races as the nineteenth century progressed. I argue that there was a relationship among science, class, and race that produced an environment that curbed the earlier humanitarian emphasis on liberty and opportunity and replaced it with a picture of static and inferior darker-skinned races that justified withdrawing economic, social, and professional opportunities. Although I certainly agree with Lorimer that class held a significant role in this transition, I argue that scientific racism, especially in light of Knox's popular lecture tour, was certainly an influential part of the discursive mix circulating at the time.

Of central importance throughout this discussion is the flexibility of race to accommodate the particular social changes taking place within the culture. Racism was a strategy by which to manage the social and ideological contradictions at the heart of English culture. It justified repressive action in a culture motivated by Christian and Enlightenment ideologies. In addition, racial and class distinctions overlapped in an attempt to shore up social structures that were cracking under the influence of agitation by working-class and women's groups. Although anthropological discourse may have exerted limited influence on the culture at large, Knox and the doctrine of physical anthropology were certainly crucial factors (Stocking,

*Victorian Anthropology,* 65). In a society in which the need for a clear delineation of class structures was an increasing source of anxiety, and imperialist and nationalist ideas gained strength, "educated men," Lorimer argues,
"found the ideas of the scientific racists attractive." Race and physical determinism were remarkably close to the idea of superior aristocratic blood,
and for a segment of the population "lacking an aristocratic lineage, and yet
seeking the trappings of gentility, pride of race formed one substitute"
(*Colour, Class and the Victorians,* 159). Racism buttressed historically established social power. Racial background provided the rising middle-class,
educated Englishman his opportunity to claim hereditary superiority.

This overlap between hereditary power structures and biological determinism is central to Knox's argument. Stocking characterizes Knox's *The
Races of Men* as "hereditarian racial doctrine in an extreme form"
(*Victorian Anthropology,* 64). "With me," Knox writes, "race, or hereditary
descent, is everything; it stamps the man" (*Races,* 6). Knox finds it curious
that so many in the population do not acknowledge the crucial importance
of race in the development of social hierarchies:

> the statesman, the historian, the theologian, the universalist, and the mere
> scholar, either attached no special meaning to the term, for reasons best
> known to themselves; or refused to follow out the principle to its conse-
> quences; or ascribed the moral difference in the races of men to fanciful
> causes, such as education, religion, climate, &c.—and their physical dis-
> tinctions sometimes to the same haphazard influences—sometimes to cli-
> mate alone—sometimes to climate aided by a mysterious law. (7–8)

Knox denies the importance of many traditional ethnological explanations
for the distinctive characteristics of different races, such as geographical
location, climate, education, social position, and religion. Although Knox
argues that each of these issues had an impact on racial development and
historical progression, the basic and immovable nature of racial identity
remains permanent, and has been so from the point of creation. Social
stratification is rooted in biology. Race, increasingly in Victorian culture, is
not an influence that can be overcome.

## The Role of Form: Political, Biological, and Fictional

For Knox, monogenesis and humanitarianism divert the public from a
true understanding of the central importance of race in history and social

organization. Taking on the doctrine of monogenesis directly, Knox asserts that "the illustrious Prichard, with the best intentions in the world, has succeeded in misdirecting the English mind as to all the great questions of race" (*Races*, 23). The result of the inaccurate and misleading doctrine is that it educates the English subject to see racial distinctions as an element of colonial geography rather than as a part of the everyday lives of citizens in the metropolis:

> As a consequence of its misdirection, on the mere mention of the word race, the popular mind flies off to Tasmania, the polar circle, or the land of the Hottentot. Englishmen cannot be made to believe, can scarcely be made to comprehend, that races of men, differing as widely from each other as races can possibly do, inhabit, not merely continental Europe, but portions of Great Britain and Ireland. And next to the difficulty of getting this great fact admitted to be one, has been an unwillingness to admit the full importance of *race*, militating as it does against the thousand-and-one prejudices of the so-called civilized state of man; opposed as it is to the Utopian views based on education, religion, government. (23–24, original italics)

Knox breaks down the distinctive nature of the colonizer/colonized relationship in English culture, with its profoundly geographical component represented in the establishment of limited freedom for slaves while on English soil in the late eighteenth century. Instead, Knox suggests that racial difference manifests itself in the streets of England by focusing not only on the darker-skinned races of the colonial context, but also on the racial distinctions evident within England, Wales, and Scotland.[11] Robert J. C. Young notes that Knox, with a colleague, "liked to analyse racial types" while walking "about the streets of Paris or London" (76). Thus, Knox uses the more expansive definition of race, frequently evident in the nineteenth-century use of the term to impart hereditary relationships, to describe not only the colonial subject, but also the everyday English citizen. Just as class was part of the English construction of the "Negro," according to Lorimer, Knox wanted to make race a broader part of the construction of the Englishman. For Knox, race is the crucial element in distinguishing among the hierarchically defined social groups composing the general English population.

Moving into larger social groupings, Knox further expands his discussion of race by confronting what he regards as the problem of nationalism. The overlap of conceptions of race and understandings of nationalism was critical in the mid-nineteenth century. Definitions in Victorian culture about what constituted a national body, what defined citizenship within a particular nation, and what characterized the relationships among different nations, all became vital concerns. Tensions among nationalities, according to David Wetzel, were the result of shifting definitions for the nation-state's cohesive force: "Previously theoreticians had invoked 'language' or 'collective conscience' as the basis of national claims. In the 1850s these fell increasingly by the wayside. 'Race' took their place" (14).[12] Read in the light of Lorimer's discussion of the diminishing opportunities for black citizens to achieve the status of gentlemen in England, social and national definitions arguably began to display a deterministic certitude that excluded those who did not fit the racial criteria, regardless of individual ability.

Knox found in the 1848 revolutions clear justification for his argument that mid-Victorians needed to transform the paradigm through which they viewed social interaction to one exclusively based on race.[13] Describing the 1848 revolutions as the "war of race against race, which has convulsed Europe during the last two years" (*Races*, 16–17), Knox argues that his work creates an outline of the history of what has been considered the nation-state by "viewing them, not as *nations,* but as *races*" (76, original italics). He notes that when he first offered these ideas five years previously, the "opinions they contained were opposed to all the received opinions of the day. The world was so *national,* and *race* had been so utterly forgotten, that for at least two years after delivering my first course of lectures at Newcastle I had the whole question to myself" (76, original italics). But in the space between the lecture tour and the publication of the book, "the press, even in insular England, has been, most reluctantly I believe, forced to take it up; to make admissions which I never supposed could have been wrung from them; to confess it to be possible that man, after all, may be subject to some physiological laws hitherto not well understood; that *race,* as well as 'democracy,' or socialism, or bands of peripatetic demagogues, or evil spirits, may have had something to do with the history of nations, and more especially with the last revolutions in Europe" (76–77, original italics)."[14]

*The Races of Men* is a work caught in an ideological struggle between the construction of the nation state as a geographically and linguistically determined entity, and one where the only significant defining factor for a particular population is its race.[15] And changing attitudes in the reception of Knox's ideas suggest a culture increasingly receptive to the more biologically deterministic way of understanding current events.

Knox vigorously criticized the structure of the nation-state because he believed that it was built on the false foundation of culture rather than on race. Margot Finn argues that nationalism is a discursive strategy that "first gained currency in the spiritual and institutional upheaval of the Protestant Reformation" (15). Nationalism gained strength as a concept in the late eighteenth century for three reasons: "the Enlightenment revolution of intellect, the industrial revolution of the economy, and the French revolution of 1789" (Finn, 23). Knox argues that this late-eighteenth century nationalist fervor was a misguided way to organize populations into functioning administrative units; it was a failed political strategy. Nationalism helped control populations by alluding to fictional, grandiose roots: "it is and always has been the practice of every race and nation, whose intellectual faculties were sufficiently elevated, to connect their history with the origin of all time, and, under one denomination or another, to identify themselves with the great creative Power" (*Races*, 386). Nations, according to Knox, achieve preeminent status as the determining structure of social interactions because they are constructed as historically destined for greatness. Moving away from a geographically and historically determined nation to a racially determined, transtemporal grouping, Knox contradicts the 1850s idea of the nation by posing a series of questions: "Forget for a time the word *nation,* and ask yourselves whence come the people composing any ancient assemblage called a nation, a state, a republic, a monarchy, an empire? Ask yourselves this plain question, are they indigenous to the soil, or have they migrated from somewhere else? and if so, have they altered in structure, in character?" (*Races,* 10, original italics). This issue of geography ties in with one of Knox's most persistent criticisms of the national system, the idea of passports and their incompatibility with human liberty (374). Thus, nations emerge against the current of nature, and work against the appropriate path of human survival and organic progression that defined the lifespan of a certain race of people. They are discursive and administrative constructs working against the true—that is, "natural"—order of things, thus they often revert to force to retain their cohesion.

Knox argues that the 1848 revolutions resulted from the disruptive friction of different races trying to form racially mixed nation-states. Knox's biographer Lonsdale asserts that Knox believed that peace "prevailed in a community consisting of one race only, and there public sentiment was respected" (319). For this reason, "empires like Austria, composed of many and diverse ethnological elements . . . must in the course of time go apart, or succumb to greater and more lasting disintegrations" (319). As Knox puts it, "Woe to the empire or nation composed of divers elements, of different races, and discordant principles!" (*Races,* 292). The reason that collections of races cannot form stable national units is that different races apparently have different "natural" propensities for social cohesion: "Each race has its own form of civilization, as it has its own language and arts; I would almost venture to say, science," and so the structure of each society provides "the result and test of the qualities of every race" (57). Lonsdale asserts that Knox "looked upon the homogeneity of Race as the only reliable basis of a well-founded nationality" (290). Knox's most pervasive example is "Hayti" because in that nation's development, an African race tried to take on the social structures of a European country. "Look at Hayti" Knox suggests, "with a deepening colour vanishes civilization, the arts of peace, science, literature, abstract justice" (*Races,* 107). The culture brought to the island by the French, Knox argues, disappeared with the white inhabitants, in much the same way as the mixed-race individual apparently reverts to one race with the passage of time. Social organizations have the same organic components as biologically based racial distinctions.

Knox's references to other points of view help us to understand the discursive climate in which he advanced these ideas. He knew his readers would not be entirely receptive to his view of nationalism: "that human character, individual or national, is traceable solely to the nature of that race to which the individual or nation belongs, is a statement which I know must meet with the severest opposition" (*Races,* v). But, he asserts directly that "*nationalities,* however strong, could never in the long run overcome the tendencies of race" (317, original italics). Because the construction of the nation-state works against the natural force of race, governments apparently must resort to drastic measures in order to maintain their boundaries: "Empires, monarchies, nations, are human contrivances; often held together by fraud and violence" (4). The figure for which Knox had the most contempt is the statesman: "to mystify, to job, to rob, to plunder. It is a portion of the organized hypocrisy which marks the statesman wherever he exists" (309). Therefore, claims that nationalism is the way to liberate people leads a population down the road to oppression because, Knox argues, a nation unnaturally yokes together unsuitable races under one governmental entity, thus requiring force to establish unity.[16]

Even if humans were separated into homogenous racial units, however, racial conflict apparently is inevitable. The author argues that the predictability of this animosity is "wonderful" because it is universal: "There is, there can be, nothing more wonderful in human history than this dislike of race to race: always known and admitted to exist, it has only of late assumed a threatening shape" (*Races*, 332–33). This mutual dislike is "innate" (89), not modifiable by social or political policies, and perhaps relates to what Knox identifies as "man's" natural ability to destroy. "Man's gift is to destroy, not to create" (464–65); and though we have already seen Knox argue that men cannot create anything new, Knox takes this idea a step further here to say that man tries to eradicate what is in front of him. Yet although man tries to destroy everything, ultimately he is unsuccessful in his goal: "he has not yet succeeded in destroying all nature's works, although he labours hard to effect this" (41). The colonial enterprise, then, is just the result of the natural impulses that drive men toward destruction.[17]

In fact, for Knox the need for alignment between political structure and racial characteristics is what made the dynamics of colonial domination detestable. "When the race attempts the civilization of another," he argues, "the whole affair becomes a ludicrous farce, and even grave men laugh at it" (*Races*, 452). Again, he refers to Haiti as an example of the folly of the enterprise, because the new black government took an emperor for its leader. Instead, "each race must act for itself, and work out its own destiny; display its own tendencies; be the maker of its own fortunes, be they good or evil. A foreign civilization they cannot adopt; borrow they may, and cunningly adapt, calling it national, native; but the imposture, like all impostures, becomes manifest in time" (452).

When a race acquires an inappropriate social structure as its own, the interesting result for Knox is that the enterprise takes on a fictional quality. The process becomes a performance that lacks genuine reality: "The whole is a farce when acted in Hayti; a melodrame with tragic episodes when Gaul is the stage; and so it is ever with the most skilful and able of impostors, that is, of imitators; sooner or later the trick comes out" (*Races*, 453). Knox creates an elaborate drama in which races interact in an eternal crisis enacted by their racial origins; this drama is determined entirely by race. The line between racial fiction and valid racial reality, therefore, becomes the appropriateness of the cultural form adopted by the group. The criteria for discerning the line between fiction and validity in Knox, however, are not properly established.

Therefore, in this enactment of global racial dynamics, Knox occupies the ambiguous position of both an advocate for the oppressed colonial "other" and a committed racist. When he observes that the statesman acts with cold assurance as he carries out his diplomatic "act of appropriation," Knox suggests that it is a method "quite unparalleled in the history of aggressions" (*Races*, 222). Using the example of the acquisition of New

Zealand, he argues that "a slip of parchment signed officially is issued from that den of all abuses, the office of the Colonial Secretary, declaring New Zealand to be a colony of Britain, with all its dependencies, lands, fisheries, mines, inhabitants" (222). He mocks language, suggesting that the "aborigines are to be protected!" (222–23). And he suggests that "if the Crown will let them alone, they can protect themselves; but this would not suit the wolf who took care of the sheep" (223). Instead, the state functioned as caretakers for those they wished to dominate, and Knox makes it very clear that he views this policy as "organized hypocrisy . . . the aborigines are not declared Britons; they are merely to be protected!" (223). The colonial administration does not bring those conquered into national citizenship; it acts as a caretaker, a role that masks the true dynamic of oppression.[18]

In Knox's critique of the nineteenth-century reverence for progress, however, the author seems to lose his sympathy for the victims of colonial oppression. Knox appears decisive in his views about progress when he says, "no greater error was ever committed than that of supposing that *the mass* of men change or progress" (*Races*, 405–6, original italics). However, the group included in this statement is narrowly restricted to the non-European races, because he suggests that the reader "look all over the globe, it is always the same; the dark races stand still, the fair progress" (222). Further complicating the issue, he argues in another section that "neither nations nor individuals stand still; onward they must go, or retrograde: there is no middle course; no fixity, no finality, in that sense" (262). Although the author seems vehemently against the idea of progress, as with his attitude towards colonialism, a contradiction appears. Knox both criticizes progress as an ideology he attributes to a British disregard for the real forces shaping human existence, and he makes clear that in the hierarchy of races, lighter-skinned people are superior because they strive and reach beyond the point at which they stand.

Knox's emphasis on history, rather than progress, makes clear that the main concept at work is physical determinism. As we saw earlier, distinct races and species do not vary from the point of their origin: "so far back as history goes, the species of animals as we call them have not changed; the races of men have been absolutely the same" (*Races*, 36). History becomes predictable and decipherable by reference to the static nature of living creatures. This predictability becomes important in Knox's references to art. Nationhood and history overlap in Knox's reflection on the relationship of the arts to social development: "Human history cannot be a mere chapter of accidents. The fate of nations cannot always be regulated by chance; its literature, science, art, wealth, religion, language, laws, and morals, cannot surely be the result of mere accidental circumstances" (5–6). Race is brought into the equation as the baseline structure of history because it is the force of permanence in human interactions. For Knox, race seemed to be the immovable force that gives structure and reason to the study of human social and physical natures. History—once the emphasis shifts from politics and nations toward physical determinism, toward what Knox called "the physiological history of man" (45)—provides a record of the essential natures of each of the differing human races.

For Knox, therefore, conventional history "offers us no guide, no data, for the composition of a systematic work on man; chronologies are mere fables" (*Races,* 150). The lens through which conventional history views human events offers a tainted perspective. Knox is particularly hard on English travelers who explore other cultures and governments. Rather than providing a resource for those like himself who wish to study the races, he says that travel writers "are so occupied with their personal adventures, and French with political intrigue, that there is no getting a single new or valuable fact from their silly books" (179). This critique becomes interesting in light of the reality that many Victorians did, in fact, derive their understandings of different races from this material. As Christine Bolt argues, misconceptions about race were related to a lack of direct contact between the races, because people found their information about other populations through biased and sensationalized narratives (5–6). Knox wanted data from these studies that would contribute to his theory that "the history of man is included in the history of the organic world. He is of this world; he did not create it, he creates nothing; you cannot separate his history from the organic world" (*Races,* 11). History, then, becomes an organic process of birth, achievement, and decay, in which all human, natural, cultural, and social forms participate. It seems a logical conclusion for an anatomist that structure is the window through which the answers to human history and development could be understood. What Knox called "the unity of organization" suggests that man is "connected with all life— past, present, and to come" (11). But a slight difference occurs in distinguishing animal history from human history, for "animals have but one history, their zoological; man has two, the zoological and the intellectual. The latter must ever, to a certain extent, be regulated by the former" (11–12). In Knox's formulation, physical and structural elements determined the intellectual or artistic nature of a race.

The unifying concept in Knox's emphasis on physical structure is the idea of "transcendental anatomy." Ironically, he replaces the idea of a unitary creation of all human races with the idea of the connectedness of all living creatures' anatomical structures within the polygenesis framework. Transcendental anatomy seeks "to explain in a connected chain the phenomena of the living material world; to connect the history of living plants and animals with those which now lie entombed in the strata of the crust of the globe; to explain the mysterious metamorphoses which occur in the growth of animals and plants from their embryonic state to their maturity of growth and final decay; to trace a plan of creation, and to guess at that plan—these are the objects of transcendental anatomy" (*Races*, 167).

Blending history, geography, anatomy, and embryology, Knox suggests that the basic anatomical structure of all animals and humans is the same, and that they differ in the point where they achieve developmental maturity. Therefore, Knox places their limitations or abilities on a hierarchical structure of physical development. The hierarchy of structures is transcendental, Knox argues, because it never changes, and it has been the way that it is from the point of creation. Variations within a species "proceed only to a certain length—they are constantly checked by two laws, the laws maintaining *species as they exist*," which are "the tendency to reproduce the specific form instead of the variety" and the "non-viability or non-reproduction, that is extinction." This stability is what "checks deformations of all kinds" (*Races*, 102, original italics). Race, biology, and anatomy are constant and unmodifiable attributes of the human animal.

Progress, then, takes place along a hierarchy of structures visible in the development of the embryo. Within the embryo, there appear to be an infinite number of structural plateaus at which each of the forms of life takes its place:

> We discover structures in the embryo . . . that the individual is in fact passing through a series of metamorphoses, expressed briefly by the term development; passing through forms which represent the permanent forms of other adult beings belonging to the organic world, not human, but bestial; of whom some belong to the existing world, whilst others may represent forms which once existed, but are now extinct; or, finally, forms which may be destined some day to appear, running their destined course, then to perish as their predecessors. Thus in the embryonic changes or metamorphoses of man and other animals, are shadowed forth, more or less completely, all other organic forms. (*Races*, 29)

Progress is the action of passing through each of the developmental stages of embryonic growth. The embryo becomes a window into all the forms of life—past, present, and future—that exist at any time. This transtemporal vortex explodes the idea that beings develop or change, because at each point in the developmental ladder a particularized and individual creation comes into existence, and then remains there forever.[19] The force that determines the forms—or determines when the form will come into existence—is not identified.

In Knox's text, what results is a tension between the forces of unity and the forces of particularity. All living things share the same collection of structural qualities, and have throughout all time (*Races*, 30). Particularity exists in the individual manifestations of these structures, which differentiate species and races. However, Knox removes darker-skinned races from this universal grouping when he denies the African races any history:

> The past history of the Negro, of the Caffre, of the Hottentot, and of the Bosjeman, is simply a blank—St. Domingo forming but an episode. Can the black races become civilized? I should say not: their future history, then, must resemble the past. The Saxon race will never tolerate them— never amalgamate—never be at peace. (244)

History, then, begins to lose clarity in Knox's writing, as do many of his principles, because he uses it in contradictory ways. We just saw that Knox locates history in the embryo, which holds the key to all life. But the African races do not have a history, except in a momentary blip, when the race achieved autonomy in Haiti by winning independence from France, an action that Knox alternately celebrates and denies ever occurred. And even if the distinction of the races implies a different developmental scale in their separate embryonic growth processes, the African race would apparently still have its own particular history. Civilization is the litmus test for the ability of a race to actually achieve a history—certainly a common nineteenth-century belief—and civilization resulted from contact with the lighter-skinned races. When the French (as well as the British and the Americans) withdrew from Haiti, they took civilization and history with them. Along with the white men goes history and civility. Therefore, when Knox argues that all beings are connected, the African races appear to hold a liminal position on his ontological scale.

Knox, however, does not limit himself to the colonial context in his discussions of race, nationhood, progress, and history. As noted earlier, his scientific gaze focuses as much on the metropolis as on the colonial context, which brings Knox's views to bear on not only the colonial site, but also the domestic site, and, by extension, on women (Young, 75). Stocking argues that in the nineteenth century there was "a close articulation, both experiential and ideological, between the domestic and the colonial spheres of otherness" (*Victorian Anthropology*, 234). The architecture—both urban and domestic—of the nineteenth-century metropolis was devised deliberately to keep different social spheres distinct and apart: "the segregation of social classes into different urban and suburban residential areas helped to keep the slum world out of sight and mind" (*Victorian Anthropology*, 215). The arrangement of different communities into a spectacle of historical development occurred as much in the metropolis, then, as in the colonial sphere. The separation of groups into discrete entities characterized by their development on a unitary developmental scale—which, in the case of Knox, is characterized by embryonic developmental stages—came to serve the needs of social control both in the colonial context and the metropolis. Wherever communities needed watching, the temporal and spatial sequencing provided the tools to justify separation and study.[20]

## Form, Gender, and the Aesthetic

Knox's primary consideration is form—physical, political, and architectural. This emphasis leads him to develop an aesthetics of surface and appearance that engages with all of the previous issues discussed in his work—science and art overlap. Knox's biographer, Isobel Rae, argues that in 1849, Knox lived in London and "spent many of his hours of enforced leisure in the British Museum, studying [the] Greek sculptures with the keen eye of the artist and the anatomist" (Rae, 147). For Knox, Greek culture represented the height of civilization (*Races*, 408), and he believed that through Greek statues it is possible to discern the perfection of human form: "The perfect type of man was discovered by the ancient sculptors of Greece: it cannot be surpassed; all attempts to improve on it have failed. Towards this, nature constantly tends" (446). In the history of humanity, the perfect man appeared early in Western culture: "When the world was yet, as it were, in its infancy, a race of men appeared in the stream of human history, with intellects and frames so glorious, that no parallel to them was ever found in history. That race was the ancient Greek" (395). The figure representing this perfect form in art is the Venus statue (413).[21]

Knox consistently emphasizes the beautiful particularity of form over the horrific universality of content. Because the internal structures of living animals and humans are generally unified, the exterior or the outward form is where "we must look for the more remarkable characteristics of animals; it is it alone which nature loves to decorate and to vary" (*Races*, 227–28). Everything within form "is frightful and appalling to human sense—never beautiful, but the reverse; always horrible. In proportion as any figure, whether human or bestial, displays through the exterior, that unseemly interior, which has no form that sense comprehends, or desires, so in the same proportion is that figure beautiful or the opposite" (415). Thus, the body acts as a kind of empty signifier, like the concept of race itself, which creates meaning only in its surface presentation. Beauty, then, signifies an act of concealment that is rooted in anxiety about "dissolution and death" (415). The signifier "race" ends up also concealing the multivalent nature of issues of racial stratification that are much more about the need within the capitalist and imperialist imaginary to create discrete and manageable communities than about any essential nature or definition.

This aesthetic philosophy, which seems nothing less than bizarre for an anatomist who studied passionately both the internal and external structure of animals and humans, leads, in his writing, to a celebration of external characteristics. However, in *Great Artists and Great Anatomists*, he seems to argue exactly the reverse. There, Knox suggests that knowledge of the interior as well as the intellectual facets of the human form provide the basis of a theory of art (*Great Artists and Great Anatomists*, 144, 192). He first says that "a knowledge of the interior of man's structure is essential to the surgeon and physician, to the zoologist and to the transcendental anatomist; it furnishes to the artist, as its highest aim, a *theory of art*" (144, original italics). In distinguishing between great portrait artists and poor ones, for instance, he argues that "the great artist looks through the material mask and reads the nature, that is, the truth, which lies beyond it" (192–93). Here, he seems to be arguing that the truth of man's mind is some kind of abstracted understanding of the nature of subjective essence, rather than the literal insides of the person, which he finds horrifying. However, this abstracted essential identity seems to contradict a rather anti-Platonic emphasis on the empirically discerned "real" throughout his work.

But perhaps by understanding the word "nature" as containing elements of both God and the natural world, as existing as a kind of liminal scientific term that lives in a space between science and theology, we can see that Knox argues for art to explain something about life essence: "There is but one school of art—Nature. But, to read her volume profitably, artists must study profoundly the antique Greek, and ancient Italian school, formed by the era of Leonardo, Angelo, and Raphael" (*GAGA*, 202). He also argues:

> The relation Anatomy holds to Art is to explain—first, how far the shapes
> and figures of the inward structures modify the external forms of man and
> woman;—second, it informs the artist of the meaning of such forms;—
> third, it explains to him the laws of deformation; that is, of variety in exter-
> nal forms; the causes of these varieties, and the tendency to which they
> lead. As an artist he must represent them, no doubt; but in doing so let him
> wisely follow Nature rather in her intentions than her forthcomings, and
> return to the perfect or to its approximation, whenever time and circum-
> stances permit him to do so. (*GAGA*, 203–4)

Knox thrives on delineating the particular variations in the external structures of different beings, with relatively few—and these are generally
offensive—references to internal qualities. But when Knox places his
observations within the hierarchical structure of his own racially stratified
opinions—and these observations are reflected on many different discursive planes in mid-Victorian culture—Knox's thought becomes a radically
derogatory racialism.

Further refining his connection between structure and the beautiful,
Knox asserts that "man alone is beautiful; the human *form* alone satisfies
the *human mind*" (*Races*, 410, original italics). He narrows this definition
by suggesting that "*woman* presents the perfection of that *form*, and, therefore, alone constitutes 'the perfect'" (411, original italics). In the female
form, Knox sees "the perfection of Nature's works: the absolutely perfect;
the beautiful, the highest manifestation of abstract life, clothed in a physical form, adapted to the corresponding minds of her race and species"
(38). It is not surprising that the white female form came to represent such
a point of perfection or centrality in this text about race. Mary Poovey
argues that in "the Victorian symbolic economy" (*Uneven*, 12), the representation of white woman could be included among issues defined as
under "cultural contestation during the middle of the nineteenth century"
(9). And in scientific discourse, in particular, and scientific institutions in
their general practices and policies, this contestation took a very practical
and visible place. Evelleen Richards notes that "Mid-Victorian science was
an all-male preserve, which women entered, if they entered at all, only as
spectators—at the most as fashionable dabblers, not to be taken seriously"
("Huxley," 257). The Anthropological Society arose partly because of dis-
agreements over women's attendance at scientific discussions, as was noted
earlier. The exclusion of women from these meetings implies an overlap in
contemptuous attitudes toward women and darker-skinned races, because
"Hunt and his fellow Anthropologicals were as scientifically certain of the

intellectual and cultural inferiority of the female as they were of the Negro" (Richards, "Huxley," 265). In his 1865 essay, "Emancipation—Black and White," Thomas Henry Huxley himself equated the emancipation of blacks with giving full equality to women, arguing that giving full opportunity to those who will never rise to the level of the white male would prove only more clearly their inferiority. For Knox, however, it is the abstract female form as embodied in the Greek marble statues, rather than the character or intellectual capacity of individual living women, which signified perfection.

Knox uses the figure of the woman in four significant ways. As I already stated, the Venus statue represents the height of formal perfection. His more general discussion of women's form takes on racial distinction in his delineation of Hottentot women who "are not made like other women" (*Races*, 236), a common misconception developed over the previous 200 years of exploration and in the resulting narratives, and which fueled the inhuman degradation of Sara(h) Ba(a)rtman(n)'s body by scientists and voyeurs alike. He also uses images of women as prominent examples of the inability to transmit physical changes genetically: "For four thousand years have the Chinese been endeavouring to disfigure the feet of their women: have they succeeded in making the deformation permanent? Corsets have been worn time out of mind: Galen complains of them; he ascribes to them all sorts of bad results, deformities of spine and chest. Have such become hereditary? All matrons still produce virgin daughters" (*Races*, 100–101).

Finally, Knox presents women in a more abstract sense as the opposite of man, just as black seems the opposite of white, so indicating women's subservient position on the developmental ladder: "Mind is everything: the history of man is the history of his mind. What is the quality of mind which most distinguishes one race from another; one individual from another; man from woman; the dark from the fair portion of mankind? It is the power of generalization; of abstract thought; of rising from detail to general laws" (341–42).

Therefore, the overlap between race and gender categories takes on institutional, intellectual, and social components. Poovey argues that this type of denigration of female intellectual capacity was used to prevent women from entering "the economic and political fray" (*Uneven*, 11), thus suggesting a connection between Knox's racial arguments and the greater issue of women's increased agitation for opportunity at midcentury. This connection was commonly made during the period: It has been argued that "this equation of woman and black is one of the most important features of the Woman Question" (*The Woman Question*, 2:91). The relationship between blacks and women is "tirelessly discussed by transatlantic anthropologists after 1865" (2:57). Not only were the mental capacities of the two groups made analogous, but physical similarities were also drawn between the white woman and the black male (2:91). The discourses of race and gender suffused the meaning of "race" in mid-Victorian culture, influencing the valences of the term as much as did considerations of skin color and geographical locale.

Therefore, although Knox argues that the female form is perfect, he does not suggest that women, in general, are morally or intellectually perfect. The perfect Greek Venus statue represents no extraformal qualities in its nature, and Knox removes the figure from historical specificity: "It is not youth, nor intellect, nor moral worth, nor associations of any sort, which constitute the beautiful and the perfect; nor is life required, nor complexion, nor motion; it is *form* alone which is essential" (*Races*, 411, original italics). The effectiveness of form was that it "satisfies *the eye for form*, and by so doing the highest and deepest of all human feelings; for on form depends the living world in as far as we are concerned. The material world itself—the stellar universe itself—all is *form*" (414, original italics). What we see becomes paramount to our appreciation and access to the beautiful, because it is essentially a structural and visual attribute. And biological form, as we saw earlier, is the window through which the history of both creation and the individual races becomes discernible. This move also resolves the problem of history with which Knox struggles throughout the text. By moving into what he constructs as the static world of aesthetics and understanding the ideal Greek Venus statue as a finite and extinct figure, Knox temporarily resolves the struggle over historical paradigms between race, nation, and time. Like Rae's description of Knox sitting in the British Museum, the narrative rests for a moment, taking a break from the ideological fray of nineteenth-century racial ideologies to relax in the realm of the beautiful.

## Knox's Legacy

Praising Knox's work eight years later,[22] Lonsdale argued that *The Races of Men* "can hardly fail to obtain a place in history; and when it comes to be read by the light of another century, by which time human prejudices, now very much on the wane, will no longer affect a free expression of thought on all matters affecting the social and religious position of our species" (330).

Although Knox's notorious work is better known for its racism than for its wisdom, *The Races of Men* helps us to understand the late-1840s cultural environment in England, when humanitarian racial arguments held diminishing power, and racist anthropological arguments flourished. The conflicted and contradictory nature of the text reflects the contested nature of the category "race" at the time. Violent rhetoric in the work suggests the reality of the relationship between colonizer and colonized, a relationship further strained by the 1857 Indian Rebellion, an event allegorically presented in Charles Dickens and Wilkie Collins's "The Perils of Certain English Prisoners," the subject of the following chapter. Knox's interweaving of race, history, nation, progress, gender, and, finally, aesthetics reflects the way in which Victorian writing about race became a layered discourse encompassing various discussions of these topics. *The Races of Men* stands as a compelling example of the fractured and often irrational meanings attached to the term "race" in mid-Victorian England.

# CHAPTER 3

⮑

# The Dialectic of Scapegoat and Fetish

## FAILED CATHARSIS IN CHARLES DICKENS
## AND WILKIE COLLINS'S
## "THE PERILS OF CERTAIN ENGLISH PRISONERS" (1857)

"*T*he Perils of Certain English Prisoners" (1857), a Christmas story written collaboratively by Charles Dickens and Wilkie Collins, differs quite dramatically in structure and ideology from Harriet Martineau's *The Hour and the Man*. In stark contrast to Martineau's revisionist biography, and more in line with Knox's virulent, irrational, and ambivalent racism, Dickens and Collins's Christmas story engages with racial conflict by addressing the contested boundaries distinguishing British subjects from various colonial "others." Mid-Victorian arguments about race, especially in texts dealing explicitly with racial conflict, often center on the problem of reasserting clear and impermeable boundaries between people and ideas from different communities. Boundaries of gender, genre, class, nationality, authorship, and architecture become zones of anxiety in Dickens and Collins's story, which struggles to resolve these crises in its resolution of the two plotlines.

"Perils" is set in 1744. A regiment of Marines arrives on the island of Silver Store in South America, having been ordered there to protect the British subjects from pirates in the area. Davis, the hero of the story, is an uneducated foundling. Self-described as "a subject of his Gracious Majesty King George of England, and a private in the Royal Marines" ("Perils," 175), the rough and bitter Davis resents having to protect a group of affluent colonials. Early in the story, Davis meets Christian George King, a character the narrator describes as a "sambo"—half negro and half Indian. His name provides an ironic comparison between Davis, who becomes a proud subject of George II, and the first of the story's villains, who has taken—and implicitly usurped—the monarch's title as his name. Pirates attack the British and take them captive, but the British eventually escape by raft. Christian George King is shot and killed, and after a description of the deaths of the pirates offstage and a picture of the future friendship of Davis and the heroine of the story, Marion Maryon, the tale ends.

The two villains in Dickens and Collins's Christmas tale—the traitorous black servant Christian George King and the pirate captain Pedro Mendez—both violate the trust of a band of British colonials on the fictional island of Silver Store. Written as a response to the events of the recent Indian Rebellion, "Perils" suggests in its depictions of these two figures the anger and frustration felt by an English public reading accounts of atrocities committed especially against British women, many of whom, as Jenny Sharpe discusses in *Allegories of Empire*, turned out to be fictional themselves. Rather than engaging with events by writing a biographical study, as Martineau chose, or a "scientific" treatise, as Knox preferred, Dickens instead aestheticized the events of the rebellion in its totality, such that connections with the historical incidents remain allegorical and metaphorical. Rebellion represents an act of ideological and political transgression—it is a crossing of the lines of authority and order. The emphasis on boundaries evident in "Perils" speaks to its allegorical relationship to the historical events of the Indian Rebellion. In this chapter, I will first discuss the tale's assertion of boundaries in its context, form, and content. Then, I will use this discussion to argue that the fate of each of the villains represents a differently conceived catharsis of cultural rage felt in response to transgressions of the imperial order, such as the Indian Rebellion. These historical transgressions are implied in challenges to social and physical boundaries within the tale. Christian George King is sent into the wilderness and killed with one clear shot, suggesting the Biblical scapegoat strategy of Christian theology. Pedro Mendez, a figure laden with the conflicted ideologies of Victorian racial discourse, is humiliated and abandoned, functioning in the text as a fetish, left unfinalized and metonymically referencing the complications inherent in the conflicted Gil Davis, the story's hero. The dialectic created by the two resolutions disempowers the story's potential catharsis, leaving this representation of Victorian racial anxiety unfinalized.

## Dickens, Christmas, and the Christmas Tale

The formal and thematic parameters of the Christmas tale suggest predictable similarities between middle-class domestic ideals and social boundary conflicts evident in mid-Victorian discussions of race. "Perils" both adheres to the formal requirements of this genre, which Dickens developed, and reflects the historical mutations that took place in Victorian celebrations of the holiday. The story first appeared in the 1857 Christmas edition of Dickens's journal *Household Words*. After the success of Dickens's first four Christmas books, the most famous of which is *A Christmas Carol* (1843), Dickens began writing an annual Christmas story for publication in his weekly magazine. The Christmas stories, according to critic Ruth Glancy, were "written between 1850 and 1867 for the Christmas numbers of his two weekly magazines, *Household Words* (1850–1859) and its successor *All the Year Round*." They were "unique experiments in journalism for Christmas, written in collaboration with other writers and taking many forms from autobiographical essay to ghost story to comic monologue" (xxi). Like many of the Christmas tales, however, "Perils" does not specifically mention the holiday. Instead, the stories became part of the entertainment people provided their friends and relatives during the festivities (Carolan, 195). Rather than reflecting the celebration, the stories became integral components of the domestic holiday ritual. So not only does "Perils" represent Dickens's, and to a certain extent Collins's, attitudes toward the rebellion in allegorical and metaphorical form, but its relationship to the holiday for which the genre itself is named is ideologically reflective rather than realistic.

The popularity of the Christmas books and stories fostered Dickens's legendary relationship to the holiday, and Glancy notes that this relationship was firmly in place by 1850 (xxi). In *Daily Life in Victorian England* (1996), Sally Mitchell argues that during the Victorian period the Christmas holiday underwent significant changes, producing what we would now call the modern Christmas (211). Because of Dickens's relationship to the holiday celebration, he is often considered one of the major figures influencing these changes. Yet Katherine Carolan and Peter Ackroyd both dispute this idea: "What we now consider a 'Dickens Christmas' existed long before Dickens" (Carolan, 20). The Victorian Christmas acquired its "peculiar form," argues Carolan, from its history as a holiday once legislated out of existence because of excesses practiced in its celebration. From 1644 to 1656, the Puritans officially banned Christmas. With the return of the monarchy, "Christmas was promptly reinstated but with some lack of its former vigor" (23). Carolan suggests that after this time, a sense of loss and nostalgia followed the season that "produced a national inferiority complex about Christmas, which extends from the Commonwealth to our own time. Christmas, the refrain runs, is never what it used to be in the old days" (24). Within the Victorian Christmas celebration, this information suggests, is the shade of the older, richer, and more exuberant holiday only partly recovered after the Puritan suppression of the festival.

According to Carolan, Dickens brought to the holiday his own sense of what Victorian culture most needed: "Christmas becomes a touchstone of the communal spirit and charity Dickens found lacking in Victorian England" (7). "The attraction of Christmas," Carolan writes, "is that it provides, if only momentarily, status and individual importance for the forgotten members of society" (17–18). Ackroyd suggests that Dickens emphasized the holiday's "cosy conviviality" (413–14). Glancy argues more pointedly that the author's goal in the Christmas stories was to convey his own particular brand of morality, as well as his own personal vision of Christian spiritual renewal (xxii). For Dickens, these critics suggest, the holiday was a time for personal and spiritual reflection, achievable through solitary contemplation, shared memories, and stories read aloud. Glancy suggests that Dickens was convinced that "personal or autobiographical story-telling was morally and spiritually renewing; in reliving childhood memories the adult storyteller can regain a sense of the wonderful that makes moral regeneration possible in a world full of regret and loss" (xxiv). Tied perhaps to his own feelings of loss deriving from hardships suffered in his early childhood, Dickens turned Christmas into a time of possibility, hope, and spiritual exploration; he transformed the holiday in his works into a chance to move beyond the limitations of personal circumstances, thus making possible a wider sense of peace and community.

It would seem ironic, then, that Dickens would choose a genre associated with reconciliation, reclamation, and "cosy conviviality" in which to dramatize the symbolic defeat of Indian sepoys. However, the plots of these Christmas tales draw a connection, in the rendering of strong ideological and architectural boundaries, between the domestic Christmas scene and middle-class Victorian concerns. And it is this ideology of idealized domestic harmony with which English colonials armed themselves as protection from contaminating racial influences when they left England. We saw this domestic ideal symbolized in the work of Robert Knox in repeated visual images of the English country house. Ackroyd observes that in the Christmas books and stories,

> there is a constant contrast between warmth and cold, between the domestic interior and the noisome streets, between the rich and the poor, between the well and the ill, between the need for comfort and the anxiety

about hopelessness. And in that ambivalence he touched upon one of the real spirits of the age. In many Victorian homes the exterior world seems literally to be kept at bay by a whole artillery of protective forces—screened by thick curtains and by lace inner curtains, muffled by patterned wallpaper and patterned carpets, held off by settees and ottomans and what-nots, mocked by wax fruit and wax candles, its metaphorical and literal darkness banished by lamps and chandeliers and candles. The central idea is one of ferocious privacy, of shelter and segregation. (414)

Danger, in the Dickens Christmas tale, is symbolized by the actual or threatened rupture of these crucial domestic boundaries, and it is here that the genre becomes amenable to aestheticizing what would appear to be an inappropriate topic for the Christmas number. If Christmas is about reinforcing the sanctity of the middle-class Victorian domestic sphere, an arena most clearly represented by the figure of the English woman, what better way to enact that project than by the symbolic defeat and humiliation of threatening, non-English, racialized villains.

## Fictionalizing Race Rebellion

Dickens designed "Perils" as an allegorical rendering of his responses to the 1857 Indian Rebellion, and, more specifically, the Cawnpore Massacre.[1] The Indian Rebellion, started by a group of Indian sepoys, began in May 1857. The British distributed Enfield rifles to the army, for which the ends of the greased cartridges had to be bitten off before they could be loaded. Yet the sepoys believed that the cartridges were greased with cow and pig fat, and were thus an affront to their Hindu and Muslim beliefs. The idea that they were being forced to commit religious sacrilege led them to rebel, although the issue of the cartridges was simply the spark on longstanding political and economic grievances. English officers, women, and children were reported killed. Stories of sepoy atrocities reached the British press, and the British public read daily reports of British martyrs. Especially disturbing to British readers were tales of barbarous acts committed against British women, such as the sale of Englishwomen in the streets of Cawnpore and the bodies of women found in the Well at Cawnpore.[2]

Dickens reacted to these accounts with expressions of anger and genocidal violence that startle readers more accustomed to his liberal critique of slavery in America, and his obvious sympathy and identification with the working classes in England. In particular, Dickens raged about Lord

Canning's attempt to quell the revengeful bloodshed that the English soldiers unleashed against the Indians after the initial Rebellion. In a letter to
Emile de la Rue on October 23, 1857, Dickens wrote:

> I wish I were Commander in Chief over there! I would address that
> Oriental character which must be powerfully spoken to, in something like
> the following placard, which should be vigorously translated into all native
> dialects, "I, The Inimitable, holding this office of mine, and firmly believ-
> ing that I hold it by the permission of Heaven and not by the appointment
> of Satan, have the honor to inform you Hindoo gentry that it is my inten-
> tion, with all possible avoidance of unnecessary cruelty and with all mer-
> ciful swiftness of execution, to exterminate the Race from the face of the
> earth, which disfigured the earth with the late abominable atrocities."
> (*Letters*, 8:473)

Dickens makes similar statements in a letter to Angela Burdett Coutts
dated October 4, 1857 (*Letters*, 8:459) and in his essay "The Noble Savage"
(1853). And we see references to this rage in his last and unfinished novel,
*The Mystery of Edwin Drood* (1870).

Although Dickens's strong feelings led him to make the Rebellion the
central focus of the 1857 Christmas number, in a letter to Mrs. Richard
Watson on December 7, 1857, Dickens states clearly that he rejected the
idea of directly fictionalizing the event: "I have been very busy with the
Xmas Number of Household Words, in which I have endeavoured to com-
memorate the foremost of the great English qualities shewn in India, without laying the scene there, or making any vulgar association with real
events or calamities. I believe it is rather a remarkable production, and will
make a great noise" (*Letters*, 8:487). He struck on the idea of placing the
events in South America, and he wrote to Henry Morley for historical
background in order to make the story plausible (8:469). Dickens wanted
to stay within the parameters of the possible, not fictionalizing the events
so as to take them into the realm of fantasy. He needed a quasi-historical
grounding to mirror feelings and attitudes about the Rebellion without
being perceived as fictionalizing actual events.

Dickens's decision to take the events out of India did not diminish the
racial or imperial significance of the tale. As Brantlinger argues, "Dickens's
placement of his tale in West rather than East India does not provide the
distance needed for considering the Mutiny dispassionately. Rather, it
extends his view of the Mutiny to other parts of the Empire" (*Rule*, 207)
and stands as yet another example of a white British author turning to the

aesthetic realm to manage and represent conflicting feelings about racial conflict. By taking the events out of the original context, the story transcends historical and geographical specificity to become part of the imperialist imaginary, effectively blanketing the length of the globe with polarized racial thinking. The villains in "Perils" mirror this extrapolation by becoming not just Indians, but a "multicultural" group of pirates representing many different nations around the globe. "Perils" presents Dickens and Collins's decided determination that the English are the superior race at war with every anarchic, rebellious, and uncivilized race on the earth.

In form, "Perils" deviates from the standard construction of the yearly Christmas number. Generally, the tales contained an implicit storytelling component, which Glancy describes as "a neat format that would allow [Dickens] to blend tales, tellers and setting in the ancient story-telling manner of Chaucer's *Canterbury Tales* or, particularly beloved by Dickens, *The Arabian Nights*" (xxii). Traditionally, according to Ackroyd, the numbers would be "a sequence of linked stories, written by several hands but with Dickens composing the transitional passages as well as some of the stories themselves" (599). They would emphasize the value of participating in community, as well as the indulgent or harmful qualities ensuing from a decision to withdraw into isolation.

Although "Perils" is not told as a series of tales, it remains within the Christmas story tradition as a work of collaborative writing, a partnership mirrored in the Lady Marion/Davis team that provides the framing narrative for the text. Wilkie Collins—Dickens's collaborator on "Perils," as well as on a number of other projects—had reading interests somewhat similar to Dickens in his early years, including *Robin Hood, Don Quixote*, the novels of Marryat, and *The Arabian Nights' Entertainment* (Peters, 32). Steeped in a similar tradition of adventure stories, fantasy, and chivalric romances, Collins could draw upon a generic repertoire in keeping with that of Dickens. Collins, however, seemingly had—or at least developed—a more moderate view of the Indian race, at least by the time he wrote *The Moonstone* in 1868. As his biographer, Catherine Peters, argues, "[I]ndeed [the novel] is remarkable for its serious treatment of the Hindu faith, at a time when the violence of the Mutiny was still fresh in British memory" (309). The collaboration between the authors seems to have been genuine, with Dickens writing the first and third chapters to start, and Collins writing the middle chapter: "The Second chapter was done, on the perusal of my first and third, by Wilkie Collins. We planned it out, and it seems to me a very notable and happy piece of execution" (quoted in Glancy, 172). As Ackroyd points out, however—and this observation is true of many of

Dickens's literary and dramatic projects—Dickens probably exerted more control over the story than the idea of an equal partnership suggests.

Dickens and Collins's authorial dynamic is mirrored in the narrative presentation of authorship. Possibly in much the same way that Dickens designed, researched, and framed the story for Collins's participation, Lady Marion often disrupts the narrative to suggest a different direction. This tactic is evident only through Davis's interjections: "My lady stops me again, before I go any further, by laughing exactly in her old way and waving the feather of her pen at me." They then go on to debate a passage, discussing whether Lady Marion should "scratch it out" ("Perils," 175). Collins was concerned about being overshadowed and controlled by his friendship with Dickens. Although the relationship between the older man and the younger Collins was certainly beneficial to the young man's career, Peters describes Collins in the 1860s as beginning to ease "himself away from the Dickensian embrace" (281). "Perils" perhaps retains some of the tension inherent in this collaboration. The power differentiation between Lady Marion and Davis reflects the gulf between the firmly established literary giant Dickens and the younger Collins. The text inscribes directly the struggle—however playful and amicable—between Lady Marion and Davis in their debates about the direction of the story, but Lady Marion has the power of literacy, and thus the power to write down what she ultimately chooses. Although he did not edit Collins's contribution to the number, Dickens did create the genre, the story, and the narrative, and invited Collins to write the second chapter. He is the ultimate controlling authority over the text. Thus we must add to the growing collection of narrative, ideological, and spatial fissures within and around this text the element of authorial collaboration inside the story and in the shaping of its creation.

In this authorial tension, we see elements of gender and class contributing to the creation of a narrative deliberately structured to convey a certain tone or ideological stance toward races other than the English. My intention is not to prioritize these categories in any way, or to suggest a kind of progression from one to another. Instead, I agree with Anne McClintock, who argues in *Imperial Leather* that "race, gender and class are not distinct realms of experience, existing in splendid isolation from each other; nor can they be simply yoked together retrospectively like armatures of Lego. Rather, they come into existence *in and through* relation to each other—if in contradictory and conflictual ways" (5, original italics). My argument is that an examination of the interdependence among race, class, and gender in "Perils" reveals sites of boundary tension that illustrate both an obsession with limits within Victorian culture, and an emphasis on strict lines of demarcation within nationalist and imperialist ideologies. For example, the Indian Rebellion suggests an attempt of the colonized to fight back, perhaps challenging the boundaries between themselves and their oppressors. The challenge was met, however, with swift and sure force. In terms of the transgression of the colonizer into the territory of the colonized, however, the imperialist project argues the necessity of crossing into the world of the colonized, in order to bring in the supposed light of civilization and to derive economic benefits. The boundary markers nonetheless remain highly policed, largely to maintain the separation between British women and "native" men.

In "Perils," the figure that bears the burden of Davis's (and Dickens's) prejudices is Christian George King. Davis hates Christian George King. From their first meeting, Davis conveys his loathing for both King and natives in general: "I have stated myself to be a man of no learning, and, if I entertain prejudices, I hope allowance may be made. I will now confess to one. It may be a right one or it may be a wrong one; but, I never did like Natives, except in the form of oysters" ("Perils," 182). It is scarcely possible that King could be portrayed as more annoying, evil, sycophantic, or untrustworthy in the tale. King betrays the colonials to the pirates, and he is complicit in their being taken deep into the colonial territory, away from the comforting familiarity of the settlement. He is described as "a double dyed traitor, and a most infernal villain" ("Perils," 193). An analysis of Dickens's use of King as a scapegoat for public frustration over colonial unrest convincingly explains one-half of the dynamics of racial representation in the story. Lillian Nayder's work[3] on the displacement of class and gender distinctions onto race in "Perils" suggests this argument, but leaves out the second crucial component of this dynamic: the pirates. By looking more closely at the pirates—and more particularly, at the depiction of the pirate captain—we see that this story moves beyond the project of displacing class and gender distinctions onto those of race. The tale presents a complex mapping of nationalism, race, class, and gender differences onto the motley crew of the pirates, a transfer that becomes displaced again, first in the escape of Pedro Mendez, and finally in the preeminent moment of the text: the killing of Christian George King.[4]

## Pirates and Racial Otherness

From the point where they are first introduced into the narrative, the group of pirates is described, from the British perspective, as a startlingly diverse collection of non-English people:

> From a spy-hole, I could see the whole crowd of Pirates. There were Malays
> among them, Dutch, Maltese, Greeks, Sambos, Negroes, and Convict
> Englishmen from the West India Islands; among the last, him with one eye
> and the patch across the nose. There were some Portuguese, too, and a few
> Spaniards. The captain was a Portuguese; a little man with very large
> earrings under a very broad hat, and a great bright shawl twisted about his
> shoulders. They were all strongly armed, but like a boarding party, with
> pikes, swords, cutlasses, and axes. ("Perils," 199–200)

Pirates represent the overlap of racial and national signifiers. They are usually an international grouping, and they represent lawlessness and transgression. In works of fiction, they are traditionally identified by their
nationality rather than by their racial composition.[5] The group in "Perils,"
which later Dickens will describe as the "scum of all nations" ("Perils,"
247), represents in one brushstroke elements of "otherness" as fearful,
dangerous, anarchic, and bent on the destruction of the British colonial-
ists. They threaten the British subjects and they represent the rebellion of
all those who should remain under the control of colonial authority.

Pirates were staple figures for the British reading public. Among the
most popular works was *A General History of Pirates*, reputed to be written
by an unknown Captain Charles Johnson. David Cordingly, in *Under the
Black Flag*, traces a debate about the author of this famous treatise on
pirates, in which authorship is variously given to the mysterious Captain
Johnson and by others to Daniel Defoe. Collections such as *A General
History of the Robberies and Murders of the Most Notorious Pirates* (1724)
or a later revision of another of Captain Johnson's works, *Lives and
Exploits of English Highwaymen, Pirates, & Robbers: Drawn from the Most
Authentic Sources, by Capt. Charles Johnson. Revised and Continued to the
Present Time by C. Whitehead, Esq.* (1842), present individualized biogra-
phies of the most famous criminals such as Robin Hood and Blackbeard.
These volumes went into multiple printings, and fed readers with stories
of romantic and dangerous outlaws. In popular novels such as Sir Walter
Scott's *The Pirate*, first published in 1821, and *The Pirate* by Captain
Frederick Marryat, first published in 1836,[6] we find a more fully elaborat-
ed picture of the pirate world as it intersected with the lives of ordinary,
more conventional characters. By using accounts of actual pirates, as well
as fictional constructions of both pirates and pirate captains, we can locate
the ways Dickens and Collins use the figure of the pirate to convey the

racial degeneracy of colonial "others" within the cultural climate raised by accounts of the Indian Rebellion.

After the initial battle, the pirates in "Perils" take the remaining colonists prisoner, forcing them to make a long journey first across to the mainland, and then into the jungle. The journey into the interior is a common facet of racial narratives, made most famous perhaps in the much later novella by Joseph Conrad, *Heart of Darkness* (1899; 1902). The colonists enter the world of the racialized "others," constructed as before time, and before history. The group is brought away from civilization, away from safety, and away from familiarity, subject to the whims of this eclectic group of racialized bandits. The prisoners arrive at a holding area deep within the vegetation of the mainland. The structure, called "The Palace," is the destination reached after going by a number of enormous idols. Here, we have another of these ruin sites that I will discuss more fully in my final chapter. Miss Marion suggests that the structure is a place where there lived "a lost race of people . . . I believe we are close to the remains of one of those mysterious ruined cities which have long been supposed to exist in this part of the world" ("Perils," 221). It is run-down, missing a roof in many places, retaining indicators of its former splendor, but with vegetation growing within the rooms. The structure is separated into different spaces where the prisoners and their captors all sleep. Here, we see the spatial realization of the crisis in boundaries that the story represents. Encroaching into the interior, domestic space of the palace is the exterior, natural world. Pirates from a variety of different races have free access to the living space of the English colonials, especially that of the women, thus triggering fears of miscegenation and rape. Potential transgression of the boundaries between the English and the pirates, and between the inside and the outside spaces, is made the height of the horror for this group of prisoners. The threat of ruptured boundaries—the breakdown of clear distinctions—is the result of the journey into the interior of the mainland and into the horror of racialized anarchy.

The depiction of the pirates in "Perils" becomes focused specifically on the pirate captain, Pedro Mendez, Collins's villain and the story's racialized fetish. His depiction focuses the anger, conflict, and fear created by racial pluralism (represented in the story as the pirates, and in English culture as the frequent eruptions of racial violence in British colonies) and creates a distraction or substitution for it. Both Christian George King and Pedro Mendez can be read as representing English racial hostility at the time of the Indian Rebellion. However, they each hold slightly different roles. Christian George King, the focal figure in the chapters written by Dickens, becomes the vehicle for the author to vent his rage at his powerlessness in the face of accounts arriving from India. We see these reactions in the letters referred to earlier. The figure of Pedro Mendez is central in the story's middle section, written by Collins. And, far more than Christian George King, it is Mendez who receives the most elaborate and extensive depiction in the story, thus perhaps suggesting Collins's more psychologically and culturally complex reactions to the rebellion.

## Scapegoat and Fetish

The scapegoat and the fetish have much in common. Both are physical objects that attempt to manage cultural, economic, and psychological anxieties. Both bear the burden of sins, fears, and conflicts held by an individual or a culture. The Biblical roots of the scapegoat speak to its origin in a community ritual based on a need to alleviate feelings of guilt. The Biblical scapegoat, described in the book of Leviticus, is actually two goats: the first is killed as atonement for sins, and the second is used as a vehicle for confession and then sent into the wilderness. In a figurative transition, the community symbolically transfers unacceptable transgressions onto the two goats, and then removes them from the community through death and geographical displacement.

The dialectic set up between these two different types of cultural purgation, as represented by the two goats, suggests a similarity with the internal dynamics of the fetish. The fetish is a concept that straddles the economic, colonial, and psychological realms in quite startling ways. In his exhaustive series of articles, William Pietz argues that the term "fetish" emerged out of conflicting epistemological structures resulting from sixteenth-century trade relations in West Africa: "The fetish, then, not only originated from, but remains specific to, the problematic of the social value of material objects as revealed in situations formed by the encounter of radically heterogeneous social systems" (Pietz, (i) 7). It was in the colonial environment, in the confrontation between different value systems and understandings of causality, that the fetish emerged as a way to bridge differences between cultures. Later, Karl Marx and Sigmund Freud developed the classic understandings of the fetish, speaking to different aspects of the complex structure. Marx used it as a way to describe the magical transformation of labor within the commodity to a universal standard capable of being understood in the process of capitalist exchange.[7] Freud argued that the fetish is a stand-in for the boy's perception of the mother's missing penis, thus allaying his castration anxiety. Both of these classic explanations have been retooled, especially in recent criticism,[8] in an attempt to revise these compelling concepts in light of contemporary theoretical concerns.[9]

Two important elements of the fetish are its essential materiality and its ability to hold a subject's understanding and misunderstanding in dynamic interaction. Aligning myself with the historicized materialism of Pietz and the blend of materialism and psychoanalysis in McClintock's work, I agree that the fetish represents the crisis precipitated when a subject or culture confronts that which is "other" to its epistemological framework. What is crucial for an analysis of Dickens and Collins's Christmas story is that this crisis necessitates the deployment of figurative language to imaginatively manage the anxiety created in this confrontation. As I noted in the introduction, Hayden White argues that "Metaphors are crucially necessary when a culture or social group encounters phenomena that either elude or run afoul of normal expectations or quotidian experiences" (*Tropics,* 184). The Freudian boy witnesses the mother's lack of penis and manages his castration anxiety by creating a substitute so as to disavow his difference from her. Capitalist culture abstracts differences in labor within the commodity so as to facilitate the process of exchange. Frantz Fanon, Hayden White, and Homi K. Bhabha describe the ways in which skin color becomes a visible fetish structuring the colonial environment, both valorizing white skin as definitively human and enabling the repressive practices of the colonizer against a colonized subject deemed both nonhuman and quintessentially loyal.[10] All of these confrontations with "otherness," racial, sexual, and geographical, suggest a commonality in the deflected responses of a subject to the perception of difference and point to the necessity of creating a compensatory structure, hierarchy, or reality as a managing strategy. There is an oscillation between the subject's or community's succumbing to the fiction that mirrors the oscillation at work within figurative structures—what Laura Mulvey calls the fetish's ability to "maintain knowledge and belief simultaneously" (Mulvey, xi). This aspect the fetish and the scapegoat have in common. I argue, however, that they differ in the particular levels of closure achieved in their negotiation of what is "other" to the culture: the scapegoat represents a more finalized relationship to what is rejected by the community, whereas the fetish maintains the more ambivalent posture of disavowal. In figurative terms, the scapegoat leans towards a more metaphoric relationship, whereas the fetish tends towards the metonymic, although the latter can deploy both.

"Perils" presents both strategies for cultural catharsis, and thus speaks to the text's immersion in the social and racial conflicts experienced by many English readers in response to reports of the Indian Rebellion. The relationship here between historical events, Victorian representations of those events, and contemporary reading of this story is not a simple one. Rather, I suggest that the complexity of this relationship is exactly what contributes to producing the fetishistic and scapegoat effects evident in "Perils." By articulating the zones of anxiety in the text, we can begin to decipher the representations of Christian George King as scapegoat and Pedro Mendez as fetish, and the ways in which the dialectic between the two ultimately impedes the ability of the text to achieve fictional catharsis.

## The Fetish of the Pirate Captain

Individual pirates quickly recede into a multicultural mob, bowing in reverence to their leader. Mendez, the Pirate Captain, emerges at the intersection of the story's presentation of economic, gender, and racial crises:

> The ruler who held all the ruffians about us in subjection, was, judging by appearances, the very last man I should have picked out as likely to fill a place of power among any body of men, good or bad, under heaven. By nation, he was a Portuguese; and, by name, he was generally spoken of among his men as The Don. He was a little, active, weazen, monkey-faced man, dressed in the brightest colours and the finest made clothes I ever saw. ("Perils," 204)

Fictional pirate captains tended to be a blend of good and bad qualities, strong and commanding, yet lacking a certain moral vigor. For example, the pirate captain of Scott's *The Pirate*, Cleveland, is a sympathetic figure to a certain extent, his brutality and past explained by his economically disadvantaged childhood, his father's life as a pirate, and his need to be able to survive among bloodthirsty pirate crews. He is described as "rather above the middle size, and formed handsomely as well as strongly" (Scott, 127). He never becomes as bad as he could, and there is always a glimmer of morality in him. He falls for the heroine of the novel, and vows to change his ways. But, much like a fallen woman, the pirate captain can never go back to live the life of a respectable man.

The pirate captain of Marryat's *The Pirate*, Cain, is more traditional. He is strong, mean, ruthless, but with a weak spot for the boy, Francisco, for whom he will turn himself in to the authorities at the end of the novel:

"In person he was about six feet high, with a breadth of shoulders and of chest denoting the utmost of physical force which, perhaps, has ever been allotted to man. His features would have been handsome had they not been scarred with wounds; and, strange to say, his eye was mild and of a soft blue" (434).

Collins's use of the terms "little" and "weazened" to describe Mendez suggests that the pirate captain of "Perils" will not be drawn from within the tradition of the dangerous yet powerful and attractive pirate captain, who at some point sacrifices himself to save another. Rather, Mendez is rendered thoroughly unlikable, vicious, and unattractive; he is potentially more in keeping with the actuality of the pirate captain, rather than the romantic fictional counterpart.

Clothing was a central element signifying pirate-captain status. It served to create a clear demarcation between pirate captains and more "legitimate" members of the business of trade. In "Perils," Mendez is described as dressed in the following manner:

> His three-cornered hat was smartly cocked on one side. His coatskirts were stiffened and stuck out, like the skirts of the dandies in the Mall in London. When the dance was given at the Island, I saw no such lace on any lady's dress there as I saw on his cravat and ruffles. Round his neck he wore a thick gold chain, with a diamond cross hanging from it. His lean, wiry, brown fingers were covered with rings. Over his shoulders, and falling down in front to below his waist, he wore a sort of sling of broad scarlet cloth, embroidered with beads and little feathers, and holding, at the lower part, four loaded pistols, two on a side lying ready to either hand. ("Perils," 204)

Marryat's Cain certainly follows this pattern of the captain wearing colorful and dramatic attire.[11] As with the description of Mendez, his costume blends together bright colors, stripes, and gold buttons, with the markers of violence—the pistols and the knife. Scott's Cleveland mirrors the costume of Marryat's Cain, although perhaps not quite so flamboyantly.[12] Scott notes that it is the presentation of the visual excess that excites the admiration of the crew, and helps to ensure loyalty and servitude. By modeling the object of their actions, the captain stands as a kind of visual reminder of the promise of piracy: riches, finery, gold, jewels, and money. The captain is a figure of excess: excessive violence, excessive color, and excessive splendor.[13]

But the association of Mendez with ladies' lace, with dandies, and with feathers suggests an effeminacy that we do not see in other depictions of the pirate captain. This effeminacy possibly suggests the way in which the authors mark this figure as a symbol of biologically and socially degenerative qualities, suggesting a kind of racialized emasculation more commonly associated with representations of "oriental" men.[14] It also suggests a latent homosexuality in Mendez's relationships with his crew. Contributing to this sense of veiled homoeroticism is the mysterious reason the pirates have for wanting to take the male prisoners further into the country. In a note to potential rescuers regarding their intentions towards the prisoners, Mendez writes that he is taking the women and children and several of the men for an unarticulated reason: "'They will be taken up the country, with fourteen men prisoners (whose lives the Buccaniers have private reasons of their own for preserving)'" ("Perils," 207). Gill reflects on the question of what the pirates have in mind: "I wondered then, as I had wondered once or twice already, what those private reasons might be, which he had mentioned in his written paper, for sparing the lives of us male prisoners. I hoped he would refer to them now—but I was disappointed" ("Perils," 212). There is certainly ample reason to believe that Davis thought the pirates wanted to sell them into white slavery, or to put them to work onboard ship. And we learn later that the pirates use the prisoners to prepare materials for rebuilding their home base. But the insistent emphasis on male physicality—coupled with Davis's confusion— suggests an unspoken reference to possible sexual abuse of the men.

Cordingly argues that although pirates lived in single-sex environments, homosexuality was not more prevalent among pirate crews than it was in the larger population (101–3). In *Sodomy and the Pirate Tradition*, however, B. R. Burg argues, from limited primary sources, that men who chose life on pirate ships were quite possibly seeking out a single-sex, transgressive environment which included active homosexuality among the crew. Hans Turley, in *Rum, Sodomy, and the Lash*, further complicates the issue by arguing that the information we have on pirates blurs the line between fact and fiction, and thus we can only talk about the transgressive nature of the trope of the pirate, rather than the literal prevalence of homosexuality on pirate ships. But Turley also argues that homosexuality and strong affective bonds between men are part of fictional pirate subjectivity, albeit often cloaked, in literature dealing with pirates.

It is not my intention to suggest that Collins intended to directly portray homosexuality in the middle chapter of "Perils." What I am arguing is that the authors render Mendez, the trope of the pirate captain, unlikable and dangerous, in part by making him less traditionally masculine than other fictional pirate captains, and by suggesting a homoerotic component in the "mysterious" and "private" reason that the pirates have for wanting to take away the men.[15] What Collins's depiction lacks is the strong masculinity and admirable presence attributed to Cain and Cleveland. Further evidence for this racialized emasculation is evident in the dismissive and deprecating tone of the pirate captain's "foreign" way of communicating: "I got on my feet, and saw the Pirate Captain communicating with the Indians of the village. His hands were making signs in the fussy foreign way, all the time he was speaking" ("Perils," 219–20). What blend in this description of the figure of the pirate captain are an intense and growing xenophobia and a need to dominate textually the figure of the pirate. Mendez is a much less ambivalently unlikable, unadmirable, and immoral figure than Marryat's and Scott's captains.

The degeneracy and ignorance of the crew, and of the "sambos" and "indians" who work with them, is suggested by their decision to follow so degraded a character. And, coupled with their dogged devotion to this figure, there is a certain underlying sense of physicality in their dealings with him:

> His face was mere skin and bone, and one of his wrinkled cheeks had a blue scar running all across it, which drew up that part of his face, and showed his white shining teeth on that side of his mouth. An uglier, meaner, weaker, man-monkey to look at, I never saw; and yet there was not one of his crew, from his mate to his cabinboy, who did not obey him as if he had been the greatest monarch in the world. As for the Sambos, including especially that evil-minded scoundrel, Christian George King, they never went near him without seeming to want to roll before him on the ground, for the sake of winning the honour of having one of his little dancing-master's feet set on their black bullock bodies. ("Perils," 204)

As the passage ends, we see the interjection again of a kind of homoerotic and submissive physicality that becomes a point of specific interest for the British crew. The juxtaposition of the "dancing-master's feet" with the "black bullock bodies" signifies Mendez's dominance of the natives that suggests both their lack of judgment in following such a character, and the ability of Mendez to be eventually overcome. It is also reminiscent of Dickens's words in "The Noble Savage" where he says that "I think a mere gent (which I take to be the lowest form of civilisation) better than a howling, whistling, clucking, stamping, jumping, tearing savage" (133).

The British soldiers have exactly the opposite response to the captain, as evidenced in their reaction to Mendez's need to have a separate person carry his guitar. Tom Packer, one of the British Marines, is horrified at this incident because he cannot believe that he is the prisoner of so uninspiring a man: "'I can stand a good deal,' whispers Tom Packer to me, looking hard at the guitar; 'but confound me, Davis, if it's not a trifle too much to be taken prisoner by such a fellow as that!'" ("Perils," 213). Unlike the pirates, the "sambos," and the "indians," the tried-and-true British men perceive weakness and a lack of true masculine identity in this figure.

If we take as a given that "masculinity (like femininity) is a *relational* construct, incomprehensible apart from the totality of gender relations; and that it is shaped in relation to men's social power" (Roper and Tosh, 2), we can see that the crisis in masculinity attached to Mendez is part of a greater gender problematic in the story, which includes Maid Marion's participation in battle, engagement with danger, and defense of nationalism. Marion's transgression into the more masculine realm, however, is a requirement for the preservation of the British subjects, and thus suggests her heroism and her allegorical relationship to the trope of the brave British woman, as described by Sharpe, produced in Mutiny discourse at this time. In opposition, the derogatory painting of Mendez in the context of Victorian constructions of masculinity perhaps suggests an overlap with the overall racial ideology of the text. As Michael Roper and John Tosh argue, "Dominant ideologies of masculinity are also maintained through asserting their difference from—and superiority to—other races" (13). Racial superiority is represented here as a more traditional masculinity, whereby the male British subjects work with, support, and listen to the female members of the British group, but retain their own sense of British masculinity.

## Failed Catharsis

Interestingly, rather than the angry, working-class Davis, it was Mendez that captured the hearts of audiences and readers. In the six versions of this story that "played in London and Brighton theatres in 1858," it was "Collins's flamboyant pirate captain, Mendez, stealing the leading role from Dickens's modest marine, Gill Davis" (Glancy, 173). Mendez becomes the focus of reading and viewing pleasure, because the story constructs him as a compelling figure, startlingly attired, powerful, and transgressive. His role as fetish derives from this ability to deflect the reader from the true conflict at the heart of the text: Gill Davis's divided loyalties, mended by Maid Maryon before the battle caused by Christian George

King, but nevertheless vulnerable. Davis's realization of his liminal position regarding the silver on Silver Store leads him to an analysis of his subject position, and his role in offering his life for its protection. By drawing him into an ideology of nationalist identification, and forcing him to defend himself from a mob of racialized attackers, Davis (and the reader) is diverted from the real problem—class—and refocused on a new villain—Pedro Mendez. Mendez's questionable relationship to Victorian ideals of masculinity only reinforces his power to draw the reader's attention and encourage the reader to disavow the text's true conflict.

The story attempts closure by moving away from the colonials' rather anticlimactic escape from Mendez (he is left sleeping), and back into a direct engagement with the simplified figure of Christian George King. The group escape on rafts in the middle of the night and are eventually rescued by Captain Carton, Maryon's future husband. It is Carton who spies Christian George King alone in the brush, and who kills him in what seems earmarked as the dramatic resolution to the story. We learn that it is Christian George King who has betrayed them by helping the pirates, thus valorizing Davis's initial dislike of him. In the final pages, we learn of the events that took place offstage, including the defeat of the pirates. Thus, the climax is not a bloody battle where all the pirates are killed, but one clean shot killing the ultimately hated betrayer, Christian George King. The scapegoat—set up as a symbol of all the rage, betrayal, and hate pent up in the mind of the contemporary British reader steeped in accounts of the Indian Rebellion—is thus both found in the wilderness and killed in a clean moment of vindication.

But is it effective? As a moment of cultural catharsis, the final point in the story is actually a failure, because of the diffusive power of the middle chapter. In effect, Collins's fetish, the easily deceived Mendez, remains unfinalized and thus inhibits the ability of the text to solve the problem of Davis's class conflicts. At the end of the text, all of the traditional limits and boundaries remain in place: "Having proved his 'nobility,' private Davis is rewarded—but not in the manner that we might expect. He is not promoted to the rank of sergeant; instead, he is transformed into a subservient 'vassal,' who pledges himself to his 'lady,' Miss Maryon, in chivalric fashion" (Nayder, 701). Davis does not marry Marion; he becomes her loyal servant in the way that is appropriate for his social standing. And this reassertion of authority is mirrored in the manner of the story's production: "Unable to read or write, Davis needs the help of Lady Carton to tell his story; she puts his oral account of the pirate attack into writing. In this way, the regressive social ideal of 'The Perils' is inscribed in its narrative form. In this double-voiced narrative, Lady Carton controls written language, the narrative's mode of production" (Nayder, 702).

But this reassertion of the dual narration—the dual manner of the text's production—reaffirms that this story is about contested boundaries, limits, and fissures, as well as the inherent issues of power which exist in all of these areas. For this story presents a remarkable encapsulation of the complex system of forces that participated in the mid-Victorian construction of race. As we have seen, generic, spatial, authorial, ethnic, national, gender, and cultural fissures riddle this text and keep it from achieving the moment of catharsis that Dickens arguably sought when he first conceived of his tale of pirate adventure in Silver Store. Rather than providing a moment of closure, the reemergence of the dialogic nature of these categories after the death of Christian George King, represented metonymically in the fetishized figure of Pedro Mendez, undermines the power of the story to express an effective moment of xenophobic catharsis.

Moving from the overt fictionalizing of historical events evident in "Perils," we turn now to a text that announces itself as an extreme representation of reality: the transcript of the Royal Commission's inquiry in the 1865 Morant Bay Rebellion. What we will find, however, is that even within this text, which consists of hundreds of pages of records of question and answer sessions held with numerous people in Jamaica in an attempt to recreate the events of the rebellion and discern Governor Edward Eyre's guilt or innocence in the violent retribution, we find that the narrow line of questioning obscures the true economic and social motivations for the uprising. Even within a genre so overtly focused on transmitting facts, we find that the parameters of the discourse deflect the reader from a direct engagement with the events. The ambivalence and conflicted nature of white British engagement with racial conflict, and the recourse to the comfortable solace of generic requirements, survive even this extreme example of empirical inquiry.

CHAPTER 4

∽

# "So Help Me God, the Truth
# and Not the Truth"[1]

## HYPER-REALISM AND THE TAXONOMY OF
## TRUTH SEEKING IN THE ROYAL COMMISSION'S INQUIRY
## INTO THE 1865 JAMAICA REBELLION

> 41645. Did you think they would tell you the truth?—
> I know we have got an untruthful community.
> —Royal Commission questioning Rev. G.R. Henderson

Governor Edward Eyre's brutal response to the 1865 Morant Bay
Rebellion in Jamaica sparked fierce controversy in England.
Strong voices on both sides of the issue fueled public discussions about the
proper role of colonial authority that continued years after the original
incident. In the transcript (1866) of the inquiry into the way Governor
Eyre quelled the rebellion, we find an account of face-to-face discussions
among agents of the English government, West Indian planters, and members
of both the black and "coloured" communities in Jamaica. The Royal
Commission's charge to determine what happened during the Rebellion
and the subsequent imposition of Martial Law produced hundreds of
pages of interviews. Although the majority of the text conveys the stark
rationalism of administrative inquiry, momentary eruptions within the
text suggest English and Jamaican frustration and antagonism. This chapter
will first present a discussion of the events of the rebellion itself, its precipitating
factors, and the reception of the news of the uprising in England,
in order to convey a sense of the atmosphere in which the Commission
conducted its inquiry. After establishing the context in which events took
place and the expectations surrounding the inquiry especially in England,
I will conduct a close examination of the transcript's rhetoric and argue
two key points. First, the cultural conflict precipitated by this event is, in

part, a rhetorical crisis regarding the transparency of realism—the governmental inquiry's extreme adherence to a visually based empirical taxonomy often lapses into absurdity as it attempts to recreate events. However, this absurdity, although disavowed, actually serves the project of imperial administration by helping cloak the realities of imperial brutality. Second, and related to the first point, when individuals exist in an unequal and oppressive power relationship, the category of "truth" becomes not a vehicle for an accurate and just version of events and motivations, but rather an illustration of the pressures and constraints on all the participants. Instead of providing a catharsis inspired by justice, the Government's search for the truth was yet another imposition of imperial authority on the colonized.

## Two Cultures in Crisis

Details of the uprising itself are well documented both in the transcript and supporting documents, and in historical and cultural studies of the event. Briefly, the Morant Bay Rebellion took place on October 11, 1865. Incensed by what they felt to be an unjust series of legal decisions, several hundred black farmers and laborers marched on the Bay to disrupt a vestry meeting. To obtain arms, the rebels first broke into the jail, and then moved on to the courthouse, where they met a small group of militia volunteers protecting the meeting. The custos, Baron von Ketelhodt, warned the mob to keep back, and then proceeded to read them the Riot Act. Accounts differ as to which group attacked first, but in either case the volunteers were hopelessly outnumbered and they took refuge inside the courthouse. The rebels set the building next to the courthouse on fire, which spread to the courthouse itself and drove the group out of the building. Some escaped, but at the end of the day the rebels killed eighteen people and wounded thirty-one others, including the custos and several members of the vestry. In subsequent days, bands of rebels murdered four more persons and wounded another three. The official response to these events was Martial Law, declared everywhere on the island except for Kingston. Martial Law would last much longer than the original Rebellion and cost many more lives.[2]

Jamaica's controversial Governor, Edward Eyre, quickly and fiercely contained the rebellion by declaring the state of Martial Law, which lasted from October 13 to November 13, 1865. Under the administration of Gordon Ramsey, the brutal officer in charge of Martial Law in Morant Bay,

British forces killed 439 people, often without a trial. In addition, soldiers flogged 600 men and women and destroyed upwards of 1,000 homes. Most provocatively, George William Gordon, a popular "coloured" politician, was captured in Kingston, an area not bound by Martial Law, and brought back to Morant Bay to stand trial under Martial Law. Gordon was tried, convicted, and hanged for what was perceived to be his part in provoking the uprising. This decision to bring Gordon back to Morant Bay plagued Governor Eyre for the rest of his life, and split the English population into those supporting the Governor's decision, and those who were determined to have him prosecuted for Gordon's murder.

Studies of the economic and social situation in post-Emancipation Jamaica suggest that tensions on the island were the result of longstanding issues of economic policy that favored sugar plantation labor policies, limited access to justice for black and "coloured" residents, intensified a social hierarchy that was based in many cases on color, and aggravated planter frustration about the ever-worsening sugar market (Heuman, *Between*, 190). From the late eighteenth century on, the "coloured" population of Jamaica was stratified into blacks who were primarily slaves, but sometimes earned their freedom; and a free "coloured" population, which "increased rapidly during the remainder of the eighteenth and early part of the nineteenth centuries" (7). Many of the free population had immigrated from St. Domingo at the end of the eighteenth century. In general, planters feared this population because they felt that they might incite the slave population to rebel, thus destroying the slave system and the sugar industry (23). Some planters recognized the potential to co-opt the free "coloured" and black population, however, by giving them an economic and social stake in the existing system (11).

After British Emancipation, the basic tripartite social structure remained virtually unchanged. The white planter population retained primary control of the economic, political, and judicial systems of the colony. The free "coloured" population was granted enough of a stake in the community to keep them faithful, and the freed slaves were pressured to remain on the plantations as laborers, frustrated in their desire to become small landowners. Relations between the black and "coloured" populations on the island were strained, as efforts to improve the lives of the poorest of the populations remained unsupported by the new "coloured" bourgeoisie. This inequality of opportunity created ongoing tensions throughout the years before the Morant Bay outbreak (Heuman, *Killing*, 77).

Also contributing to social tension was the erosion of the sugar industry after Emancipation. When the British Whig Government equalized the sugar duties in 1846, it was, Heuman argues, "an economic as well as a psychological blow to the West Indian planters" (*Between*, 141). Rather than change their economic situation, however, the planters stubbornly determined to retain their system intact (149). In his study, *The West Indies* (1862), Edward Underhill, Secretary for the Baptist Missionary Society, provides an especially vivid description of the Jamaican situation in the early 1860s. Underhill was an outspoken critic of the economic and social system of Jamaica, and his letter to Colonial Secretary Edward Cardwell sparked meetings of black laborers and farmers all over the island in the 1860s, which many argue were the catalyst for the explosion of Morant Bay.

In conversation with various passengers on the voyage to the West Indies, Underhill found that even though the economic transition caused by Emancipation had been a struggle, there was no general desire to return to the system of slavery. In fact, except for Jamaica, all the English islands were actually prospering under the free system (Underhill, 5). Underhill argues, in response to those such as Thomas Carlyle—who suggested that if productivity had sunk on the islands after the elimination of slavery, perhaps the decision should be reconsidered[3]—that "the rights of humanity demand that they be left to work out their own destiny, even though it be obtained through anarchy and civil strife. Men are not made fit for liberty by oppression or servitude. Freedom alone is the true school in which men's faculties can be trained for the higher purposes of life, and the black is as capable of attaining them as the fairer-skinned peoples of more favoured climes" (Underhill, 176). In other words, although the transitional system on Jamaica may not have worked to an optimum level of productivity, what was of primary importance was the need to allow the population to learn the trade, one might say, of freedom and how to thrive under it.

During his visit to Jamaica, one of Underhill's most striking observations was that truth and information were understood relative to social position. Differences of opinion regarding the enfranchised population "met us at our first step," which led the party "not only to look at *what* was said, but to inquire *who* says it, in order to arrive at an impartial judgement" (182, original italics). Underhill notes that "there were very few disposed to take a hopeful view of the prospects of the country. The newspapers, with scarcely an exception, represent things in the darkest light; and if we may believe the statements unceasingly made, Jamaica is hopelessly ruined" (183). Startled by the lack of any pride or loyalty in the general population regarding their home, Underhill notes the criticisms generally made:

Nothing is right. The Government is extravagant and bad. The officers are venal. The legislature is governed by class interests, and addicted to "log rolling." The planters are poor, their estates worthless, and their cultivation thriftless and unskilful [sic]. The people are idle, vain, improvident, unchaste. Their religion is hypocrisy. Their social condition is one of African barbarism and dark superstition. In short, the island is in a state of irretrievable decay. Such is the picture which is held up to a stranger, and no little pains are taken to make him believe it to be a faithful representation. (183)

The relationship between the different classes and colors is poor: "the intercourse of the white with the black is often marked by hauteur, by peremptoriness, by indifference, and not seldom by contempt" (192). Underhill argues this alienation between the classes "will continue to exist until the intelligence and wealth of the black, shall place him more on an equality with the white" (192). Although Underhill reduces the relationship of color to one between black and white, he goes on to discuss the tensions between the black and the "coloured" population, arguing that "the presence of the white is the chief security for order and good government, for the antagonism between the brown and the black is greater than that of either against the white. The brown element has of late largely influenced the Assembly, and with no advantage to the country. The brown people are eager for place, and the number of offices of emolument under the Government is perfectly astonishing" (225).

Underhill specifically addresses many of the complaints that are later involved repeatedly in the investigation and in the papers regarding this disturbance. Planters complain that workers do not want to work past midday because they are lazy. The laborers argue that if they work past midday, they are often not paid for the extra work they perform (259). The rate of wages over the previous thirty years had been steadily declining, and the laborers could make more money working their own land (264–65). Rather than acknowledge the economic roots of the laborers' work ethic, Underhill comments, planters will argue that "generally the people of Jamaica are great deceivers and liars. It might be a remnant of slavery influences; but it seemed, in most cases, inherent in their character, almost a natural peculiarity" (267). Using the classically racist, biological explanation of the inferiority of a particular group, decisions made on the reality of economic conditions were dismissed by planters in favor of hereditary weakness.

Ultimately, Underhill depicts the horrendous state of social and economic relations as resulting from old resentments and an inability on the part of the planters to achieve a new labor philosophy (270–71). Coupled with obstinacy is the sense among the laboring class that they are not treated fairly or respectfully by the planters, and that the planters have not moved beyond feeling that the workers are their property (330). A man on the island explains to Underhill,

> When the slaves were made free, they were a "little obstinate" about wages and their provision grounds, which belonged to the estates; the overseers were a "little obstinate" too, and wished to do as they had been accustomed during slavery. So the overseers pulled down the people's houses, and discharged them. The people having thus become quite free, went to the mountains, obtained land, made themselves independent, and now they won't come back; they do better on their own land than at estate work. (387)

Coupled with this state of mistrust was a periodic slump in sugar prices, as well as the outbreak of the American Civil War which "led to a substantial rise in the cost of importing food and clothing" (Heuman, *Between,* 171). Therefore, as Heuman argues, "the riot at Morant Bay occurred at a time when conditions were especially difficult in the colony. Economic distress had affected the island generally, and the meetings to discuss the Underhill letter had broadcast the people's grievances over a wide audience" (190). The number of "black and brown representatives declined during the early 1860s," and so it was "far less possible" for these populations "to remain a significant political force in the island" (Heuman, 171). Added to the mix was the arrival on the island of the new governor, Edward Eyre.

Heuman argues that Eyre came into conflict almost immediately with an outspoken Radical "coloured" politician on the island, George William Gordon (*Between,* 176). Gordon was born a slave, the son of a planter attorney and a slave woman. Freed by his father, "the younger Gordon eventually opened a produce store in Kingston which proved successful and enabled him to purchase large plots of land all over the island" (61). Gordon intended to sell these plots to the laborers who worked the land, and thus to expand the pool of voters in the black population (61). He had become an increasingly outspoken advocate for the poor, and was at the same time becoming part of the Native Baptist population of the island that encouraged the poor to organize and better themselves. More specifically, as magistrate of Morant Bay, Gordon had complained about the atrocious

condition of the parish jail. When Eyre arrived on the island, his immediate reaction to Gordon's activism was to censure Gordon and dismiss him
from the magistery (61). Heuman observes that Eyre generally blew problems out of perspective through a stubborn adherence to his own point of
view (179). This legacy of mistrust, political turmoil, and tension erupted
on October 11 with the Morant Bay Rebellion.


## Reception in England

Coming soon after the 1857 Indian Rebellion and the American Civil War,
the reception in England of news of the insurrection, by a British public
increasingly impatient with the problem of colonial unrest, kindled familiar arguments about the nature of darker-skinned people, the English role
in the colonies, and the problem of colonial uprisings. As with the Indian
Rebellion, initial reports from planter papers in Jamaica contained inflat-
ed accounts of the size and scope of the conflict. These accounts portrayed
heinous crimes being committed against British citizens reminiscent of
reports coming out of India just a few years before.[4] Although authorities
put down the Morant Bay Rebellion quite easily, the controversy sparked
by methods the military used to control the situation lasted for more than
five years.

These initial accounts added fuel to the already growing fire of racism
in the 1860s. As Patrick Brantlinger argues, the events of both Cawnpore
and Jamaica solidified for "many Victorians that the 'dark races' were destined to remain forever dark until they perished from the face of the earth"
(*Rule*, 38). Mary Poovey adds that for many Englishmen, "the 'savagery' of
dark-skinned peoples was proved once more" (*Making*, 179). The dark-
skinned races in the colonial environment, this line of thinking suggests,
were obviously unfit for freedom, unworthy of trust, and in need of strong
management.[5] Major figures in the artistic and scientific communities
took sides on the issue of Eyre's authority to inflict harsh punishment, and
on his decision to transport Gordon from Kingston into an area under
Martial Law. Brantlinger writes that "Carlyle, Dickens, Kingsley, Ruskin,
and Tennyson all supported the Governor Eyre Defense Committee, jingoist in all but name (Eyre was in their view the hero, rather than the villain,
of the Jamaica Rebellion of 1865)." Opposing these figures were "Mill,
Huxley, Darwin, Tom Hughes, and other liberal intellectuals who wanted
Eyre to stand trial for murder" (*Rule*, 28–29). Although Dickens did not
match the unadulterated racism advanced by Carlyle in "Occasional

Discourse on the Nigger Question" (1853), he was far from liberal or progressive on issues regarding populations under colonial authority.
Dickens's support for Eyre stemmed largely from his basic mistrust of
administrative systems and his belief in the bumbling nature of governmental information structures. The revolutionary nature of the uprising
was yet another incidence of racial rebelliousness to add to the Indian
Rebellion, illustrating, for Dickens, the injustice of addressing the plight of
free blacks rather than the suffering of British laborers.

Carlyle and the Eyre Defense Committee focused on creating an image
of Eyre as the heroic leader who saved Jamaica from anarchy and ruin,
placing Eyre within the tradition of heroic figures such as Cromwell and
Frederick the Great. The committee justified Eyre's use of force by alluding to the memory of both Haiti and the Indian Rebellion, events that
came to function as tropes in an ever-deepening rhetoric of racism circulating in mid-Victorian culture. As Catherine Hall argues, "the double
spectres of Haiti (when the blacks had driven out all the whites), and of the
Indian Mutiny (when, according to the collective English myth, the
Indians had brutally massacred, in the most treacherous circumstances,
English men, women and children) were ever present in both the Jamaican
and the English consciousness, shaping expectations and raising hopes and
fears" (*White, Male and Middle-Class*, 282).

The Eyre Defense Committee was able to use the tropes of "Haiti" and
the "Indian Mutiny" to garner support. They combined events: Eyre's
actions and those of his officers prevented what happened in Haiti and
India from occurring in Jamaica. Even though the validity of the accounts
initially describing both events was suspect, the images described in them
were lodged in the English psyche and thus easily evoked. The horrors of
Haiti and Cawnpore were recognized widely enough to provide support
for Eyre's actions.

Not surprisingly, many in the reactionary scientific community supported Eyre's actions. According to Robert J. C. Young, radical racialist
James Hunt, president of the Anthropological Society, "announced his
'intense admiration' at the conduct of Governor Eyre, who was himself a
member of the Society, in his brutal suppression of the Jamaica
Insurrection in 1865" (136). George Stocking notes that the organization
responded with "a public meeting at which Captain Bedford Pim gave a
paper on 'The Negro and Jamaica.' Pim's racist diatribe was greeted 'with
loud cheers' and a unanimous vote of thanks, after which one member of
the audience after another got up to offer comments on 'the true art of governing alien races.' One even advocated killing savages as "a philanthropic

principle"—when trouble broke out, there was 'mercy in a massacre'"
("What's in a Name?" 379). Eyre garnered support from a variety of different communities and populations, the common element amongst them
being a growing frustration with increasing violence both on the part of
communities of color in the colonies, and of working-class Englishmen in
the metropolis.

Support for Eyre was met with outrage on behalf of many politicians
and intellectuals, because of the perceived injustices perpetrated on behalf
of the nation. Hall argues that as accounts of the events began to arrive in
England, humanitarian, Radical, and governmental figures became concerned "about some of the apparent irregularities which had taken place,
particularly around the court martial and execution of George William
Gordon. Gordon had been a member of the Jamaican House of Assembly;
he was the illegitimate son of a white planter by a slave-woman but had
himself become a landowner and married a white woman" (Hall, *White,
Male and Middle-Class,* 276).[6]

In his *Autobiography,* John Stuart Mill describes this change in public
opinion during this time. He says that initially,

> [t]he perpetrators of those deeds were defended and applauded in
> England by the same kind of people who had so long upheld negro slav-
> ery: and it seemed at first as if the British nation was about to incur the
> disgrace of letting pass without even a protest, excesses of authority as
> revolting as any of those for which, when perpetrated by the instruments
> of other governments, Englishmen can hardly find terms sufficient to
> express their abhorrence. After a short time, however, an indignant feeling
> was roused: a voluntary Association formed itself under the name of the
> Jamaica Committee, to take such deliberation and action as the case might
> admit of. (207–8)[7]

Harriet Martineau, in a letter to Fanny Wedgwood dated November 5,
1866, expressed her hope for the activities of the Jamaica Committee. She
called its work "the best test of what we are worth, as English citizens, that
has been offered in my time. It is a wonderful way of separating the sheep
from the goats,—and the muddle-pated from the clearsighted, and the
superficial from the wellgrounded" (273). Beyond issues of justice, governmental and popular reactions to the accounts came to represent for
Martineau a way of gauging the temper of her times.

What became central to the discussion was the role of authority and
the limits that should or should not be put on the exercise of that author-

ity in times of rebellion, whether at home or abroad (Lorimer, *Colour*, 197). Mill declared,

> There was much more at stake than only justice to the Negroes, imperative as was that consideration. The question was, whether the British dependencies, and eventually, perhaps, Great Britain itself, were to be under the government of law, or of military license; whether the lives and persons of British subjects are at the mercy of any two or three officers however raw and inexperienced or reckless and brutal, whom a panicstricken Governor, or other functionary, may assume the right to constitute into a so-called Courtmartial. (208)

And Christine Bolt argues that increasingly the "defense of the rights of Negroes was equated with defense of the rights of British working men, and of labour the world over" (83), an equation that galvanized Liberal and Radical support for more rigorous inquiry into exactly what happened on the island during the Rebellion and the extended imposition of Martial Law. Government authorities felt the pressure of this growing feeling of concern about what happened on the island. Heuman notes that "almost immediately Cardwell came under pressure to withhold support for the actions of the authorities in Jamaica" (*Killing*, 164). As time passed, it became increasingly evident that some kind of official inquiry into the situation was necessary (165). Finally, according to Hall, "the government announced that a Royal Commission would investigate what had happened and Eyre was called back to London" (*White, Male and Middle-Class*, 276). This inquiry and Eyre's defense of his actions would produce hundreds of pages of information, the ultimate value of which lies in its display of the limited utility of an empirically-based fact finding project for the imperial enterprise.

## Information and Control

> An endless task, the cataloguing of reality. We accumulate facts, we discuss them,
> but with every line that is written, with every statement that is made one has
> the feeling of incompleteness.
> —Frantz Fanon, *Black Skin, White Masks*

The documentation of the Royal Commission's investigation into the events of the Morant Bay Rebellion provides a curious record of power imbalances, evasion, and misspent labor. Central to the project is the assumption that an organization sent from the mother country, armed with the tools of an empirically based visual taxonomy of governmental administration, can determine the truth. Underpinning this taxonomy is an understanding of truth as an entity to be discerned by physical and visual contact with the situation and people. If they go to the island and speak with the different communities, they should be able to discern what happened. However, the text produced by the inquiry presents a virtually postmodern collection of manipulations of subjectivities that ultimately problematizes the concepts of realism, identity, and order far more than it discerns the truth of any of these categories.

The emphasis on visual information speaks to the challenge of geographical detachment that strains the efficacy of the imperial project. The geographical distance between the center of power and the colony required the creation of an illusion of knowledge in order to satisfy a need for perceived control over the Empire's holdings. Data and information became the mediating force that yoked together the British Empire. In *The Imperial Archive* (1993), Thomas Richards connects the British need to control the empire with the Victorians' obsession with facts and documents. Richards observes, "An empire is partly a fiction. No nation can close its hand around the world; the reach of any nation's empire always exceeds its final grasp. An empire is by definition and default a nation in overreach, one nation that has gone too far, a nation that has taken over too many countries too far away from home to control them effectively" (1).

In this situation of fictional control, Richards argues, "[the British] often could do little other than collect and collate information, for any exact civil control, of the kind possible in England, was out of the question. The Empire was too far away, and the bureaucrats of Empire had to be content to shuffle papers" (*Imperial,* 3). Papers, inquiries, and information were partial mediators between the metropolis and the colonies, and when this relationship disintegrated, it had to be buttressed by violence and by the fictional ability to truly know what is occurring in those distant outposts.

A positivist belief in the "fact" as a pure and value-free category of knowledge underpins the government's faith in the ability of Commission members to understand the dynamics of the island. As Richards argues, this ideology "had also led most people into believing that the best and most certain kind of knowledge was the fact. The fact was many things to many people, but generally it was thought of as raw knowledge, knowledge awaiting ordering. The various civil bureaucracies sharing the administration of Empire were desperate for these manageable pieces of knowledge. They were light and movable. They pared the Empire down to file-cabinet size" (*Imperial*, 4).

This project of Victorian data collection reduced the world to facts, which were considered value-free, linguistic items; when collected together, they would produce the "truth." The problem, Richards suggests, "was that facts almost never added up to anything. They were snippets of knowledge, tiny particularized units responsible for our current idea of information. It took a leap of faith to believe that facts would someday add up to any palpable sum of knowledge" (*Imperial*, 6). Conclusions derived from collections of facts, Richards argues, would be incomplete at best.

Close examination of the documents ultimately presented by the Commission, however, reveals a pastiche of forms and perspectives that, far from providing a clear picture of events and motivations, present an opportunity to address the connection between formal structures, ideological perspectives, and the assumptions underpinning a governmental taxonomy of truth seeking. The official governmental "facts" describing the Morant Bay Rebellion are contained in a long document divided into three sections: papers submitted by Governor Eyre in response to the inquiry into the events on the island, including letters, accounts, testimonials, and a report; the report of the Royal Commission summarizing its findings after its inquiry; and the extensive transcripts of the interviews conducted by the Commission. This collection of texts transforms the Rebellion into a rhetorical event that certainly endorses Richards's claim that the governance of a colony geographically situated so far away from the home government is liable to failure. But this gap between epistemology and ideology created by the limitations of information gathering also serves as an effective tool for imperialism, because it provides an obscuring filter in the guise of hyperrealistic truth seeking.

The documents attest to, and intensify, the divisions existing among white, "coloured," and black populations on the one hand, and between citizens of the metropolis and the colony on the other. Themes that recur throughout the texts include the prominent role of women in the Rebellion; the black rejection of established church religion, which was used by whites as a diagnostic criterion for future unrest; and the repeated dismissal or limited acknowledgment of labor issues as a motivating factor in the rebels' decision to attack.

The formal qualities of the documents vary widely. There is frequent repetition, evident, most prominently, in Governor Eyre's obsessive explanation of his actions. Summaries of the events of the rebellion recur throughout the text, as does analysis of the events primarily based on the hereditary or biological explanation for black behavior. There are innumerable transcripts of court martials, question-and-answer sessions, testimonies, and depositions; additionally, the documents include official and personal correspondence, maps, innumerable lists of flogging victims and hangings, official notes for debts, announcements, newspapers, dispatches, and records of oaths forced on different individuals by the rebels or by the government. Although the diversity of materials gives us a polyphony of voices participating in the search for answers, the formulaic nature of the documents creates a hypnotic effect, making it difficult for a reader to absorb the material after a certain point.

Both the documents provided by Governor Eyre and the documents of the inquiry include raw data and analysis. The Commission Report synthesizes into a narrative the isolated, individual accounts found in the Eyre papers. Most curious in these papers are the two models of text that make up the Governor's defense of his actions. In the Eyre Papers, letters of support from many of the island's white citizens appear in their original form. Eyre then seemingly pulled a couple of sentences from each letter, and then strung these bits together to create yet another text summarizing what the Governor thought to be the most pertinent points. From the original documents, more documents were created by a kind of discursive pastiche. This second text creates the sense of multiple voices, but rather than speaking in unison, they speak in succession. The rhetorical dynamics of this text attempt to enhance the Governor's support by metonymically referencing an imaginatively limitless pool of information proving the correctness of his actions—a pool itself partially signified by the full-text letters included in the documents. Immediately, however, we see that this collection of governmental materials functions at least as much as rhetorical battleground as container of factual information.

The Eyre Papers begin with a January 1866 dispatch from Governor Eyre to Edward Cardwell, M.P., justifying his use of extreme force to quell the rebellion. Four key arguments, echoing Underhill's presentation of the planter perspectives on the island, make up Eyre's defense of his actions. First, Eyre addresses the increasing conflation of colonial and English labor interests in mid-Victorian discourse by arguing that the "negroes from a low state of civilization and being under the influence of superstitious feelings could not properly be dealt with in the same manner as might the peasantry of a European country" ("Reports from Commissioners," 1). He goes on to explain that "to produce any adequate effect upon such a population, numbering as they do some 350,000, as against about 13,000 whites who are scattered amongst them in isolated and unprotected positions and widely separated from each other, it was of paramount importance that punishment for such serious offenses as rebellion, arson, and murder, should be prompt, certain, and severe" (1). Because of black Jamaicans' limited understanding of the workings of advanced civilization, Eyre suggests, a form of punishment commensurate with their social level was necessary.

Eyre's second reason for using excessive measures was that "as a race the negroes are most excitable and impulsive, and any seditious or rebellious action was sure to be taken up by and extended amongst the large majority of those with whom it came in contact" ("Reports from Commissioners," 1). The third reason was "that as a race the negroes are most reticent, and it is very difficult to obtain from them full or specific information upon any subject; hence it is almost impossible to arrive at anything like correct details of their plans or intentions" (2). Information was difficult to obtain, not because of firmly entrenched dynamics of mistrust and violence, but because the blacks were constitutionally reticent. Tied to this issue of obtaining information is the fourth reason: "the negroes exercise a reign of terror over each other which deters people from giving information of any intended outrage, or from assisting in any way to frustrate its perpetration" (2). Again, concerning the issue of garnering information, black Jamaicans were not only constitutionally reticent, but they encouraged further reticence by means of violent acts committed on one another. Eyre closed his response by asserting that the Rebellion was universal throughout the island, and that there were only one thousand troops to respond to the problem.

Three themes recur throughout the letters in support of the Governor. First, predictably, is the threat of Haiti as an example to the population. Eyre admits in his statement that innocent people may have been killed, or had their houses burned, but in the heat of the moment, with the threat of Haiti in minds of the rebels, drastic measures had to be taken. Eyre supporters also assert that Haiti influenced the rebels. Doctor John Stothert Gerrard claims that "at one meeting in particular the negroes '*were advised to do as the Haytiens had done*,' we could not but make sure that if an outbreak did occur, it would be of a most sanguinary and merciless character" ("Reports from Commissioners," 34, original italics). And in a letter from Rector Charles T. May to Mr. Myers, on the state of the island on January 4, 1866, May states that "I further believe that there are now, at the present moment, Haitiens [sic], who pretend that they cannot speak English, going about the Island, endeavouring to inculcate the same seditious spirit. I have grave suspicions that this is the case" (142). The trope of "Haiti" stands here as a testament to the absolute necessity of committing many violent acts in order to ensure that the revolution of that island not recur in Jamaica.

Second, the Eyre documents are full of accusations that the British Press fueled the fire against Governor Eyre, thus putting the lives of the British on the island in danger. In a letter to Governor Eyre, dated January 16, 1866, Dr. McCatty writes, "I hasten to sympathize with your Excellency in the treatment you have received by the fanatical portion of the English press" ("Reports from Commissioners," 19). The Rev. Heneage Guid, Rector of St. David's, concurs, in a letter to Mr. Myers, on the state of the island on January 2, 1866: "I believe the spirits of G. W. Gordon and Paul Bogle to be still active, and the elements of insubordination still fermenting, but to what extent I will not pretend to say; but if they should hereafter show themselves in overt acts, Mr. Chamerovzow and his coadjutors of the English press could hardly escape the charge of having pandered to and inflamed them. That their writings are carefully communicated to the negroes, it cannot be doubted from certain rumours which are at present current among them" (87). Liberal and Radical writings that evoked Haiti created a threat which, when disclosed, justified Governor Eyre's actions. The discourses, produced by Liberal organizations in the metropolis, had the power to influence the citizens beyond the immediate reality of their livelihood. This power is reminiscent of the determined work of abolitionist writers earlier in the century.

Finally, the letters accuse the Baptist missionary Edward Underhill of inciting the population to riot by sending a letter to the Colonial Office regarding the extreme poverty in which the vast majority of the island's population lived. Captain Kent, R.N., Stipendiary Magistrate, writes Mr. Myers on January 4, 1866 that he feels that "the injudicious and intemperate conduct of Dr. Underhill is mainly to be attributed this fearful outbreak and loss of life. For that gentleman to state that the negroes were starving and could not obtain work was false in the extreme" ("Reports from Commissioners," 94). Kent claimed that religious reasons, rather than economic and survival issues, had created discontent among the Jamaican farmers:

> the conduct and bearing of black people [is] . . . less industrious, less orderly, and less respectful than formerly, and as often exhibiting gratuitously offensive, insolent or defiant demeanor. They speak of the utter disregard of right, law, truth, honesty, or morality, of sullen vindictiveness

and savage brutality, of excitement caused by imaginary wrongs sedulous-
ly preached to them by others, of agitation stimulated by designing demagogues, of statements calling their attention to their numerical strength as
compared with the white population, and of the holding up to their view
the results accomplished by the black race in the neighbouring republics of
Hayti [sic] and St. Domingo. (18–19)

The writers of these letters represent black Jamaicans as easily led and
manipulated for the purposes of Liberal and religious forces that are
unaware of the true nature of the black race. There was apparently no
threat that the black population held the power of self-determination in
these events; they were merely pawns.

Haiti is not the only trope for colonial violence evoked in support of
Governor Eyre. Repeated references to the Indian Rebellion, juxtaposed
with accounts of the behavior of the Jamaican rebels toward British
women on the island, imply that the threat of rape justified severe, violent
retribution. In his statement, Edward William Major, health officer of Port
Morant and Morant Bay, says that he believes "there has not been one lady
killed, but the purpose for which they were spared makes the rebellion still
worse than the Indian mutiny, and it is now admitted that orders were
given by the leaders to kill all the males and to save the females, as they
would take them for themselves" ("Reports from Commissioners," 30).
India joins Haiti in the colonial imaginary as a site where the rebellion of
colonial populations resulted in British suffering. Conspicuously absent
from the discourse of the Eyre papers is any examination of the economic
or social dynamics of the island. Instead, the rhetoric employs theories
about the biological disposition of the black Jamaicans, evokes the specter
of black violence, and castigates the rhetoric of metropolitan discourse and
intervention. Universal qualities, as well as historical precedent, are confi-
dently asserted to justify the outrages committed by colonial authorities
and undermine the authority of black or "coloured" testimonies.

Eyre uses classic imperialist reasoning to justify his actions during
Martial Law. In *The Colonizer and the Colonized*, Albert Memmi discusses
how colonials often use violence to justify the intrinsically oppressive
nature of the colonial system. In his Introduction to Memmi's text, Jean-
Paul Sartre describes colonialism as a system that "denies human rights to
human beings whom it has subdued by violence, and keeps them by force
in a state of misery and ignorance" (xxiv). Memmi himself suggests that
"[c]olonial racism is built from three major ideological components: one,
the gulf between the culture of the colonialist and the colonized; two, the

exploitation of these differences for the benefit of the colonialist; three, the use of these supposed differences as standards of absolute fact" (71). Echoing the words and justifications used by Eyre and his supporters to defend the Governor's position, Memmi describes a "mythical portrait of the colonized" (79) that includes a disposition to be lazy, wicked, backward, evil, thieving, ungrateful, and sadistic, all characteristics which the colonizer uses to justify "his police and his legitimate severity" (82). Colonials deny individuality, liberty, and humanity to the colonized (85–86). Finally, Memmi argues that the most serious offense imposed upon the colonized "is being removed from history and from the community. Colonization usurps any free role in either war or peace, every decision contributing to his destiny and that of the world, and all cultural and social responsibility" (91). All of these tactics are used in the Eyre papers as a way to disarm any kind of humanitarian explanation for the struggle for human rights and basic dignity in the colonial context.

The treatment of violence is one of the primary differences between the papers submitted by Governor Eyre and those submitted by the Royal Commission. In the Eyre papers, rebels commit violent acts upon the colonists. A reader can walk away from this collection of papers with the impression that the island's colonial government did not exact any retribution for the Rebellion. When the reader moves into the papers documenting the Royal Commission inquiry, however, frequent and graphic descriptions of military violence emerge. The most powerful impression one receives from a careful examination of the documents is the formal tension that exists between the detached, dispassionate, and depersonalized tone of the text, produced by a sterile question-and-answer format, and the content that contains a level of violence so destructive that it is often difficult to read. For example, Richard Sherrington, a black laborer, describes the murder and dismemberment of another man:

> 12,102. Did they not carry the body down the hill?—No; the soldiers took their feet and capsized him down the hill. 12,103. Was the head on then?— Not till after they came down, and then they cut his head off. They loosed him when he received one shot and could not finish him, but as he fell down they gave him another close shot, and then they capsized him down the hill, and I saw the men pitched him down to the market. (Report II:239)

The matter-of-fact presentation of much of the testimony regarding flogging, torture, murder, and sadistic treatment of prisoners paints a stark picture of extreme colonial authority. The form in which the information is presented, however, limits the impact of the violence. A reading of this text suggests several questions: When is narrating vast numbers of violent assaults an act of psychological violence in itself? When does the recounting of innumerable acts of violence lead to the impression of absurdity or sublimity? And how does that absurdity come into contradiction with the hyperrationality of the text's organizational structure?

## Factual Excess

Truth is that which hurries on the break-up of the colonialist regime; it is that which promotes the emergence of the nation; it is all that protects the natives, and ruins the foreigners. In this colonialist context there is no truthful behavior: the good is quite simply that which is evil for "them."
—Frantz Fanon, *The Wretched of the Earth*

By far the largest section of the document is the record of the question-and-answer sessions conducted by the Commission with countless citizens from the island. Of obvious priority to the Commission members was the reconstruction of an exact picture of the actions that took place during the extended imposition of Martial Law. Detailed questioning about people's activities, actions, and locations suffuses the text, providing the illusion of absolute visual accuracy in renditions of the events. The rational, unemotional air created in the text gives the impression of a bank of data, unencumbered by solipsism or emotion. This emphasis on visual reconstruction, however, ultimately fails to produce a clear picture of the events. Rather, the apparent absence of rhetoric functions as a rhetorical strategy that ironically obscures the social dynamics of the event in question. Although we can see where individuals were and what they did, readers lack a clear understanding of motivation for those actions, and thus cannot go beyond an illusion of knowledge about the events created by a sense of visual immediacy. Underhill's injunction to understand not only what is said, but who is saying it, when dealing with complex social communities in the West Indies becomes reduced by the Commission to a racist disregard for the complicated subject positions of Jamaican black and "coloured" residents.

The Royal Commission, a Liberally and Radically inspired investigation, "held its first meeting on 20 January [1866]. In addition to the president of the Commission, Sir Henry Storks, there were two other members, the Recorder for Leeds, J. B. Maule and the Recorder of the City of London, Russell Gurney" (Heuman, *Killing*, 167). The stated purpose of the Commission was "to make inquiry into the origin, nature, and circumstances of certain late disturbances in the Island of Jamaica" (Report I:7). At the end of their investigation they produced a nine-hundred-page text containing a report and a list of 49,158 questions with answers. Notable differences exist between the testimonies of white and "coloured" individuals, and those made by black individuals. As in the letters used by Eyre, white and "coloured" witnesses generally criticized blacks for their insolent and defiant manner, lawlessness, and laziness. Witnesses repeatedly refer to black Jamaicans' use of seditious and threatening language, and they report that the younger blacks lack respectfulness. White and "coloured" witnesses state that the rebels threatened to kill all white men and keep all white women for themselves, were armed with cutlasses and hatchets—all laborers required these implements for their work—created fictions of economic hardship, and organized an insurrection. They also complain of the Underhill meetings and of the activities of George William Gordon and Paul Bogle. Blacks would have been peaceful if not stirred up by Underhill and other Baptists, these testimonials suggest. There are repeated references to blacks constructing their own government and courts including levying fines—accounts always tempered, however, by differing views on the ability of blacks to organize. White and "coloured" witnesses describe black rebels using traditional military titles for their leaders in the Rebellion, using drums, carrying flags, and professing loyalty to the cause as they engaged in military training and drilling to prepare for the Rebellion.

Conversely, the black witnesses complain of primarily economic issues: low wages, not getting paid, failure to receive land promised to them, not having money earmarked for fighting smallpox, excessive tariffs, and not receiving land and money they thought the Queen had sent especially for them. The black witnesses also complain of a lack of judicial equality. They worried that slavery was returning, and worried that representatives sympathetic with their situation, like Gordon, would be run out of government. In fact, as Heuman notes, "when the Commission concluded its efforts on 9 April there was a great deal of conflicting evidence. Moreover, it was not always clear who was telling the truth. Some witnesses lied; as *The Colonial Standard* pointed out, this included men and women who exaggerated the flogging they had received" (*Killing*, 170). More significantly, the Commission's ability to determine the validity of facts being reported to it often seems impossible, especially in several extreme cases.

The first involves a woman supposedly killed while delivering a child. John Elish Grant, a stillerman at the Albion estate, testifies that he was taken away by the soldiers, and that the following incident took place on the march:

> 2440. What happened as you went along?—When we got to a house a person was grunting in the house, and directly a soldier went up to guard the house, and when the woman was grunting he said, "You bitch, I will let you grunt for something," and directly I heard "Oh, oh." I went to the door and saw a female naked in the house, and a baby came out from her in the house, about this (*about a foot*), and at that time the soldier shot an old lady and a little boy in the house.
> 2441. Were they shot do you mean?—The soldier shot the old lady and the woman, and a little bit of a boy in the house. (Report II:55)

The Commission, after hearing this account, asks for and receives confirmation from the witness (Report II:56). Later in the testimony, however, the evidence of three witnesses, Edward Gillespie, Emily Davis, and Thomas Miller, refutes the story (Report II:335). The question becomes: how does this government inquiry determine the validity of an account such as this one? Often in the transcript, vividly violent moments such as this one appear in the midst of conflicting accounts and testimonies. The visual spectacle of the moment becomes paramount, especially when brought out by the Commission's emphasis on visual detail. And although the spectacular nature of the event remains, the Commission's overt project of discerning validity becomes seemingly impossible. As the ability to gain accuracy recedes in the documentation, the text begins to read more like the details of a James Grant or H. Rider Haggard novel than an official truth-seeking project.

In the final Report, produced by the Commission and submitted to Edward Cardwell on April 9, 1866, the members of the Commission point to the problem of establishing a true picture of the events. They note, "in many cases the witnesses manifested a singular ignorance of the nature and value of evidence, as well as a misconception of the proper scope of the Inquiry" (Report I:8). They continue, "it is enough to recall the fact that they were for the most part uneducated peasants, speaking in accents strange to the ear, often in a phraseology of their own, with vague conceptions of number and time, unaccustomed to definiteness or accuracy of speech, and, in many cases, still smarting under a sense of injuries sustained" (I:8). Finally, "many of them, again, misconceived the object of the

Commission, and came to tell their tale of houses burnt or property lost, in the undisguised hope of obtaining compensation." Much of the evidence, they conclude "on being sifted by us, proved of but little value" (I:8). The Commissioners suggest that they "should have been glad if we, who witnessed the deportment of witnesses, and had the opportunity of comparing their evidence with one another, could have distinguished those upon whose testimony we could not rely. To have done so, however, we must have entered minutely and at length into details which seemed to us to be inconsistent with the character of our Report" (I:8). Three issues become critically important in this conclusion. First, evidence is discarded because of linguistic confusions that obscured meaning. Second, the Commission members could not evaluate truth-telling, or discern the effect of oath-taking on those testifying. Third, the irony that the Commission concludes that their ability to discern the truth of events would require further detailed inquiry when the evidence of the transcript suggests that it is less an issue of detail and more an overemphasis on visual information. In other words, in place of complex ideological engagement, such as is found in Underhill's examination of the island's economy and populations, the Commission worked from an ideal of visual hyperrealism that obscured issues of agency and motivation.

Several exchanges vividly illustrate the language barrier to which the Commissioners refer in their report. For example, the panel has difficulty understanding Ann Mitchell, a black woman from Harbour Head. When first questioned, Mitchell denies seeing the rebel, Paul Bogle: "4785. Before the Saturday had you ever seen Paul Bogle?—No; I never saw him. I don't live near him at all. I live quite in another district entirely." But soon after this point, she reveals that she attended his church regularly. The Commission member questions the discrepancy:

> 4793. How do you know that Paul Bogle could not write?—Because I always been to his chapel.
> 4794. But you said some little time ago that you had never seen Paul Bogle?—I never saw him for three or four months before the row commence.
> 4795. You said a little time ago that you had never seen him; then you did know Paul Bogle?—I know him; but before the war commenced, about two or three months ago, we never met together. (Report II:103)

Because dialect is not transcribed in the text, it is difficult to glean the nature of the linguistic barrier between questioners and witness. Although in this interaction Mitchell seems to have trouble understanding the questions, she may be simply trying to keep herself from being associated with one of the presumed leaders of the rebellion. Why should this woman trust an administrative body sent by the same authorities as those soldiers who have run roughshod throughout the island? What become key to understanding this moment are the issues of agency and motivation. Does Mitchell use the language barrier to intentionally obscure her intentions? The Commission's report seems to place the answer on the obvious lack of understanding on the part of the "native." What seems equally plausible, however, is a manipulation of the linguistic confusion as a barrier to clear understanding, so as to make use of the lack of clarity desired by the Commission's underlying belief in a taxonomy of truth and visibility.

It is in a more extended situation, involving the death of a man dragged from his house, that the obscuring effect of the visual basis of lines of questioning becomes most clear. In this vignette, there appear to be both recognized and silent influences on the participants. Explaining how his brother-in-law was killed, George Bryan, a black laborer living in Long Bay, gives confusing testimony about whether or not he saw the killing. From the extended testimony, it appears that Bryan hid in his house and watched his brother-in-law being dragged out of the house next door, tied to a tree, and then shot by a group of black soldiers. Bryan and the Commission members repeatedly go over such details as Bryan's distance from the event, view of the event, and description of the event.[8] The Commission members belabor minute details of placement and view, as is common in a legal proceeding.[9] Often a third party would interview witnesses prior to their appearance before the Commission; these two testimonials could then be compared to ascertain if there were any discrepancies.[10]

After the Commissioners interview the executed man's wife, Mary Bryan, the story becomes even more convoluted. Mary Bryan testifies that her husband and his brother were both in the house with her, and that George Bryan was in his house next door. Questions arise over how many people were killed, where they were killed, and how they were killed.[11] The Commission takes extensive time to determine whether one man was shot through the other man. Black soldiers under command of white militia captains carried out the killings, breaking down easy color divisions in the situation. The Commission questions Mary Bryan about the whereabouts of George Bryan in an attempt to discern where George Bryan was during the act in question.[12] George Bryan is then recalled. He proceeds to give testimony about several other killings that he claims to have witnessed, and is then questioned again about killing of Mary Bryan's husband.[13] In a bizarre twist, it turns out that George Bryan was the one who helped the wife cut her husband down from the post where he was killed.[14] The interaction ends with a confusing litany about the exact nature of the familial relationships.[15]

My purpose in discussing this incident is twofold. First, this incident illustrates several rhetorical features of the governmental transcript, including the panel's focus on the minutiae of each event recounted to them, the use of initial interviews, and their repeated questioning of certain peculiar issues. Second, the incident conveys the ideological limitations of the questioning process. The presentation of this incident becomes circus-like, with George Bryan running around in the bushes, not knowing how many people are being shot, even though he is the one who apparently buried them. Is the problem one of language, or is the problem influenced by the reality of Martial Law? Is George Bryan, who supposedly testified in a background interview about the double execution before appearing before the Commission, trying to cover up for the fact that he did not really see anything? Or is this story an example of how "the terms of authority, once given voice, are far from having a direct and unambiguous effect; on the contrary, they can be reappropriated by the colonized and used against the institutions from which they emanate" (Spurr, 186)? In other words, were the black Jamaicans deliberately confusing the questioners to ensure that the Commissioners would not know what actually happened? And, were the questioners quite willing to embrace this factual indeterminacy because of its efficacy as a vehicle for an essential irony at the heart of imperial governance? The almost fanatical visual empiricism that underpins the procedures of imperial governance obscures complex and offensive ideologies on which that project depends. This factual inhibition appears most dramatically in the Bryan incident in the lack of questions about the political beliefs of the men that were killed, or about their participation in the Rebellion. The panel's obsession with details obscures the larger picture of the relationships between the soldiers and the witnesses in the events. The Commissioners then explain away this obscuring of the truth as illustrative of the barriers of language and education. Left out is any sustained investigation of economic relationships or power dynamics resulting from the abuse of Martial Law. As Richards argues, "Like power, information does not exist in a vacuum. It has to be made and used" (*Imperial*, 73). The question-and-answer format, coupled with the nature of the questions asked, illustrate vividly the power relationships involved in the production of knowledge in imperial administration.

The history of economic, political, and juridical inequality was only amplified by the sheer violence of the military action against the population, revealed most dramatically at one point in the text in testimony about the pressures that one reporter experienced. Augustus Walter Hewett Lake, a "coloured" man who was at the time of the uprising a reporter for the *Colonial Standard* newspaper, testifies that there were influences on what he wrote regarding Provost Marshal Ramsay, one of the most vicious of the colonial authorities:

> 14,436. Did you write to your employer, Mr. Levy, stating that the Provost Marshal was "the right man in the right place, and a Crimean hero"?—I did. I wrote to say he was the "right man in the right place," and if I had said he was the "wrong man in the wrong place" I knew what I would have got.
> 14,437. Then it is not strictly true?—It is not strictly true. I don't believe I committed any sin. I only saved my back from being lacerated. (Report II:282)

To survive within this dangerous environment, Lake altered the truth. Truth, in such a system, became a concept utilized for survival rather than a reliable metaphysical constant. The relativity of truth, the fixity of which undergirds the governmental taxonomy structuring the process of information gathering, problematizes the integrity of the information gathered, even though that information is presented in a format that appears to hyperemphasize the value-free nature of the facts.

## Conclusions, or the Inability to Conclude

Richards argues that during the 1860s, a belief in the "communicational transparency of knowledge" began to break down, just at the time of the Eyre controversy (*Imperial*, 75). The transcript, in form and content, speaks to this erosion of faith in the validity of linguistic realism. Its inability to produce little but the most general judgments about events on the island suggests the paralysis of discursive vision, when confronted with an absurdly large amount of a particular kind of data. The Commission concluded that the rebellion was planned, caused by hostile feelings and lack of confidence in administrative and judicial authorities; Governor Eyre's speedy response saved lives, but Martial Law lasted longer than was needed, and the punishments were excessive (Report I:40–41). And though the

Jamaica Committee in England tried to have Eyre prosecuted for murder, they were never successful. As Richards argues about the Victorians in general, "The truth, of course, is that it was much easier to unify an archive composed of texts than to unify an empire made of territory, and that is what they did—or at least tried to do, for most of the time they were unable to unify the knowledge they were collecting. It fell apart" (*Imperial*, 4). The search for the reality of events in Morant Bay broke down in the vision of hundreds of pages of minuscule type in this vast collection of interviews focused on the particulars of individual events. The Victorian imperial archive's "microepistemological project of national security" (41), a phrase particularly apt for the discourse produced by the Royal Commission, becomes "a lost horizon of comprehensive knowledge" (39).

Startlingly, only once in the hundreds of pages of exchanges between witnesses and Commission members is there a disruption of the dauntingly consistent aesthetic of impartiality created by the Commission's process. It is perhaps in this momentary rupture that we can most clearly discern the taxonomic parameters of the project of governmental inquiry. On the eleventh day of testimony, the Commission interviewed a black baker named James Bonner Barnet. Barnet recounted being flogged for no reason by a number of soldiers, and was then asked how many lashes he received. In response to his declaration that he received a dozen lashes, the questioner asked, "Was it a baker's dozen?" (Report II:172). This momentary relaxation of the posture of seriousness and integrity in a record of excessive, hyperrational question-and-answer sessions registers much more than the frustration and growing disconnect experienced by the Commission members in response to the constant narration of violent incidents. It suggests the necessity to efface the subjectivity of the questioners as much as possible to create an impression of neutrality. In this moment, both in the obvious insensitivity of the questioner and the economic basis of the "joke," we have a glimpse within the text of the limits of this governmental taxonomy. This moment speaks to the Commission's understanding of the need to create an impression of impartiality by focusing on the visual nature of the events and disavowing politics and ideologies. This crack in that project reveals the radical constructedness of that position and the limitations of visual empiricism as a viable basis on which to create faith in imperial administration. In this momentary eruption, subjectivity emerges, problematizing the impartiality of the process and undermining the power of this inquiry to fulfill the hopes of those like Mill and Martineau who sought justice for those wronged in Jamaica.

An analysis of James Grant's jingoistic fictionalization of the Indian Rebellion, *First Love and Last Love,* provides me with the opportunity to tie together many of the issues I have addressed thus far. In particular, my discussion of this text looks at the role of ruin structures in the novel, in which the single scene of ruin we saw in both *The Hour and the Man* and "Perils" becomes an almost anxious, repetitive return to the sites in Grant's novel. This narrative phenomenon suggests the importance of these structures in representations of race in the nineteenth century. They allow, in spatial form, the communication of anxieties about time, history, degeneration, aesthetics, home, and danger within a plot that reads very much like the fictional rendering of the events outlined in the transcript. Although many of the issues involved in aestheticizing this historical event will have much in common with the dynamics evident in "Perils," Grant's novel, written after the Morant Bay Rebellion, conveys an extreme rage and confusion in its use of the techniques of the Gothic in the rendering of these ruin scenes.

CHAPTER 5

〜

# Race, Ruins, and Rebellion

## SPATIALIZING RACIAL OTHERNESS IN JAMES GRANT'S
### *FIRST LOVE AND LAST LOVE* (1868)

> We gave him a skin-deep civilization; we took a leopard from the jungle
> and apparently domesticated him, but so that on the first opportunity he should
> turn and rend his keeper: our strong controlling hand withdrawn, every devilish
> passion was at once unchained; every one who wished for plunder or power, took it.
> —"Extent of the Indian Mutinies"

> Women are the slates, memsahib, on which men write the history of the world.
> —Jane Robinson, *Angels of Albion*

$T$he violence evident in the transcript of the Royal Commission's inquiry into the Morant Bay Rebellion threads its way through most mid-Victorian race narratives, especially those concerned with colonial unrest. James Grant's *First Love and Last Love* (1868), one of the most graphically violent mid-Victorian racial texts, presents the events of the 1857 Indian Rebellion in more directly realistic terms than does Charles Dickens and Wilkie Collins's "Perils." However, the central themes remain the same: the violation of English womanhood, the sense of betrayal, and the need for vengeance. In Grant's novel, the association of women with the domestic, with a sense of home, becomes centered on the trope of the ruin site. Mid-Victorian fictions representing racial conflict in the colonial context often contain scenes in which the protagonists of the story escape to, or are confined in, a consciously stylized ruin site. We have already seen two of these structures. In Harriet Martineau's *The Hour and the Man* (1841), L'Etoile, the dilapidated mansion, is re-envisioned to represent the rising new black nation of Haiti.[1] The ruin site in Charles Dickens and Wilkie Collins's "Perils," The Palace, is a prison in which dangerous pirates keep English colonials captive. Grant's rendering of the ruin site includes a Gothic atmosphere that intensifies images of sexual violence found so frequently in Mutiny discourse. And a key trope of the Gothic, as I will discuss, is the site of the ruined, inadequate, or dangerous home. In this chapter, I will explore the further development and elaboration of the ruin scene in Grant's novel and suggest that there is a relationship created in this text between the Gothicized ruin space and the body of the rebelling racial "other." We saw this connection between structure and the racialized body in Knox's obsessive use of the English country house to convey the Anglo-Saxon character, an image that becomes crucially important in Grant's novel.[2] The additional element of a Gothic atmosphere intensifies the sense of English rage and confusion in the face of challenges to colonial authority.

In *First Love and Last Love,* the romance plot becomes firmly established before the opening of the Rebellion, and the overlap of an adventure plot and a romance plot provides the basic structure of the text. Grant's novel begins just a few weeks before the outbreak of the Rebellion. The hero, Jack Harrower, is a British officer stationed in India. Jack is in love with Lena Weston, a young woman whose family has just arrived in India. Jack and Lena were engaged at one time, but she broke off the relationship to become engaged to another officer. When that officer broke their engagement to marry a woman with more money, Lena was abandoned. Jack desperately wants to reunite with Lena, the heroine of this novel. The romantic element becomes primary, and much of the violence, although graphic, is narrated offstage.

Jenny Sharpe argues in *Allegories of Empire* that the violated body of the white British women was the central trope of representations of the Indian Rebellion. As I discussed in my analysis of Dickens and Collins's "Perils," accounts of high numbers of women killed in the Indian Rebellion, and the reports of mass raping of white women, later found to be without basis or evidence, brought out a chivalric rage in the officers in India at the time, as well as in the British public at home. Sharpe asserts that "there is no evidence pointing to a *systematic* rape and mutilation of English women, and that the Mutiny reports reenact that absent violence in its place" (Sharpe, 67). Dickens and Collins decided to render this anger metaphorically by constructing a historically divergent situation upon which to place the feelings elicited by accounts arriving from India in 1857. Grant, writing in the midst of the Governor Eyre controversy, by contrast places his novel in India at the time of the Rebellion and directly renders the violated female body, so graphically created within the accounts to which Sharpe alludes.

The actual situation of white women in India before the Rebellion was complicated. Often these women were blamed for rising tensions in the colony; scholars debate the validity of this charge. Penelope Tuson argues that the large female presence in the Anglo-Indian community in India was a relatively recent development at the time of the Rebellion: "In the 1850s, women had only just begun to go out to India in large numbers, either to accompany civilian or army husbands, or, to a much lesser extent, as independent missionaries and teachers. Even before the outbreak of the Rebellion, this created an atmosphere of anxiety among many of the almost exclusively male governing elite who had grown used to a lifestyle away from domestic responsibilities and who accepted, as a way of life, local sexual liaisons and friendships" (293).

The presence of middle-class white women bridged the gap between the freer, less restrictive colonial culture and middle-class metropolitan mores. No longer was India a place where men could live beyond conventional social norms. English women arrived, bringing with them the social restrictions of England, thus taking away a great deal of the freedom formerly associated with living in India. Tuson suggests that Englishwomen were supposed to embody the morals of middle-class culture, much as they were to be the purveyors of this type of morality in the metropolis:

> European middle-class women in India were represented in public discourses in the same general terms as those in Victorian Britain and they were expected to bring with them to the imperial territories those same qualities of domestic virtue that were required of them in the home country. In return they were similarly accorded an exalted status and, increasingly, as notions of Britain's imperial civilizing mission developed, they were protected, nurtured, and, at the same time, disempowered, as its gentler and more fragile representatives. They were to be the velvet glove on the iron fist of colonial aggrandisement. (294)

The women in Grant's novel embody this moral and domestic symbolism, but without the complications evident in the historical events. They also display little of the pluck and bravery of Dickens and Collins's Lady Marion. Unlike Lady Marion's superior fighting skills in "Perils," the Weston girls struggle to endure the loss of their privileged lifestyle, a loss that Grant dwells on at considerable length. They do not contribute markedly to the fight against the rebels. Instead, the women represent what the fighting men protect and reinstate.

In *Angels of Albion: Women of the Indian Mutiny* (1996), Jane Robinson argues that the response to English women in India was mixed. Many argued that the women were, in fact, responsible for creating a rift between the English officers and the Indian sepoys, because the women's presence confirmed the boundary between the groups of men. The arrival of English women also created anxiety about miscegenation, which in turn created a still greater need for limits. And as women tried to carry out their prescribed role of spreading the light of civilization, they created anxiety in the Indian population. English women often reached out to Indian children and women, but this caused problems because they were perceived as trying to change the indigenous way of life (Robinson, 11). So, on the one hand, the English women's contact with Indian women and children provided a moral pathway to carry out a religious and cultural mission that caused tension between the two communities. On the other hand, the women inhibited the relationship between the Anglo-Indian men and the Indian community, which had brought a sense of closeness between officer and sepoy and established an avenue for both interracial relationships and exploitation of Indian women by Anglo-Indian men.

Any ambivalence felt regarding the English female presence in India disappears in accounts representing the violence committed against white women during the Rebellion. And Grant's representation of the events is more violent and shocking than is Dickens and Collins's, because he depicts the violence done to women, both real and imagined, in graphic, disturbing, and sustained ways. Nancy Paxton argues that "the most extraordinary feature of Grant's *First Love and Last Love,* one of the earliest novels about the Mutiny, is that it violates perhaps the most powerful literary taboo of the Victorian era which prohibited the description of the naked (white) female body and silenced mentions of rape in polite literature" (254).When one considers the historical context of the work, however, the violent images seem less of an aberration. Of particular importance to the English public in the metropolis that read about the event, and the Anglo-Indian community in India experiencing the events, was the violence that English citizens suffered. Reading about the brutal acts committed on English men and women created a sense of rage in the English psyche, especially when it came to the horrific Cawnpore massacre: "Cawnpore was not merely a matter of military affront: it struck deeper than that. It was all that was most vicious about the Mutiny stripped bare: the first time the women of England had ever been slaughtered in the history of battle. The British response was a tribal one—even atavistic—and still fuels bitter debate both here and in India itself" (Robinson, 98).

The publication date of Grant's novel further fueled the rage expressed in its pages. Grant's novel was first published in 1868, during the height of the Governor Eyre controversy, an event, as we saw in the previous chapter, suffused with violence at every level by the English troops and rebels. The English reading public may have been overwhelmed with the frequency of accounts of colonial violence—accounts that were eroding the good feeling created earlier in the century with the abolition of the slave trade and Emancipation. The English were under attack, these accounts suggested, and it was time to put these ungrateful and inferior subjects in their place.

The violence experienced by the Jamaican black and colored community was, of course, also part of Indian colonial life. Rudrangshu Mukherjee argues, "Violence . . . was an essential component of the British presence in India" (93). Regarding women in particular, he notes that British colonials committed violent acts of punishment on Indian women in much the same way that British soldiers inflicted violence on Jamaican women during the revengeful punishment for Morant Bay. Sexual violence in particular, noticeably absent from the hundreds of pages of testimony taken during the Morant Bay inquiry, was also part of life in colonial India. Mukherjee argues that "it was an era of brutal floggings and of Indian women being forced to become mistresses of white men; of recalcitrant elements being blown from cannons so that their bodies were effaced and the onlookers covered with blood and fragments of flesh. British rule thus visibly manifested itself by marking the body of the Indian" (94). The violence so feared by and experienced by the British in India, then, was an inverse reflection of what they inflicted on the colonized population.

This volatile combination of violence, women, colonial rule, morality, and boundary anxiety became focused on the representation of the English home. As Robinson argues, "The root of the problem was that women represented home. That, to put it crudely, is what the memsahibs in India were for. They were sent out as portable little packets of morality, to comfort their men, keep the blood-line clean, and remind them of their mothers" (13). And the question of home—how to create the Victorian home in the colonial context, and what that home represents—became a trope that conveys this array of issues in Grant's text. The ruins to which his characters return over and again (as opposed to the single visit evident in the earlier texts) become figurative and imaginative recreations of home as a safe space in the midst of rebellion. Catherine Hall argues that the relationship between home, nation, colony, and imperialism is fundamental and insufficiently explored in the Victorian imperial project.[3] I argue that the trope of home represents this relationship in Grant's novel, and that the image in which the discussion is most fully revealed is the ruin scene.

## Romance, Domesticity, and the Trope of Rape

From the opening of the novel, it becomes clear that home, domesticity, and romance are central concepts in Grant's text, and they are not limited to the romance between Lena and Harrower. Lena's sister Kate is about to marry a good-natured soldier and friend of Harrower's, Rowley Mellon, and so the initial moments of the text are suffused with romance and future weddings. This overlap between rebellion and domesticity is so overt that Kate's wedding night is the moment when the Rebellion breaks out. The wedding takes place, but the Rebellion erupts between the wedding and the wedding night, thus interrupting the consummation of the marriage. The scene, which takes place in a chapter called "Kate's Wedding Night," begs an interpretation of the Rebellion as an event directly intruding on the domestic sexuality of the English home. The celebration, filled with happiness and safety, ends up as a scene of violent destruction: "The brilliant bridal party which had assembled in the church of Dr. Weston on that eventful 11th of May, was now scattered far and wide, or lying gashed and gory, dead and mutilated, a prey to jackals and vultures in the streets and gardens of Delhi" (Grant, 167). Kate, taken prisoner by an Indian prince, spends the rest of the novel trying to keep from being raped by him, a fate she successfully avoids.

An irony exists between Grant's fictional use of the trope of rape to assert a particular view of the relationship between Indian men and English women, and the reality that little or no rape of English women was committed during the Rebellion. "As early as 1865," claims Paxton, "the distinguished historian George Trevelyan argued in *Cawnpore* that there was no evidence that English women were actually raped during the Uprising of 1857" (251). Mukherjee, discussing the religious nature of the Rebellion, observes, "Here was a society in open war with a foreign power; at the time when the rebels seemed to be victorious they had British women at their mercy for about fifteen days. Yet there was no rape" (115). However, even though Grant's novel was published three years after Trevelyan's account, the novel is filled with images of rape, threats of rape, and metaphors of rape.

Grant's decision to retain the trope of rape in such dramatic and insistent fashion suggests a desire to exploit the sense of outrage arising from late-1850s accounts of the Rebellion. Paxton argues that the trope of rape fulfilled several concomitant functions: "Novels written after 1857 which were organized around this narrative [rape of English women by Indian men] naturalized British colonizers' dominance by asserting the lawlessness of Indian men and, at the same time, shored up traditional gender roles by assigning British women the role of victim, countering British feminist demands for women's greater political and social equality. In short, texts which focus on the rape of English women by Indian men were used to mobilize literary traditions about chivalry in service to the Raj" (249).

The trope of rape, even when not supported by historical or investigative evidence, served to usher in conventional ideas about women's roles, the domestic English environment, and the realities of violence in the colonial context. This constellation of issues is focused in Grant's text on the idea of home, which takes many different forms, but centers primarily on ruin sites. The use of ruins allows the image of home to take on a more imaginative construction in the mind of the reader, not only because language presents the structure, but also because the incompleteness of the structure allows the reader to participate in creating and completing the vision of home.

## The Solace of the English Home

Representations of home take three primary forms in the novel: sketch, memory, and ruin. At the beginning of the novel, before the outbreak of the Rebellion, Harrower keeps a sketch of Thorpe Audley, his home in England and the place representing Lena and himself as a couple. After he has seen Lena again with her family, he returns to his living quarters and looks at the sketch: "Harrower looked at the sketch again and again, and touched it up anew with his pencil, the arch of the Lichgate and its masses of ivy—the stile that lay beyond—the square tower and the porch of the old village church, with the chimneys of the village itself, peeping up among the woodlands in the distance. Every chimney there Lena would remember, and might recal [sic] its household, their faces, and all their little histories" (Grant, 54).

Here we see the conscious use of the aestheticized English home by the protagonist as solace in the midst of racial conflict. Harrower uses this representation of his home community to recall visions of his happy times in England while in the colonial context. In *The Poetics of Space*, Gaston Bachelard argues that "Daydreams return to inhabit an exact drawing and no dreamer ever remains indifferent for long to a picture of a house" (Bachelard, 49). This moment brings us back to the repetitive use of the English country house in Knox's *The Races of Men* as a stand-in for the figure of the Anglo-Saxon man. Key to this dynamic is the replacing of body with structure, the overlapping of organic and architectural form. The sketch represents home, Englishness, and the future domestic and romantic relationship he desires with Lena.

This sketch will become his way of winning Lena back while in India, because the English home is a symbol for the colonial romance: "How fortunate it was that he had fondly preserved this little relic of those happy days, which he hoped it would bring back to her memory, in all their strength and purity" (Grant, 54). Malcolm Kelsall, in *The Great Good Place: The Country House and English Literature* (1993), argues that "the country house was the essential expression of England" (5). And we saw in Knox's text that the image of the English country house is used three times to express the fundamental ethos of the Anglo-Saxon race. Grant's novel triangulates the romance between Lena and Harrower through the image of home, and it is of primary importance that the location of this home is England. Its retention within the sketch becomes a morally virtuous refuge from the violence and from the cultural chaos produced by open rebellion.

Throughout the novel, the perfection of the English home is contrasted with the inadequacy of the Indian home, in both its domestic and ruin state. When Lena and Jack flee the violence of the Rebellion, not knowing what happened to friends and family, they begin a long process of trying to find safety and shelter in the colonial wilderness. Khoda Bux, father of the Westons' ayah, Safiyah, agrees to shelter the two people (although he thinks that they are married), even though it is dangerous for him to be seen helping the English. In a series of reflections on their surroundings that can strike the reader as exceptionally critical, the uncomfortable particulars of the Indian residence are continually dwelt upon, and this inadequacy is linked with the mistreatment of women, a common point of criticism in Victorian discussions of colonized societies:

> Compelled to remain close within doors, Jack and [Lena] found the house of Khoda Bux an almost intolerable residence. Like all the dwellings of the poorer ryots, it was small, badly ventilated, children, cattle, and poultry being nearly all under one roof; but this mattered little to Khoda or the women of his household, as they were all a-field by cock-crow, and at work with spade and hoe among the sugar canes and rice fields. . . . Khoda was perhaps kinder to his horses and cattle than to the women of his household. As a Brahmin he was a thorough believer in the transmigration of souls; he knew that in the next state of existence he might figure as a horse, a cow, or even an alligator, but certainly not as a woman. (Grant, 211)

Often in texts about the Indian Rebellion, both fictional and nonfictional, authors point to the treatment by Indian men of women as inferior beings as a sign of their backwardness. Here, this misogyny is tied to the spatial environment of the home that fails to retain the crucial demarcation between the animal and human spaces, and that fails to valorize woman as the queen of the sphere. Spatial, bodily, and ideological concerns overlap to suggest the inferiority of the Indian group, even though they put themselves at risk to help Harrower and Lena. It is not that the Indians are bad people, the text suggests, just underdeveloped and uncivilized.

Eventually Khoda Bux learns that he is in great danger, and tells our hero and heroine that they will have to leave. It is at this moment that ruins begin to feature most prominently in the text. Their protector encourages them to look for shelter in sites of ruin scattered throughout the countryside: "'The forest is full of ruined temples and old tombs—there you will find shelter easily'" (Grant, 214). Harrower finds this suggestion particularly distasteful: "'Ruined temples and old tombs—ugh!'" (214), to which Khoda Bux responds, "'Safe shelter, Sahib, till the present danger is past'" (214). The couple has little choice, and makes preparations to leave. Lena and Harrower take off into the wilderness with limited provisions. Lena is on horseback, and Harrower runs beside her in chivalrous fashion. Before long, they arrive at the first of several ruin sites in which they will keep shelter:

> Lena's horse began to stumble among stones or masses of fallen masonry, over which an elaborate network of creepers, the growth of many years, was spread. Some arches and fallen columns next appeared, and before them stood one of the ruins to which Khoda Bux had referred—a fragment of an old Hindoo temple apparently. Two arches of the Moorish or horse-shoe form, about eight feet high, were still entire; but the pillars from which they sprung were buried to their capitals by the stones that had fallen from above and the rank luxuriance of the vegetation of centuries. (Grant, 216–17)

In this description of the ruin site we see familiar echoes of both Martineau's L'Etoile and Dickens and Collins's Palace. Nature encroaches on the domestic ruin site, just as at L'Etoile, "ropes of creepers hung down the walls" (*Hour* 1:276). Ruins illustrate an intersection of temporal (that is, historical and nostalgic) and spatial (that is, architectural and geographical) concerns evident in mid-Victorian representations of race and racial conflict. Reminders of a past, developed, and awesome civilization remain in the decayed arches and columns, an image reminiscent of "Perils," in which "a flight of stone steps, of such mighty size and strength that they might have been made for the use of a race of giants" (222), leads to the ruin site. Grant's ruin has religious overtones in its history as a temple, and this element adds to its signifying power as a cultural artifact. This type of scene persists in racial representations of the period, and it symbolizes an ongoing discussion that took place within Victorian society about the relationship between the English and colonial home, the gendered and racial body, and the place of women in both locations.

The emergence of these questions in the ruin space becomes evident in the way our hero and heroine demarcate the area. Unlike Lady Marion in "Perils," Lena is a more traditionally passive female character, much more in keeping with the male adventure novel tradition. After they arrive at the ruin site, Harrower notices that "[r]ocks or masonry closed up those arches on one side, making each a species of vault" (Grant, 217). Harrower literally barricades Lena into the structure in order to create a wall of safety: "In one of these, Harrower stabled the horse and quartered himself; the other he apportioned to Lena, piling up in front of it, and in the entrance, several large stones as a barrier in case of a sudden attack from sepoys, or any wild animal" (Grant, 220). One could argue that this move simply creates a protective shield around Lena. But I suggest that it also reinforces certain domestic barriers so important to the Victorians, such as between the safe interior of the house and the dangerous outside, or the reliable English world and the unstable Indian world. These separations are especially important in light of the hero and heroine's unmarried status.

Further emphasizing the ways in which this structure reinforces ideas about domesticity and romance, the first evening at the ruins make Jack think of Thorpe Audley, the scene rendered in the sketch he touched up earlier in the plot:

> He was neither fanciful nor romantic, but somehow on this night there came to his mind vivid thoughts of his home in Cornwall, of his family fireside and the faces of the dead; of the bleak hills and the peak of Caddonburrow, with his little patrimonial dwelling, the tenants of which he envied at that time of peril. And then he thought of the quaint chapel hard by, built by one of his ancestors, who had been a crusader—tradition said; for his effigy was there, cross-legged, with sword at side, shield on arm, and his hands clasped in prayer; and he remembered how that grim effigy had been an object of terror in boyhood, all the more that the name carved on the tomb was the same as his own—'Johan de Harrower, Miles.'

His family had for ages been buried in and around that little Norman fane, and many monumental brasses testified to the fame they had borne among the men of Cornwall, long ago. Would he ever lie there? (Grant, 218)

Hiding at the ruin with Lena triggers this series of associations for Harrower, bringing him imaginatively back to England. The natural environment becomes enmeshed with his romantic and domestic future. And his vision of home suggests a violent, Christian familial history, loaded with moral overtones. By sharing a name with his ancestor, Harrower is directly tied to his behavior, and the text suggests that Harrower is both awestruck and intimidated by the shoes he must fill.

Ruin scenes also take on the more mundane function of travel narrative, and this element of Grant's novel once again embodies the importance of the raced and gendered body. Each of the sites is explained in some historical or cultural fashion, so giving the reader interesting facts about the original structure. Often these passages take on a digressive quality, and the tone differs vastly from the primary one in the Rebellion plot. In the explanation Harrower receives from a loyal Indian sepoy about the structure in which they keep themselves safe early in the novel, however, the connection among the domestic, the colonial, and the structure resumes:

It would appear, by what Harrower learned from the soubadar-major, Bhowanee Lall, that the ruin with the two quaint arches, which had afforded a shelter to Lena and himself in the forest of Soonput, was the remnant neither of a mosque nor a mansion . . . but it was the fragment of a once magnificent tomb, connected with the romantic story of one of the most beautiful and remarkable women who ever figured in the stirring and changing history of India—Nour Jehan, "the Light of the World," better known in many a song and tale of fiction by her softer and more loving name, Nour Mahal, "the Light of the Harem"—(the same sobriquet which, in vanity or jest, or in his pride of having a toy so new and beautiful, Mirza Abubeker had bestowed upon his poor little English captive, Polly Weston . . . ). (Grant, 248)

The story of this young sixteenth-century woman named Nour Mahal is told at length in the novel in a chapter devoted solely to that end (Grant, 248–53). It is at root a story of domestic betrayal, in which a father sells his daughter into a harem in order to pay his debts. Nour Mahal is also the name given to Lena's younger sister Polly, taken prisoner by an Indian prince, thus suggesting her possible fate as sexual slave. Eventually, in the legend, father and daughter are reconciled when he is able to save her life as an adult. This story of Nour Mahal, of domestic abandonment and reconciliation, underpins the structure in which Harrower and Lena hide. They take shelter in the architectural representation of the legend, the structural metaphor of the betrayed and violated female Indian body.

Eventually, Harrower and Lena have to leave the first site, and they remove themselves to another that is even more elaborate than the first. The repetition of ruin sites in Grant's novel is reminiscent again of Knox's use of the image of the English country house. Rather than one ruin site that stands at the center of the text, as we saw in *The Hour and the Man* and "Perils," the protagonists inhabit several different ruined structures over the course of the novel, each of which becomes more Gothic and menacing. Soon we read a familiar scene as Harrower takes control of Lena, placing her in an appropriate place within the ruin site, and then creating a safe environment for them: "Up several steps, broken, decayed, and covered with grass and herbage, and between pillars of twisted, bulbous, and fantastic form, they passed, Harrower leading the shrinking Lena by the hand, until he found a stone or fallen column, on which he seated her, while preparing to make a fire, that they might look around them and see the features of their temporary habitation—the vast memorial of unknown ages, and of a mental darkness that is yet undispelled in the land" (Grant, 311).

These ruin sites are the remnants of an ancient civilization, both awesome and primitive. Traveling into the world of the colonial wilderness entails, in a sense, traveling back in time to primitive and lost civilizations. As we read further, the Gothic overtones, suggested by the "mental darkness," are further accentuated. The ruins may be majestic, but the reader is not to forget that these are the ruins of a more primitive and less enlightened (albeit once grand) culture, far inferior to the English.

As with the previous site, the text provides a history of the structure, but this time the description includes traditional Gothic imagery. More importantly, the structure becomes personified, thus embodying a connection between history, legend, and the organic body:

This temple—one of the many magnificent Hindo fanes, rifled and ruined by Mohammed Ghora during his conquests in the twelfth century—is of vast extent and height, and out of the ghostly uncertainties of its depths and shadows, there could be seen coming forth in bold relief, while the light of the fire wavered and brightened on several pillars of bulbous outline, with flat oval capitals, and many gigantic stone figures, whose heads supported the roof: and when the unsteady glow played on their huge and grotesque faces, these seemed to become animated, and to grin, mock, and jabber at the intruders; yet the whole scene, in all its details, its bold features, its black obscurities, and unknown history, was calculated to impress the mind with awe. (Grant, 311)

This site takes on a more sinister feeling than had the previous one. The images speak to the couple as they enter and mock them as they seek shelter and safety within its walls. The darkness of the scene becomes increasingly accentuated, and the couple seems dwarfed by the size of the statues. But still the description ends by acknowledging the impressiveness of the spectacle and its ability to elicit the couple's respect.

The increasingly menacing nature of the structures provides the opportunity to display the bravery and resilience of the English character. Even though this structure takes on fearful and sinister traits, it also holds the scene of reunion between the two lovers in a quiet moment that conveys a sense of domestic peace. Successful romance becomes synonymous with English fortitude. The middle-class domestic plot will not be overrun by the personified, racialized Gothic ruin structure:

She was reclining with her left hand under her cheek; she stretched out her right to him, and he pressed its soft fingers between his own in silence, and thus they sat for a long space hand in hand, looking sometimes at each other, and sometimes at the fire which burned brightly on the paved floor; at the quaint pillars, at the quainter figures of the Hindoo idols, hewn out of marble of porphyry, on which daubings of red paint were still traceable; at the symbols on the walls, where the bull of Brahma, the serpent of Seva, the trident of Vishnu, and the noose of Kalee, were reproduced in innumerable carvings. (Grant, 312)

As with L'Etoile in Martineau's *The Hour and the Man*, different aspects of the novel blend into the structure and surroundings in which the primary characters hide. The exotic spectacle of the Indian site accentuates the moment. Rather than providing a fearful scene, the imagery vacillates between traditional symbols of the romance plot and the rebellion plot. The natives are dangerous, the previous passage seems to suggest, with their dark past and their dark civilization. But as aesthetic and historical spectacle, the specifics of the scene enhance the romantic tenor of the moment between the hero and heroine.

The scene becomes the point at which Lena finally breaks down and admits her feelings for Harrower. As this action takes place, Grant's depiction of the site continues to vacillate between suggestions of fear and sublimity. The text specifically highlights this ironic juxtaposition when it describes the physical manifestation of the feelings that have been developing between them: "and now they were reunited, lip to lip, hand in hand—but where?" the text asks. "In a Hindoo temple of Bengal—far, far away, amid the savage wilderness of Soonput Jheend!" (Grant, 316). The narrator points to this paradoxical moment for the reader, a paradox housed within the contradictory space of the colonial ruin site.

Although the site has the potential for goodness, romance, and peace, in general the couple's flight from the Anglo-Indian community suggests the inferiority of the Indian landscape relative to the English domestic environment. Pat Doyle, the goodhearted Irishman and British officer, says, "When people have a comfortable home, I wonder why the devil they ever leave it" (Grant, 331). And in an overtly jingoistic moment, the narrator reinforces the superiority of the English relative to the Indians: "For in the terrible time of the mutiny, when happy households and loving family circles were scattered far and wide, men were thankful to entrust wives, children, and sisters to the care of all, or any, who could protect them, the sole bond, the greatest tie of all, being community of race, religion, or colour" (Grant, 223). The natives—even the loyal ones—are far inferior to one's own kind, Grant's narrator implies. Grant constructs English identity in relation to family, race, and nation, and uses the loyalty evident between families, and the treachery against the English that the Indian population exhibits, to reinforce the moral and racial superiority of the colonizers.

## The Gothic Ruin Site

The connection among ruins, domestic space, entrapment of women, and sexual danger has obvious similarities with the conventions of the traditional Gothic novel. In *Rule of Darkness: British Literature and Imperialism, 1830–1914* (1988), Brantlinger outlines the development of what he calls the "Imperial Gothic" in the late-Victorian period. Brantlinger argues that the "Imperial Gothic" has three central themes: "individual regression or going native; an invasion of civilization by the forces of barbarism or demonism; and the diminution of opportunities for adventure and heroism in the modern world" (230). This development arises in works written by H. G. Wells, H. Rider Haggard, and Joseph Conrad, to name just three authors, and reflects late-Victorian cultural anxieties about the imperial project, the erosion of the importance of religion, and an increasing interest in the occult. Grant's novel is an earlier, less ambivalently jingoistic manifestation of the "Imperial Gothic" subgenre. Although Grant's novel certainly exploits popular interest in alien and exotic cultures, the manifestation of the Gothic in *First Love and Last Love* is unwaveringly nationalistic and suggests none of the ambivalence evident in later imperial fiction such as Conrad's *Heart of Darkness* (1899, 1902). In addition, as Linda Bayer-Berenbaum argues, the subject of colonial rebellion more directly mirrors themes evident in the earlier branch of the Gothic, such as fears about populist revolutions: "In terms of politics, the Gothic novel has been continuously associated with revolution and anarchy" (42).

Perhaps the strongest generic similarity between *First Love and Last Love* and the early Gothic is in the overlap of danger, domesticity, and the site of the failed home. In *The Contested Castle: Gothic Novels and the Subversion of Domestic Ideology* (1989), Kate Ferguson Ellis argues that the image of the castle in Gothic literature conveys the paradox of the middle-class domestic space as both site of happiness and site of terror (x). In Gothic texts, the domestic turns fearful: "Focusing on crumbling castles as sites of terror, and on homeless protagonists who wander the face of the earth, the Gothic, too, is preoccupied with the home. But it is the failed home that appears on its pages, the place from which some (usually 'fallen' men) are locked out, and others (usually 'innocent' women) are locked in. . . . Either the home has lost its prelapsarian purity and is in need of rectification, or else the wandering protagonist has been driven from the home in a grotesque reenactment of God's punishment of Satan, Adam, and Eve" (ix).

The ruin structures in Grant's novel suggest a kinship with the Gothic castle, and the centrality of women in positions of vulnerability reflects the overlap of the domestic and the dangerous so prevalent in the early Gothic novels. The "fallen man" becomes the colonial soldier, officer, or administrator, and the vulnerable female his wife or sweetheart. The colonial environment takes the place of the mountainous Italian terrain. Rather than the Italian, Catholic castle, the protagonists must first find shelter in, and then escape from, the exotic colonial ruin. The newfound home in the colonial territories becomes terrifying, and images of the true home in England shepherd the English hero and heroine to safety.

Bayer-Berenbaum points out in *The Gothic Imagination: Expansion in Gothic Literature and Art* (1982) that ruins were a central element of early

Gothic texts. She argues that the development of the Gothic in the late-eighteenth century suggests a connection between its development and growing interest in time, archaeology, and historical ruins: "soon any ruins—the process of decay itself—became associated with the Gothic as did wild landscapes and other mixtures of sublimity and terror" (19). And of course ruins were central to the picturesque aesthetic and abound in Romantic literature. Later, Thomas Carlyle would use the ruined Abbey at Bury St. Edmunds as his "Past" in *Past and Present,* thus using a ruin site as a repository for a state of mind and way of living that Carlyle saw as necessary for the salvation of England. Carlyle uses ruins as spatial metaphors for his temporally based argument to look to the past for remedies for present social ills: "For the Present holds in it both the whole Past and the whole Future" (Carlyle, 42). Ruins exist at the intersections of times, as a way of marking both the passing of organic time and the persistence of the past in current life.

The colonial ruin conveys conflicting ideas about the clash of cultures that transcend the moment at hand. Ruins suggest time, past and future time, as well as the power of time to erode greatness, structure, and civilization. In his classic work, *The Past is a Foreign Country,* David Lowenthal argues that ruins force a culture to confront its own possible mortality in the ruined scene of fallen greatness: "Exemplifying the transience of great men and deeds, the consequence of depravity, or the triumph of justice over tyranny, ruins inspired reflections on what had once been proud and strong and new but was now decrepit, corrupt, degraded. And as reminders of the evanescence of life and the futility of effort, ruins became a staple of eighteenth- and nineteenth-century response to the past" (Lowenthal, 148). Ruin sites are a trope of "Imperial Gothic," whereby, like the castles of the late-eighteenth and nineteenth-century Gothic novels, ruins become central to the creation of a uniquely frightening atmosphere existing at the center of some form of domestic or cultural unrest. But rather than evoking images of populist revolution or social unrest within the European continent, the early Imperial Gothic develops in response to increasing fears regarding the colonial uprisings and bloodshed. For, as Edmund Burke argued in his discussion of the sublime: "I know of nothing sublime which is not some modification of power" (Burke, 59). Power exists in the ruin site in complicated fashion, in that it represents both power degraded or passed and power currently contested. The heroes and heroines of this genre find themselves at the mercy of a dangerous and exotic colonial subject in a state of rebellion, and dragged into the wilds of the colonial landscape, away from metropolitan protective forces and social norms. It is a genre born out of developing racial theory, fueled by increasing colonial unrest, and feeding public antagonism for the subjects of British authority in the colonies.

The racial "others" that invade the ruin site in which Harrower, Lena, and now Pat Doyle hide harken back to the Indian banditti so common in the early Gothic novel. Grant's narrator describes the scene as a moment of supernatural terror as Harrower, Lena, and Pat observe the marauders from a hiding place deep within the ruin site:

> The glare of several torches and Indian fireworks (particularly the flaming trident of Vishnu) elevated on poles, and shedding blue, green, purple, and yellow glares, alternately ruddy or ghastly, or mingling and blending together in rainbow hues, now lighted up a most wild, picturesque, and striking scene, bringing out in bold relief the quaint carvings and details of the ancient Hindoo temple, its wondrously decorated and twisted pillars, wreathed with stony garlands and seven-headed snakes, and more than all, the gigantic figures of the triple gods, each four-armed, with high conical caps, thick flabby lips, depressed noses, staring eyes, and girdles of lotus leaves. (Grant, 332)

The flickering torchlight, demonic villains, sense of entrapment, and awe inspiring surroundings all create a conventionally Gothic atmosphere. Time is central to this moment, because the degradation of the structure and the ancient writings on the wall combine to give a sense of oppressive danger and claustrophobia. The negative characterizations of the Indian figures speak to the directly racial nature of the terror employed in the scene. Religious figures add a supernatural or otherworldly tenor to the site, but they also allow the element of irrationality, so prevalent in racial thinking, to find a voice. Much as the early Gothic novel is associated with anti-Catholic sentiments, the early Imperial Gothic reacts against the perceived pagan heathenism of the Oriental world. The protagonists need to escape from the temporally displaced world of the past, and, this novel suggests, into the light of English civility.

What becomes crucial here is the overlap of Gothic structures and racialized, dangerous bodies. Judith Halberstam suggests that "Gothic fiction is a technology of subjectivity, one which produces the deviant subjectivities opposite which the normal, the healthy, and the pure can be known" (Halberstam, 2). Grant's bringing of a Gothic atmosphere into the description of the ruin site, an atmosphere missing from Martineau's use

of the trope and muted in Dickens and Collins's text, suggests a preoccupation with deviant subjectivities in the overlap of structure and racial
identity. And, as Henri Lefebvre argues in *The Production of Space,*

> Before *producing* effects in the material realm (tools and objects), before
> *producing itself* by drawing nourishment from that realm, and before
> *reproducing itself* by generating other bodies, each living body *is* space and
> *has* its space: it produces itself in space and it also produces that space. This
> is a truly remarkable relationship: the body with the energies at its dispos-
> al, the living body, creates or produces its own space; conversely, the laws
> of space, which is to say the laws of discrimination in space, also govern
> the living body and the deployment of its energies." (Lefebvre, 170)

In Grant's novel, the overlap of organic body and physical structure, the
connection between the creation of space and the living human form,
becomes accentuated in the repetition of the image and the Gothic nature
of the rendering. The relationship between the African subjectivity negotiated in Martineau's L'Etoile and in Dickens and Collins's Palace becomes
overtly personified in Grant's living ruin site that jeers back at the colonials. But what they face in the personified structure is the product of their
own consciousnesses, their own bodies. They confront the spatial realization of the racial "other" produced in scientific and colonial discourse.

The heroism of the colonials is suggested by their immunity to the
scene, by the ability of the romance plot to continue in the face of the site.
If, as Halberstam suggests, the "Gothic . . . is the breakdown of genre and
the crisis occasioned by the inability to 'tell,' meaning both the inability to
narrate and the inability to categorize. Gothic, I argue, marks a peculiarly
modern preoccupation with boundaries and their collapse" (Halberstam,
23), then we can see Grant's deployment of the trope as a further intensifying of the situation we found in "Perils." These texts create conflicting
plotlines that break down around the ruin site as they engage with ideologies of race circulating in mid-Victorian culture. The ability to decipher
breaks down in Martineau's text as the monkeys stare at the renderings of
French political authorities. In "Perils," Collins's ambivalence conflicts
with Dickens's rage in the decision to leave Mendez sleeping and kill Christian George King. In Grant's novel, the romance narrative and the adventure tale become most firmly delineated in the face of the most striking personification of the ruin space. Race, for the Victorians, precipitated an
obsession with boundaries. Racialized rebellion became a crisis of form and
limits, an interweaving of different times, different identities, and different

geographies. As a barrier against the influence of the Gothic ruin site, Harrower turns pleadingly to the representation of the English country house for solace in the confusing world of racial conflict, structural degradation, and romantic frustration. It is to structure, as with Knox, that the protagonist turns, and it is an aestheticized structure that will ultimately embody the conflicted and irrational nature of imperial policy and the racial ideologies upon which it was built.

᠅

The trope of architectural ruin in mid-Victorian racial fictions conveys several overlapping ideas: dangerous colonial natives, romantic civilizations lost in history, adventurous travel, and colonial expansion into unknown worlds. English characters in these texts respond to the unknown, dangerous quality of the sites by attempting to impose a specifically British domestic environment onto the scene. The result of this interaction between domestic and exotic space, gender, and entrapment, and time and safety, is the production of a branch of the Gothic genre centered on colonial conflict. This branch represents mid-Victorian cultural anxieties about colonial rebellion, much as late-eighteenth and early-nineteenth century Gothic writings reflect anxieties about populist revolution and social unrest. Exploration of these spatial sites is the exploration of the past, and thus it suggests the intersection of spatial and temporal considerations so common in Victorian discussions of racial distinction. Supernatural and religious images within the sites reflect the irrational and imaginative aspect of racial thinking. The danger of racial rebellion, Grant's novel suggests, is the loss of domestic and national control, as embodied in the ruin space. But in Grant's text, British control is ultimately regained and vengeance won; ambivalence about expansionist policies remains at a minimum; and the English remain steadfastly English until the end.

The drawing of Harrower's English home provides a temporary canvas on which Grant projects that image of safety and happiness, a picture that helps the hero and heroine to survive the danger. The solace found within this aestheticized emblem of Englishness is our final example of the pattern within the texts under consideration in this study; these texts move toward aestheticized environments or questions regarding the aesthetic as a way to manage, escape from, or reconcile anxieties and confusions produced in the texts by white English confrontation with racial otherness. Harriet Martineau's L'Etoile provides a more romanticized, natural, and hopeful ruin site in which she stages an engagement with politicized racial conflict that ultimately ends in a vision of indecipherability. Robert Knox obsessively returns to the structure of the English country house as he constructs his irrational and contradictory taxonomy of racial otherness. Ultimately it is aesthetic form in which he, like Harrower, rests as he gazes on the Greek Marbles in the British Museum. Dickens and Collins aestheticize the Indian Mutiny itself, taking events away from the realm of historical accuracy and moving into a metaphorical engagement with imperialism and the problem of racial rebellion. The use of the "Palace" in that text becomes, as in Martineau, another inconclusive scene as the fetish figure of racial otherness, Pedro Mendez, is left sleeping at the ruin site. And finally, in the Royal Commission transcript we see the obsession with form that motivated Knox made evident in the Commission's meticulous adherence to the generic parameters of empirical inquiry. Taking Halberstam's observation on the breakdown of genre in Gothic form and the creation of the racialized other, we can see that the momentary break with generic convention created in the "baker's dozen" comment brings into relief the obscuring nature of these generic parameters. As we turn now to the present day and the return of Sara(h) Ba(a)rtman(n)'s remains to South Africa, we will look at what is involved in reversing the process—what is required to de-aestheticize the racial "other" of white British discourse.

# CONCLUSION

༄

# De-Aestheticizing
# Sara(h) Ba(a)rtman(n)

"I've come to take you home—
home, remember the veld?
the lush green grass beneath the big oak trees
the air is cool there and the sun does not burn.
I have made your bed at the foot of the hill,
your blankets are covered in buchu and mint,
the proteas stand in yellow and white
and the water in the stream chuckle sing-songs
as it hobbles along over little stones.
—Diana Ferrus, "A Poem for Sarah Baartman"

*I* n the spring of 2002, a delegation from South Africa traveled to France to escort the remains of Sara(h) Ba(a)rtman(n) back to her homeland for burial. The resolution of the struggle between the South African and French governments over the Khoi-Khoi woman's remains becomes a site from which we can engage with the issues of agency, reconciliation, and restitution central to beginning a process of healing cultures suffering under a legacy of racist destruction. The extrication of Ba(a)rtman(n)'s skeleton, brain, and genitals from museum curators at the Musée de l'Homme in Paris and French government officials was intended, in the words of poet Diana Ferrus, "to restore—to make good what was bad" (*The Return of Sara Baartman*). Ferrus's poem, the first nine lines of which are the opening epigraph to these concluding remarks, played a central role in breaking the stalemate in the battle to return Ba(a)rtman(n) to South Africa. By employing an ethic of care, Ferrus disrupts a racist ideology predicated on ideals of rational observation and examination by focusing on the ideals of empathy rather than of rationalist knowledge-gathering. This movement from objectification to engagement, although complicated, holds the seeds of a strategy to disrupt a legacy of hatred.

142

Up to this point, this book has examined the processes by which white British Victorian writers represented race as an arrangement of competing tropes that led, ultimately, paradoxically, and seemingly unintentionally, to an unraveling of the rational basis of the category. The narrative crisis in each text results in an aesthetic turn, whether it is in the decision to fictionalize historical events while at the same time insisting on their accuracy, to dramatize the process of narrative interpretation, or to nostalgically reflect on an aesthetic remnant of home and of the British domestic realm. Sara(h) Ba(a)rtman(n) has functioned throughout this study as a shadow figure, a woman who represents the literal human destruction produced when a culture chooses to aestheticize otherness in whatever form it appears. Ba(a)rtman(n) became the emblematic, aestheticized racial object or spectacle in early-nineteenth century England, the living embodiment of the social and racial metaphor. Her suffering stands as testimony to the destruction that can be produced when the aesthetic collides with oppression and returns to its origins in the body. In *The Ideology of the Aesthetic,* Terry Eagleton asserts that "Aesthetics is born as a discourse of the body" (Eagleton, 13). Her body was used both to construct and to modify the existing metaphor of racial and gender otherness, a process that has continued, even as her remains were brought back to South Africa, in the recent spate of fictional representations of her life. As South Africa's ambassador to France, Thuthukile Skweyiya, suggested when asked about the return of Ba(a)rtman(n) to her homeland, Ba(a)rtman(n) became "the symbol of a nation's need to confront and acknowledge its past, and of a nation's overwhelming desire to restore and reaffirm dignity and honour to all its people" (qtd. in Hearst, 13). I want to suggest that it is in the ethic of care and love embodied in both Ferrus's poem, and in the political act of Ba(a)rtman(n)'s return to South Africa, that we glimpse a way to enact the reconciliation required to begin to heal the wounds of ethnic violence and oppression, even as we recognize the danger that we may be simply recasting the terms of Ba(a)rtman(n) as a symbol or reverting to a simple sentimentalism in celebrating the return of her remains.

In a variety of fictional renderings of Ba(a)rtman(n)'s life, authors struggle with how to give this woman voice and agency within circumstances that reveal powerless victimization, loneliness, and misguided allegiance. All studies of Ba(a)rtman(n)'s experience agree that her life illustrates, in extreme form, how the positivist ideal of Western science fails to produce any real knowledge of another, the "other." With all the microscopic data obtained about her body, we still do not know who she really was—and writers work to ascribe agency on her, to her, and from her.

Suzan-Lori Parks's play *Venus,* Stephen Gray's poem "Hottentot Venus,"
and Elizabeth Alexander's collection and poem *The Venus Hottentot* all cel-
ebrate the woman, express outrage, and attempt to dramatize the struggle
for agency embedded in the severe exploitation of this woman. Perhaps
most powerfully, Ferrus's "A Poem for Sarah Baartman" and Barbara Chase
Riboud's *Hottentot Venus* portray the rage felt when one engages with this
woman's story and the act of rescuing her remains.

But does she become any less of a figurative construct in these texts
than she was in Baron Georges Cuvier's narrative of her anatomization, or
in any number of outrageous or farcical treatments of her display in early-
nineteenth century England and France? As I have argued throughout this
book, the figurative nature of mid-Victorian racial discourse in narratives
of racial conflict permitted the transmission of complex debates in con-
centrated moments. In a variety of different narrative forms, Victorians
discussed such topics as the nature of the African subject, their fears about
the eradication of slavery, and white panic over black self-determination.
Fictional and nonfictional writings about race and colonial rebellion at the
time used abolitionist, adventure, and gothic plot structures and themes
that later evolved into the conflicted and ambiguous presentations that
Patrick Brantlinger named the "Imperial Gothic" and H. L. Malchow
termed the "Racial Gothic." Each of these formal choices conveys different
facets of debates about race in mid-Victorian England. The abolitionist
narrative suggests the ideals of Enlightenment humanitarianism and
Christian egalitarianism. The adventure tale represents the excitement of
colonial travel, growing English nationalism, and intensifying arguments
for white racial superiority. And, finally, the Gothic helps communicate the
fears, anxieties, and uncertainties of a community experiencing changes in
the hierarchical structures by which they ordered their lives.

Representations of Ba(a)rtman(n) cross the boundaries of scientific,
popular, and gothic genres. As Malchow argues in *Gothic Images of Race in
Nineteenth-Century Britain,* the display of Ba(a)rtman(n)'s anatomy as
"aberrant" was cast in discourses crossing a variety of generic lines and
served to fuel anti-egalitarian arguments in an environment grappling
with the question of the slave trade: "The exhibition of this indentured
black woman, Saartjie Baartman, to curious crowds in Regency London,
the extraordinary interest taken in her physical form by the press, and the
way her body, after death, was literally disassembled to prove spurious theories about Negro nature, is a reminder of the way the cultural prejudices,
fears, and deep-seated neuroses of the observer may impinge on 'science'
and literature, and wander from one arena to another" (13).

It is not surprising that one element of the aestheticizing of Ba(a)rt-man(n) found her victim to a process by which the Gothic was used to enhance racial characteristics that buttressed increasingly reactionary and jingoistic ideologies of race and colonialism. Early Gothic writers such as Ann Radcliffe and Matthew Lewis referenced, commented on, and manipulated fears of social unrest, domestic insecurity, and sexual danger felt by many readers in the late-eighteenth century. Reports from a virtually continuous stream of colonial uprisings after Emancipation sparked similarly intense public reactions and anxieties that reached a zenith of concern with the safety and plight of white women in the 1857 Indian Rebellion. These events became part of the narrative palette used in the "Imperial" or "Racial" Gothic.

As the Victorians read about racial violence in the colonies over the first half of the nineteenth century, narratives become increasingly concerned with dramatizing the creation of ethnic and racial distinctions among different human communities, a process in which the public obsession over Ba(a)rtman(n) played a critical role. In Charles Dickens and Wilkie Collins's fictionalizing of the 1857 Indian Rebellion, "The Perils of Certain English Prisoners" (1857), the authors created a story fraught with putative boundary violations and focused on the problem of reasserting those limits. My analysis of this quite conventionally racist text shows how Victorian racial discourse often enacted the process of creating safe distances from other communities perceived as dangerous. In "Perils," racial "others" are collected together into a band of renegade pirates who, in one image, combine all that is fearful and that threatened the English way of life. Although the killing of the story's villain, Christian George King, conveys all the earmarks of literary catharsis, I argued that the story ultimately fails to release fictional and cultural racial anxieties. For reasons I also enumerated, the parallel humiliation of the pirate captain also failed to provide a clean cathartic release for the Victorian reader. These failures suggest the frustration and rage experienced by the authors in response to initial accounts of the 1857 Indian Rebellion, as well as their perception of sympathy from the reading public.

My analysis of James Grant's *First Love and Last Love* (1868) in this study's final chapter returns to many of these same issues in its representation of the Indian Rebellion. However, Grant's text works with the actual historical events rather than an allegorical representation of the dynamics involved. I argue that the novel illustrates how the confusion, anger, and frustration experienced by many English readers in response to colonial rebellions found expression in the use of gothic themes and patterns in mid-Victorian fiction. *First Love and Last Love* is a particularly vivid example of the overlap of colonialism, violence, gender, and nationalism. The ruin sites in which the English found shelter become spatial metaphors for conflicts underpinning much Victorian racial thinking: past civilizations, exotic religions and cultures, strange natives, and terrifying violence. Ultimately the sites become representations of the racial others themselves—inanimate symbols of the dangerous rebelling Indian Sepoys and an important trope for the "Imperial" or "Racial" gothic. In this genre, the social upheaval caused by rebellions in the colonial context—coupled with anxiety experienced by the metropolitan public's reading of sustained, inaccurate, and inflammatory accounts of the events of these rebellions—finds expression and realization.

## Resensitizing the Viewer

Readers may find my reluctance to repeat the details of Ba(a)rtman(n)'s life and anatomy frustrating. In studies of Ba(a)rtman(n)'s experiences, the details of what was constructed as her "aberrant" physicality, as well as the dissection of her body post-mortem, are endlessly repeated in the ostensible service of unmasking the horror of her life and death. In a way, what happens in these narratives becomes another act of violence. Pictures of her genitalia litter articles. Yuko Edwards's short film, *Politics from a Black Woman's Insides,* brilliantly resensitizes the viewer to this violent act by interlacing discussion of Edwards's attempt to gain access to Cuvier's monograph on Ba(a)rtman(n), narratives of contemporary African American women negotiating the medical establishment, and film from an actual autopsy. What this film does is to add the element of time to the drawings of Ba(a)rtman(n)'s anatomy, which triggers horror in the viewer. This short documentary suggests that, as we wince at the graphic, close-up, violent still images of Ba(a)rtman(n) represented in numerous articles, we find ourselves, at the same time, placed unavoidably in the position of voyeurs, examining materials that we should not have ever been allowed to see.

The central studies of Ba(a)rtman(n)'s life all recount the details of the woman's exploitation and violation, whether in pictures or in narrative, with varying degrees of sensitivity. Presenting the specifics of her treatment and perceptions of her otherness in these early treatments is justified by the relative paucity of information regarding her life. In three of the first studies of Ba(a)rtman(n), Sander L. Gilman, Richard D. Altick, and

Stephen Jay Gould each discuss the horror of this woman's experience. Gilman's account, perhaps the most frequently cited of these studies, reproduces drawings of Ba(a)rtman(n), even the most graphic ones of her genitalia drawn after her death. Gilman asserts that "Sarah Bartmann's genitalia and buttocks summarized her essence for the nineteenth-century observer" (235). Although the shock of these images can make one turn away from the page, the frequency with which Ba(a)rtman(n) appears as pieces of her body is both representative and disturbing. Altick, identified by Abrams as "the modern rediscoverer of Sara Bartman" ("Images," 221), describes her as "a heavy-arsed heathen" and then goes on to make the "joke," "She may be said to have carried her fortune behind her, for she was steatopygic to a fault" (269). He later refers to "her monumental haunches" (272).

These off-hand remarks, described by Abrams as "markedly lacking in both racial and gender sensitivity" ("Images," 221), are reminiscent of a question posed by a member of the Royal Commission inquiry into Governor Edward Eyre's handling of the Morant Bay Rebellion. In my discussion of the transcript of that inquiry, I looked at the moment when a black baker, while recounting his experience of being flogged, was asked if he had received a baker's dozen lashes. That question represented a crack in the formidable generic façade of empirical fact finding that obscures all but the most fleeting glimpses into the real motivations behind actions on all sides. In the transcript (1866) of the inquiry into the way Governor Eyre quelled the Morant Bay Rebellion, we find a vivid record of English imperial truth seeking, the same kind of positivist ideology that motivated the examination and anatomization of Ba(a)rtman(n). At first glance, the documents would seem to provide a transparent window through which to view mid-Victorian exchanges between white Englishmen, West Indian planters, and members of both the black and "colored" communities in Jamaica. However, in the document's record of the stark rationalism of administrative inquiry, we find a paradoxical blindness to the economic realities of this post-Emancipation sugar-growing community. That blindness in the face of monumental detail mirrors the ways in which the specifics revealed about Ba(a)rtman(n)'s body get us farther away from her complexity as a woman. Details such as her motivations, likes and dislikes, and feelings of homesickness remain illusive, even as we stare into the renderings of her genitalia.

But noting the insensitivity of the remark to the Jamaican baker or the use of the brutal images of Ba(a)rtman(n)'s genitalia does not necessarily guarantee that we do not repeat the same dynamic of exploitation. In "Which Bodies Matter?: Feminism, Poststructuralism, Race, and the Curious Theoretical Odyssey of the 'Hottentot Venus,'" Zine Magubane argues that "although most studies that discuss Baartmann (or Gilman's analysis of her) are scrupulous in their use of words like *invented, constructed,* and *ideological,* in their practice, they valorize the very ground of biological essentialism they purport to deconstruct" (Magubane, 817, original italics). However, Gould argues that a reading of Cuvier's monograph of the Ba(a)rtman(n) dissection reveals a limited construction of the anatomist that says more about our reading of the text than about reality. Gould suggests that Cuvier had a more complex understanding of his subject than others have acknowledged: "Cuvier states again and again (although he explicitly draws neither moral nor message) that Saartjie was an intelligent woman with general proportions that would not lead connoisseurs to frown. He mentions, in an offhand sort of way, that Saartjie possessed an excellent memory, spoke Dutch rather well, had some command of English, and was learning a bit of French when she died. (Not bad for a caged brute; I only wish that more Americans could do one-third so well in their command of languages.)" (296). Interesting here is the attempt by Gould to redeem both Cuvier and Ba(a)rtman(n) simultaneously. Cuvier, he seems to suggest, saw more than we give him credit for. Ba(a)rtman(n), he argues, is more than simply a "caged brute"—after all, she could speak several languages and was aesthetically pleasing to the eye. The trappings and values of liberal bourgeois civilization are ushered out here to validate her humanity.

Yvette Abrams speaks to the problem of reproducing these images in her article on Ba(a)rtman(n), as she explains her decision to include one plate: "However, it is crucial to remember that the illustration reproduced in this essay does not bear any relation to Sara Bartman as she was in real life" ("Images," 224). Even as she includes them in her study, she reads them as evidence of a twisted psychology that reveals more about those who originally rendered the figure than about Ba(a)rtman(n) herself: "The illustration of Sara Bartman in this chapter could best be characterized as a sketch from the nightmares of the melanin-deficient. As such it may be upsetting. But it should not be viewed as a picture of Black people" ("Images," 224). These images support a particular construction of Ba(a)rtman(n) that I was not interested in perpetuating any further. I am concerned with beginning to examine in this conclusion the ways in which the space between the woman, Sara(h) Ba(a)rtman(n), and the images of her body shifts as a result of her remains leaving France and returning to

South Africa, and how that event brings into relief the scientific ideals of observation and anatomization that served literally and figuratively to disassemble this woman's life.

What becomes clear is that we are dealing with circulating representations rather than an understanding of a human person. We are engaging with the tropification, if you will, of this woman's experience, both initially as a circus "freak" and now as a symbol of reconciliation and healing. Abrams goes so far as to suggest that both the representations and the original spectacle of Ba(a)rtman(n) were constructed events. In "Images of Sara Bartman: Sexuality, Race, and Gender in Early-Nineteenth-Century Britain," Abrams states, "My own research has shown that there was in fact a considerable degree of manipulation involved in creating both the physical exhibit and the discursive myth" ("Images," 222). She goes on to explain: "What is important about the myths built around Sara Bartman is precisely how the myth building became an increasingly conscious, and public, process. Before the exhibition of Sara Bartman, sexual analyses of Black people may have been a minor theme in dominant discourses. Afterward, ideas about the essentially deviant sexual nature of the Khoisan spread to include all Africans" ("Images," 224). In other words, the "evidence" so frequently circulated as explanation for why Ba(a)rtman(n) became a spectacle may not represent the characteristics of the actual woman at all. Thus, our ability to identify, understand, and analyze the psychosis surrounding Ba(a)rtman(n) as a spectacle becomes limited to a process of identifying the importance of the traits (color, primitivism, and genitalia) that were chosen for manipulation.

The separation that is so important here is between the physical body and the psychological spirit. Ba(a)rtman(n)'s body was appropriated, circulated, and denigrated in the service of a racial ideology that required the emptying out of her spirit to deploy the representation most effectively. Using feminist theory and disability studies, Janell Hobson, in "The 'Batty' Politic: Toward an Aesthetic of the Black Female Body," refers to the work of Rosemarie Garland Thomson when she argues that "as a 'deviant' body—by virtue of skin color, femaleness, and body shape—Baartman becomes a 'freak' in Europe precisely because she is a 'type' of Khoisan woman of South Africa. In this construction of her sexualized and 'disabled' body, Westerners can prescribe racial and cultural differences—and, hence, their 'superiority' as Europeans in comparison with African people and cultures" (Hobson, 91). Ba(a)rtman(n) became a spectacle, an aberration, and a commodity, while at the same time providing evidence for a scientifically rendered examination of global races. Discourses surrounding her body brought together the burgeoning market economy, jingoistic colonial policies, systems of gender stratification, and changing attitudes towards the aesthetics of color difference. Ba(a)rtman(n)'s body was central to this process.

Questions of property, commodification, and their relationship to race, then, become central to the critical history surrounding Ba(a)rtman(n). Magubane argues that in the representation of Ba(a)rtman(n), issues of property intersect with race, putting the discourse surrounding this woman in line with early-nineteenth century debates about slavery: "When many people looked at Baartmann, they saw not only racial and sexual alterity but also a personification of current debates about the right to liberty versus the right to property [ . . . ] The contemporary debates about slavery provided the context to the Baartmann controversy, and it is within their parameters that it must be understood. Many individuals who opposed slavery on humanitarian grounds, nevertheless, were reluctant to infringe on the property rights of slaveholders" (Magubane, 827–28). The intersection of aesthetics, the body, and property becomes important in understanding the circulation of Ba(a)rtman(n), the sign, in a climate debating the question of slavery.

Harriet Martineau understood this connection of bodies, property, and policy, and she tried to focus her anti-slavery writings on solving the problem of this confluence and its relationship to racial violence. This study has engaged closely with signs of impatience and ambivalence, as well as the Victorians' growing desensitization to violence, in genres ranging from government discourse to a Christmas tale. The ambiguity evident within Victorian racial discourse was not limited to texts advocating a harsh, racist view of racial distinction. As we saw in Martineau's historical romance, *The Hour and the Man* (1841), ambiguity can surface in texts that display a wide range of political and social viewpoints. The indeterminacy of Martineau's interpretive dynamics suggests that there was an implicit irrationality or inexplicability at the heart of her and other Victorians' attempts to understand and categorize people racially. Although Martineau certainly advocated a humanitarian view of African people, her text is laced with moments that suggest her immersion in a complex discourse of race beyond which she could not move. She was, however, able to work within many of the conventions of Victorian racial discourse to create a text celebrating both the slave victory in Haiti and the establishment of a new government based on the needs of that community.

Martineau's novel gives voice and agency to all of those participating in an unresolved debate regarding issues of slavery, nationhood, and color.

That narrative decision separated her from the bulk of abolitionist writers who dramatized the saving of African slaves by benevolent white figures. In studies of Ba(a)rtman(n)'s life, questions of agency often stall as descriptions of this woman's victimization suggest a figure at the mercy of unscrupulous and cruel English and French people. In particular, narratives flinch when addressing the court case brought by abolitionists, after seeing her initial display in London, to "free" her from the clutches of her oppressors. Complicating easy understandings of choice and agency, Ba(a)rtman(n) refused to be "rescued" from her arrangement. Rosemary Wiss speaks to the confluence of issues of agency, the Enlightenment construction of the rational self, and the court case over Ba(a)rtman(n)'s treatment as suggesting concepts at the heart of racist thinking:

> In the court case which questioned Saartjie Baartman's 'owner's' sexual access to her, and later attempts by racial scientists to discover the 'secret truths' of Hottentot female sexuality, Saartjie Baartman was effectively silenced. These were not discourses within which she had the right to represent herself. It is not a process of constructing subjectivity through confession, which therefore applies to Saartjie Baartman, but of extraction. Her body was a text which was read by her colonial viewers; it was not the site of her own discourse. Her lips could not tell/speak. (Wiss, 37)

The court case, according to Wiss, illustrates the ways in which the courtroom situation became yet another environment in which Ba(a)rtman(n)'s aestheticized and silenced body was read by those participating in a positivist rational system of regulation and evaluation. Within that site, Ba(a)rtman(n) was silenced. The truth of her situation could not be rendered—the complexity of her feelings, situation, positionality, and spirit would not fit into the prefigured paradigms and tropes offered for her expression.

We have, then, several related paradigms, all working within the same array of representative tropes and positivist, commercialized, and jingoistic discourses. Science, law, and marketplace all converge on the silent body of Sara(h) Ba(a)rtman(n) as we continue to examine her life, her pictures, her decisions, and her anatomy for evidence of colonial exploitation or cloaked agency. In T. Denean Sharpley-Whiting's *Black Venus: Sexualized Savages, Primal Fears, and Primitive Narratives in French*, the author defines "the concept of the (white) male gaze as a desire to unveil, 'to dissect,' 'to lay bare' the unknown, in this case the black female. The gaze 'fixes' the black female in her place, steadies her, in order to decode and comfortably recode her into its own system of representation" (6). In her discussion of Cuvier's examination of Ba(a)rtman(n), Sharpley-Whiting argues that "[e]ven in Bartmann's nakedness, Cuvier had yet to decipher her body, to undress the body. In the nineteenth century it is only through dissection that the hidden secrets of the body are fully revealed to the medical gaze, and Bartmann still wore the veil of her skin" (27). To decipher, in this case, is to search for origins, explanations, and answers in an almost frenzied scientific endeavor to get to the smallest and most bare unit of observation. What becomes interesting is the paradoxical movement away from any kind of true, complex understanding of subjectivity in the results of this impulse to taxonomy.

But am I simply carrying on a tradition of searching for truth in the dismembered minutiae of discourses, bodies, and ideas? As I suggested in chapter two, taxonomic impulses reach extreme levels of both racism and ambivalence in anatomist Robert Knox's *The Races of Men* (1850). On the one hand, Knox's notorious text makes race the central influencing factor in history thus far, moving away from ideas of nation and civilization. Biology, this anatomist argued, determines the course of events within any human community. He went on to examine in detail all the races of the planet, as he understood them, creating a physical and psychological profile of each group, which concluded in a clear racial hierarchy. On the other hand, however, this overtly racist agenda, saturated as it was with brutally derogatory digressions on the limitations of some races, predicated on material gained from individual dissections of individuals from a variety of cultures, resulted in an inadvertent critique of imperialism. For, as Knox argues, each race is predisposed to embrace a particular governmental structure, and so the process of imposing English social structures on other races is doomed to fail. Imperialism is therefore flawed, because it does not take into account the more important factor: human biological variations.

The power of Diana Ferrus's poem derives from its movement away from this paradigm of positivist scientific "rationality" to harness a protective, maternal voice as a way to usher in the rage at the way Ba(a)rtman(n) was treated. The voice becomes one that wrenches Ba(a)rtman(n) away from those who dissected her and respects the integrity of her body, creating a sense that the spirit is still alive and the oppression continues. There is a way, suggested here, that we can all still participate in bringing her out of that world in which her remains still live and her spirit is still trapped:

I have come to wretch you away—
away from the poking eyes
of the man-made monster
who lives in the dark
with his clutches of imperialism
who dissects your body bit by bit
who likens your soul to that of Satan
and declares himself the ultimate god!
(Ferrus, 10–17)

Here we see a way out of the dead-end of positivist analysis in the simple expression of anger and the determination to care. Rather than using Ba(a)rtman(n), Ferrus positions the speaker as offering herself for succor and return. The relationship to the body becomes one of care and protection, rather than one of a frantic search for individualized agency or biologically rooted explanations for cultural differences.

This switch of perspective is dramatized in Barbara Chase-Riboud's novel, *Hottentot Venus,* by having anger expressed by Ba(a)rtman(n) herself. Chase-Riboud narrates a large part of the story, including the dissection, from Ba(a)rtman(n)'s point of view. At the point when she is brought to the Jardin des Plantes to be put on display and "explained" by Cuvier to scientists and artists, Chase-Riboud powerfully collapses the museum, the circus, the laboratory, and the freak tent into one spectacle of degradation and death. The observers become oblivious to the trauma they inflict as they simultaneously examine, aestheticize, narrativize, and anatomize this woman. As Ba(a)rtman(n) surveys the main gallery of the museum where she will be the subject of a lecture and examination, she is astounded by the variety of objects, figures, and animals that surround her. The men believe she thinks the figures are alive, and they laugh. All the while Ba(a)rtman(n) thinks of the pain surrounding her: "The white men stood in a circle like hyenas, laughing at me. I tried desperately to control myself, repeating to myself that these exhibits were only skinned and stuffed animals, not real souls . . . but what of the human severed heads?" (225–26). As the process of scientific study that will end in the rending of her body literally into parts begins, we see the relationship between narrative, aesthetic, and literal dismemberment depicted in Ba(a)rtman(n)'s dissection as told from Ba(a)rtman(n)'s own perspective.

Ba(a)rtman(n) indicts Western philosophy and science from the site of her display in the Musée de l'Homme: "Oh, shame, shame, shame on you, masters of the universe. Shame on Dapper and Barrow, Levaillant and Diderot, Voltaire, Jefferson, Kolbe, Rousseau, Buffon, and fuck you, sirs! You are no gentlemen. This is no freak show. I am on display without compensation or compassion, in the name of all mankind and the great Chain of Being. The Hottentot Venus, archetype of inferior humanity. This very last layer of the human pie. Undo all this, sirs. Undo all this. Undo me" (285). Throughout this novel, the "freak" speaks back to the observers, the anatomists, and the artists, turning the tools of decipherment back on those who value its ideals. In one moment, a rationalist tradition of scientific endeavor is accused of atrocities, made the object of great shame, and exposed as the site of an ethic of dismemberment antithetical to the ethic of care embodied in Ferrus's poem.

Trinh T. Minh-ha argues much the same point in her critique of Western science and positivist rationality. Reflecting on the methodological requirements of Western academic work, she asserts directly her intention of working within an alternative paradigm:

> Thus, I see no interest in adopting a progression that systematically proceeds from generalities to specificities, from outlines to fillings, from diachronic to synchronic, or vice versa. And I am profoundly indifferent to his old way of theorizing—of piercing, as he often claims, through the sediments of psychological and epistemological "depths." I may stubbornly turn around a foreign thing or turn it around to play with it, but I respect its realms of opaqueness. Seeking to perforate meaning by forcing my entry or breaking it open to dissipate what is thought to be its secrets seems to me as crippled an act as verifying the sex of an unborn child by ripping open the mother's womb. It is typical of a mentality that proves incapable of touching the living thing without crushing its delicateness. (48–49)

Here, Trinh T. Minh-ha unmasks a destructive vision of theorizing as a process of searching, within a model of depth, for the central, originary, and clear explanations for ideas and issues.[1] As an alternative, she suggests that "opaqueness" sometimes should elicit respect, and that within the unknowable may exist knowledge that requires the need to respect its boundaries. To charge at it, rip it open, explore its elements is the intellectual equivalent to searching within the body of Ba(a)rtman(n) for answers to racial difference that do not exist there. In fact, it is the search within individual bodies for this understanding that perpetuates the system. Only in respecting the boundaries of the body and dealing with it by respecting its integrity and understanding its "opaqueness" can we begin to see that the source of the knowledge we seek is in the culture and the ethics of exploitation developed by a system of positivist racial exploration.

## A Legacy of Violence

What then becomes the proper ethical scholarly relationship with a subject such as Ba(a)rtman(n), a woman who stands as such a clear symbol, victim, and embodiment of Western colonial violence? How do we recognize the woman at the source of the destructive discursive explosion that arose in her wake and, at the same time, analyze the constructed nature of those representations? How do we honor the fractured subjectivity suggested in the visual partitions I use in the spelling of her name, while at the same time help participate in the beginnings of a cultural and intellectual healing process? How do we intervene in the aestheticizing of individuals in order to bring the representations out from the dynamic that desensitizes and dehumanizes the representative signifiers? As a beginning, Ferrus offers a model of a way of appreciating human beauty in a spirit of care and love:

> I have come to soothe your heavy heart
> I offer my bosom to your weary soul
> I will cover your face with the palms of my hands
> I will run my lips over lines in your neck
> I will feast my eyes on the beauty of you
> and I will sing for you
> for I have come to bring you peace.
> (Ferrus, 18–24)

The main ethical impulse of this poem is caring for the other. Moving into the historical situation of Ba(a)rtman's exploitation, the speaker intervenes by participating in a wholly different kind of physical relationship. The poem sets up a comparison between the scientific, anatomizing, and conventionally aestheticizing relationship to the body and a loving and appreciative relationship to form. The body is the center of both, but in Ferrus's poem the nurturing movement is from the speaker to Ba(a)rtman(n).

My analyses have addressed instances of violence in each of the texts in this study, as well as the ways those moments suggest wider implications for mid-Victorian racial representation. Violent acts are intrinsic to fictional and nonfictional racial narratives of the period. Although Martineau shied away from direct reference to violent actions, the narrative gaps in which violence occurs, such as in the disappearance and presumed death of Thérèse's child, convey the material reality that violence permeated every facet of the colonial system. Colonialism and imperialism were violent activities that resulted in the suppression of the colonized, and the eventual eruption of that group against their oppressors. Dickens and Collins's tale conveys the public's growing post-Emancipation frustration with repeated rebellions by former slaves. Both the transcript of the Governor Eyre controversy and the irrational rantings of Robert Knox represent, in vivid detail, the violence felt and experienced in relations among different races. Finally, Grant's novel develops the theme of vengeance evident in Dickens and Collins's tale written a decade earlier. The prevalence of violence suggests the reality of colonial relations and the frustration felt by English citizens who struggled with and debated issues of race and colonialism.

Ba(a)rtman(n)'s return to South Africa represents one small and powerful instance of cultures beginning to move beyond this violence to create moments of healing from its legacy of destruction. As Abrams and others encourage us to use the spelling on the baptismal certificate, Sarah Bartmann, so lifts the divisions in her name as the divisions and pain begin to heal with her return to South Africa, for those who live in South Africa, and those of us across the racial, national, and political spectrum who participate unknowingly and unacceptably in a system of taxonomic oppression. This successful negotiation, coupled with Ferrus's powerful ethic of care, provides a compelling model for a way to move beyond and begin to heal the legacy of destruction created by colonial and imperial structures and to engage in a model of intellectual exploration that takes into consideration the ethical imperative to be part of this process. Rather than employ a logic that suggests that truth lies in the details, a belief so vividly deconstructed in the Royal Commission transcript, we need to embrace a respect for the integrity of wholeness, for the need to change perspective on the totality rather than rend it into smaller and smaller bits. For, as the final lines of Ferrus's poem point out, we all need to participate in the dismantling of the legacy of racial violence.

I have come to take you home
where the ancient mountains shout your name.
I have made your bed at the foot of the hill,
your blankets are covered in buchu and mint,

156

the proteas stand in yellow and white—
I have come to take you home
where I will sing for you
for you have brought me peace.
(Ferrus, 25–32)

# NOTES

〜

## Notes to Introduction

1. See footnote 4 on page 33 of Scott's edition of the *Journal*.

2. As Gillian Beer suggests, it is not surprising that Eliot would address racial conflicts directly: "Descent, development, and race are central to *Daniel Deronda*" (Beer, 182).

## Notes to Chapter 1

1. See "Past and Present State of Hayti," *Quarterly Review* 21 (1819): 430–60. Note that this citation information differs from that found in the Appendix to the novel. The titles are the same, however, and there are no similar articles at the location Martineau cites.

2. Her topic also suggests an affinity with Victorian writings about the French Revolution, such as Thomas Carlyle's *History of the French Revolution* (1837), Karl Marx's *The Communist Manifesto* (1847), and Charles Dickens's *A Tale of Two Cities* (1859). The influence of Carlyle is especially important considering Martineau's close personal relationship with both the author and his wife, Jane. But Martineau's treatment of racial revolution has far less of the Romantic passion so powerfully conveyed in Carlyle's language and avoids the scapegoating of former slaves in which both Carlyle and Dickens engage when arguing for a more sympathetic attitude towards suffering white workers in England.

3. Parliamentary debaters tended to assume that the words of the government could produce rebellions. Diane Roberts argues, in her discussion of the American anti-abolitionist writer Louisa McCord, that opponents of Emancipation used "the anti-abolitionists' favorite example, Haiti, to describe the murder and rapine that would be visited on whites by outraged and vengeful black 'barbarians'" (66). As with Edwards's argument in 1797, the words produced by the home country—whether in pamphlets, tracts, or parliamentary debates—had the power to incite slaves in the colonial context to rebel. Slave uprisings, this argument suggests, were discursively fueled events.

4. See Ott's discussion of the specifics of the military campaign in his chapter "Toussaint and the British Invasion, 1793–1798" and C. L. R. James's analysis throughout *The Black Jacobins*.

5. See Ott's chapter, "The French Invasion, 1801–1802" for a historical description of these events in addition to C. L. R. James's detailed account.

6. Toussaint's Catholicism very likely impeded the conventional English reader's sympathy with his brand of Christianity, however.

7. An example of a text that takes the opposite position is Frances Trollope's *The Life and Adventures of Jonathan Jefferson Whitlaw: or Scenes on the Mississippi* (1836), a novel about a Louisiana slave plantation that connects the lack of education with an ignorance of Christian morality, rather than with the importance of, or need for, freedom (see 1:172).

8. In *The Problem of Freedom*, Thomas C. Holt suggests that the freedom into which the slaves moved was more of a transition in labor practices than true freedom from institutional restraint fueled by the intersection of abolitionism and the industrial revolution: "In this way slavery helped locate the outer boundaries of freedom; it was the antithesis of freedom. If slavery meant subordination to the physical coercion and personal dominion of an arbitrary master, then freedom meant submission only to the impersonal forces of the marketplace and to the rational and uniform constraints of the law" (Holt, 26). Holt is, of course, modifying Eric Williams's more economically deterministic argument in *Capitalism and Slavery*. In that work, Williams argues the following: "In 1833, therefore, the alternatives were clear: emancipation from above, or emancipation from below. But EMANCIPATION. Economic change, the decline of the monopolists, the development of capitalism, the humanitarian agitation in British churches, contending perorations in the halls of Parliament, had now reached their completion in the determination of the slaves themselves to be free. The Negroes had been stimulated to freedom by the development of the very wealth which their labor had created" (Williams, 208). Martineau speaks to the complex social and emotional situation of sudden freedom by having Toussaint's wife in the novel experience a sense of confusion and disorientation after realizing that they were free of the slave system (1:94–118).

9. Martineau's use of literacy as a narrative tool to gain the respect of the reader makes a great deal of sense, in terms of the ways in which the acts of reading and writing signify within the Western and European mindset. As Gates argues, "Writing, many Europeans argued, stood alone among the fine arts as the most salient repository of 'genius,' the visible sign of reason itself. In this subordinate role, however, writing, although secondary to reason, is nevertheless the *medium* of reason's expression. We *know* reason by its writing, by its representations. Such representations could assume spoken or written form. And while several superb scholars give priority to the *spoken* as the privileged of the pair, most Europeans privileged *writing*—in their writings about Africans, at least—as the principal measure of the Africans' humanity, their capacity for progress, their very place in the great chain of being" ("Introduction," 9, original italics).

The issue of literacy in light of work such as Edward Said's *Culture and Imperialism* (1993), and Gauri Viswanathan's "Currying Favor: The Politics of British Educational and Cultural Policy in India, 1813–1854" (1988) and *Masks of Conquest* (1998), cannot be left to exist as a kind of liberal idealization, however. Said's and Viswanathan's works illustrate vividly the power of the project of cultural literacy to intersect directly with physical and social brutality. Thus considering the way that Martineau's novel develops, a critique of the power of education as an imposition of social control over a population becomes significant.

10. C. L. R. James identifies Charles Bellair as Toussaint's nephew, and James argues that Toussaint "destined Belair to be his successor" (257).

## Notes to Chapter 2

1. Rae discusses two incidents specific to Knox's work on the intersections of science and art: first, Knox's time in the British Museum studying the Elgin Marbles in 1848, and second, his visit at that time to the Jardin des Plantes where he viewed what I believe was the *Venus Génitrix*. This image of Venus is reproduced by Knox in a sketch in *Races of Men* on p. 401 of that work. Knox thus collapses particular Greek statues into an essential ideal racial type.

2. One of the controversies surrounding Knox was how he got hold of these black African bodies upon which he performed his work. As his biographer and contemporary, Henry Lonsdale, argues, "Of the many wicked stories told by his enemies, one had reference to his possessing so many Caffre skulls in his museum. It was alleged that when one of his students inquired of the Doctor how he got them, he replied: 'Why, sir, there was no difficulty in Caffraria; I had but to walk out of my tent and shoot as many Caffres as I wanted for scientific and ethnological purposes.' This monstrous accusation had its believers. Knox was tender to a degree, wherever humanity was concerned; he never approved of the Caffre war, and always extolled the Caffre man for his courageous conduct" (Lonsdale, 149, f. 1).

Both Lonsdale and Knox biographer Isobel Rae argue quite openly for a renewed appreciation for their subject, who, they suggest, was unfairly judged by both his contemporaries and history alike. However, Knox's paradoxical and erratic attitudes toward darker-skinned races suggest that the blind coldness evident in the above vignette was somewhat out of character for what we will see as the anti-imperialist racialist.

3. Lonsdale suggests that from the beginning of his interest in race, even before the lecture tour in the late 1840s that took his work to a broader audience, Knox worked to convince those around him of its central importance: "From an early period in his career as an anatomical lecturer, he had pointed out the import of the study of Race, and, after 1834, had indoctrinated the majority of his friends with his more advanced views; it was in the year 1846 that he ventured to appear on a public platform to address a non-medical audience. In the language of the day, these lectures caused a sensation by their novelty, and led to much talk out of doors, and no small amount of controversy in the press" (Lonsdale, 295).

Knox's professional identity as one of the foremost comparative anatomists and medical professionals positioned him to take his place at the center of the controversies surrounding race. The goal for these individuals became creating a connection between biology and racial characteristics. Douglas Lorimer argues, "Pride of place as men of science went to the medical practitioners with an interest in comparative anatomy. The purpose of their studies was to establish a correlation between anatomical features and mental traits and social behavior. In this task, the comparative anatomists were dependent upon the context of the common culture. They presumed that the psychological traits and social behavior of various races, as encapsulated in commonplace stereotypes, were known" (Lorimer, "Science and the Secularization," 213).

4. "Unsettled from 1842 to 1846, and moving to and from on both sides of the

Tweed; now living with an old pupil, now searching for employment in London, he was at length induced to give a few lectures on the 'Races of Men,' in Newcastle-upon-Tyne, Manchester, &c. This peripatetic philosophizing made him known to the general public, and helped his finances; but it was not exactly the position for a man of Knox's calibre to occupy in England, that had its 'Royal Institution' and many chartered corporations under whose wing he should have played a part equal to the best-cultured minds of the day. His letters at this period express disappointment, and no wonder. Possessing the highest gifts of intellect, he obtained to acknowledgment in the ranks of his own profession; the greatest teacher of anatomy could find no chair and no lectureship in the mighty metropolis; and the Government, not knowing the meaning of the word science, could not possibly see the merits of a man of genius" (Lonsdale, 284).

5. H. L. Malchow notes that Ralph Waldo Emerson's view of hybrid individuals was influenced for the worse by his reading of Knox (Malchow, 184), thus suggesting a wide influence and reading of Knox's work in the nineteenth century.

6. Early in the text, Knox addresses the common argument at the time that darker-skinned races must have smaller brains. When evidence emerged that some darker-skinned races have larger brains, Knox sought to explain the findings. Lonsdale reports that "Knox thought there must be a physical, and consequently a psychological inferiority in the dark races, not depending altogether on deficiency in the size of the brain *en masse,* but rather perhaps on specific characters in the quality of the brain itself" (308). Knox portrays Chinese people in a similarly contemptuous manner. Arguing against those who praise the scientific achievements of the race, Knox says, "A love for science implies a love of truth: now truth they despise and abhor. I do not believe there is an individual Chinaman who could be made to comprehend a single fact in physical geography" (283). Knox goes on to argue that "it is admitted on all hands that they are devoid of all principle, and essentially a nation of liars" (285). And he asserts that the Gypsy is "without a redeeming quality" (159).

Knox asserts that Jewish people should be classed among the dark-skinned races, and thus they deserve the most derogatory of descriptions. They have "no ear for music as a race, no love of science or literature; that he invents nothing, pursues no inquiry" (194), and they seek "callings where cunning of the mind surpasses the gifts of science, the profound knowledge of the arts, and the skill of the hands" (196). He argues that the "Slavonians" are the most intellectual race (356). The Saxon race he generally calls the most superior (46) because it comprises hard and determined workers without any artistic ability (54).

7. A mixed-race child is a "monstrosity of nature"; "there is no place for . . . a family" that could produce such a child (88). In general, "man can create nothing" that is not already produced in nature. All types and varieties are fixed: "Nature produces no mules; no hybrids, neither in man nor animals" (65). The mixed-race individual "cannot extend his race, for he is of no race" (111).

8. Stocking argues that the "roots of the APS in turn are to be found in the crusade led by Evangelical and Quaker philanthropists against the African slave trade and slavery in the British colonies" ("What's in a Name?" 369).

9. As Stocking argues, the young scientists felt that women inhibited their ability to speak freely on all subjects: "the presence of women made it impossible to discuss freely matters of human anatomy and physiology, or such questions as phallic worship and male and female circumcision" (*Victorian Anthropology*, 253).

10. Far from dominating contemporary racial discourse, the attitude of the Anthropological Society was primarily reactive. The organization waged war on the still powerful ideology of monogenesis, attempted to destroy the remains of the abolitionist humanitarian stance towards the races, and sought to retain control over racial discourse by excluding women and by belittling the work of those of the Ethnological Society. According to Stocking, the growth and popularity of the ASL were phenomenal, "despite the fact that its internal life was marred by dissension and frequent resignations. Within two years there were over five hundred members, and in 1866 constitutional provisions were made for local branches" ("What's in a Name?" 377). Darwinians, interestingly, remained members of the Ethnological Society. Many credible scientists stayed away from the ASL because they were perceived as a renegade group of scientific radicals who, as Stocking describes, "violated the canons of behaviour appropriate to a respectable scientific group." Calling "themselves 'The Cannibal Club'" and calling their meetings to order by gaveling "a mace in the form of a Negro head" ("What's in a Name?" 380) exemplified this perception.

11. This argument perhaps suggests an ideological precursor to what Deirdre David calls the "trope of invasion by the colonizer and counterinvasion by the colonized" (204).

12. See also Benedict Anderson's *Imagined Communities* (1983) for a discussion of the transition from language to race as a definitive component of national identity.

13. Stocking argues that "within Europe itself, the 'racial' nationalism of the revolutionary epoch of 1848"—commonly called the Springtime of Nations—"gave the idea of race a greatly heightened saliency, even for men of unquestioned humanitarian commitment" (*Victorian Anthropology*, 63).

14. Lonsdale also notes this change in public opinion: "Those who felt disposed to laugh in 1846 at Knox's theories of Race, were surprised at the historical endorsement they obtained in 1860" (Lonsdale, 317).

15. One element of the late-1840s revolutionary environment in Europe that perhaps contributed to a climate in which Knox's ideas could receive a more sympathetic reception was the influx of refugees into England, fleeing a number of the 1848 European national conflicts. Referring to this phenomenon as "one factor that has not been sufficiently explored" (17), Wetzel argues that three issues contributed to an environment within English culture that could nurture incipient racism. First, "in 1850 half the population of England was under twenty-six, a decrease of six and a half years over the average age ten years before" (17). This change combined with the "unprecedented movement from the countryside to the cities" (17) of rural citizens over the previous fifty years. However, when these rural citizens arrived in the city, they found life "risky and uncertain" and "competition over jobs, food, and clothing" was fierce (17). Add to this situation the final factor of "the presence of aliens" brought about by the revolutionary climate, and you have all the ingredients for creating a sense of racial "xenophobia" (17). And although Wetzel argues that it is necessary not to overemphasize the significance of this situation, it becomes important as another contributing element in a cultural environment moving away from humanitarianism.

16. England exemplifies this dynamic. Knox has special contempt for the government of England, arguing that the feudal Norman government—in what he describes as "semi-Saxon England"—imposes itself on the people, resulting in the oppression of much of the population (*Races*, 371). He suggests that "the military force at the disposal of the

government for the crushing down and intimidating the freemen of England is more effective, more insulated from the people, than in the most despotic European state" (372). So the nation becomes the vehicle in Knox's work for a government's oppression of its own people in the direction of the race that has the preeminent natural strength within the population. Government becomes the way in which the oppression of one race by another is masked by the mirage of national destiny.

17. Although racial conflict is inevitable, and one race will always try to dominate another, Knox labels the races that yearn for freedom and liberty as superior. As with Martineau's *The Hour and the Man,* the concept of liberty becomes crucially important in Knox's text, most pointedly in his dramatic presentation of Saxon superiority. For Knox, "all men love liberty, in one sense or another; but all do not attach to the term the same ideas. Each race interprets the expression differently" (*Races,* 373). Liberty, for Knox, comes to be yet another slippery term, however, introducing a linguistic relativism in the relationship between the races. "Each race has its own ideas of liberty," Knox argues, but the Saxon race is the only one whose "ideas on this point are sound." And the Saxon perspective is sound, because the political system that he most desires is democratic, and it is only the Saxon "who combines obedience to the law with liberty. But the law must be made by himself, and not forced on him by another" (374). Therefore, the Saxon resists being the object of colonial oppression because as a race, he cannot live with the imposition of external laws not natural to his racial makeup. And this reverence for liberty perhaps ties in with Knox's declaration of admiration for rebellious slaves. The desire to be free is a mark of racial superiority.

18. Knox argues that his experience studying race had shown him that avoiding the subject served the interests of dominating colonial powers who justify their subjection of races by not acknowledging the distinctions that exist: "More than thirty years ago, observation taught me that the great question of race—the most important, unquestionably, to man—had been for the most part scrupulously, shall we say purposely, avoided—by the statesman, the historian, the theologian; by journalists of nearly all countries. Unpalatable doctrines, no doubt, to dynasties lording it over nations composed of different races" (*Races,* 4).

Rae argues that "[a]lready, in 1820, Robert Knox held sufficiently advanced opinions to make him a supporter of equality and fraternity—an early and unfashionable anticolonialist" (16). In addition to his criticism of aggression masking as administrative paperwork and posturing, Knox is particularly hard on the use of the cloak of Christianity. But the "inevitable" as always blended with the "constructed" in Knox's observations: "A profitable war is a pleasant thing for a Saxon nation" he notes, and he then maintains that "a crusade against the heathen has always been declared praiseworthy" (*Races,* 4). But Christianity, which he calls "the everlasting truth," has no ability to "alter race" (367). For Knox, however, Christianity certainly does not ensure a civilized manner and agenda: "Civilization and Christianity are identical, it is true; but then it must be real, and not sham Christianity—the actual, not the shadow" (399). Here again, we see this issue of the actual and the shadow, the real and the fictional, the biologically determined versus the obscuring construct. Rather than being a vehement anticolonialist, Knox advocates for a directly aggressive manner against those a group wants to dominate: "I prefer the manly robber to this sneaking, canting hypocrisy, peculiar to modern civilization and to Christian Europe" (*Races,* 43). What he seems to find offensive is the dishonest "justification" used for aggressive colonial policy, not the reality of the actions.

19. This discussion begs the relationship between Darwinian evolutionary thought at this time and this idea of biological determinism as rooted in the development of the embryo. And although Knox delimits the role of progressive change or adaptation, certainly the development and mutations of the embryo suggests some kind of historical component. Beer's discussion of the role of evolution and the evolutionary metaphor (18) becomes important here, in that one can see Knox struggle with how to fold in the temporal nature of human biology and to configure the role of human beings in relation to the rest of the living world. Beer argues that one of the most challenging aspects of evolutionary theory was the placing of human beings in the realm of the rest of the animals (19). Darwin remained a believer in monogenesis all his life, although his theories were often seen as a way to unite the impulses of both strands of racial thinking. However, as connected as the living world became in evolutionary theory, there was still an implied hierarchy at work along a now evolutionary scale (Stepan, 55).

20. "By the latter half of the nineteenth century, the analogy between race and gender degeneration came to serve a specifically modern form of social domination, as an intricate dialectic emerged—between the domestication of the colonies and the racializing of the metropolis. In the metropolis, the idea of racial deviance was evoked to police the 'degenerate' classes—the militant working class, the Irish, Jews, feminists, gays and lesbians, prostitutes, criminals, alcoholics and the insane—who were collectively figured as racial deviants, atavistic throwbacks to a primitive moment in human prehistory, surviving ominously in the heart of the modern, imperial metropolis" (McClintock, 43).

21. See footnote 1 for this chapter.

22. Knox died December 20, 1862.


## Notes to Chapter 3

1. See Ruth Glancy's specific remarks regarding "Perils" in *The Christmas Stories* (1996), 171.

2. There are many accounts of this event. See, for example, Lillian Nayder's description in "Class Consciousness and the Indian Mutiny in Dickens's 'The Perils of Certain English Prisoners,'" (1992), 693.

3. See Nayder, "Class Consciousness and the Indian Mutiny in Dickens's 'The Perils of Certain English Prisoners'"

4. Oddie suggests that this characterization of the servant is made to bear the weight of a growing and virulent British xenophobia: "The character of Christian George King, clearly enough, is an expression of the pathological hatred of 'natives' that swept over England during the mutiny. Dickens was not, in any case, very well disposed towards dark-skinned races, and King is a kind of all-purpose 'wog', half negro and half Indian, on to whom he can fasten his loathing" (7).

5. According to H. L. Malchow, "the multicultural nature of ships' crews became analogous in the nineteenth century to a kind of miscegenation, and the white sailor, by association (and perhaps sexual liaison) with racial aliens both on ship and in exotic ports of call, absorbed some element of their strange, deviant ways" (Malchow, 103).

6. Like the pirates of "Perils," the crew of Marryat's *The Pirate* has representatives from many different nations: "The crew consisted in all of one hundred and sixty-five

men, of almost every nation; but it was to be remarked that all those in authority were either Englishmen or from the northern countries; the others were chiefly Spaniards and Maltese. Still there were Portuguese, Brazilians, negroes, and others, who made up the complement, which at the time we now speak of was increased by twenty-five additional hands" (435).

7. Karl Marx, "The Fetishism of Commodities" (1986).

8. See especially the following: Emily Apter and William Pietz, Eds., *Fetishism as Cultural Discourse* (1993); Jean Baudrillard, *For a Critique of the Political Economy of the Sign* (1981); Homi K. Bhabha, "The other question: difference, discrimination and the discourse of colonialism," *Literature, Politics and Theory: Papers from the Essex Conference 1976–84* (1986); Frantz Fanon, *The Wretched of the Earth* (1963) and *Black Skins White Masks* (1967); Lorraine Gamman, Lorraine and Merja Makinen. *Female Fetishism* (1994); Henry Krips, *Fetish: An Erotics of Culture* (1999); and Hayden White, "The Noble Savage Theme as Fetish," *Tropics of Discourse: Essays in Cultural Criticism* (1978).

9. For example, Charles Bernheimer gives a particularly lucid description of the phallocentric limitations of Freud's theory of the fetish: "Even after it is revealed to be a false front, this construct continues to determine a central truth of psychoanalysis, the truth of castration. But this truth is of course a phallocentric deceit: woman cannot be deprived of an organ that was never hers in the first place. In terms of the criterion of factual reality that Freud himself introduces in this context, the unmasking of sexual difference reveals that woman is uncastratable, not that she is castrated" (65).

10. See also the following from Hayden White: "From the Renaissance to the end of the eighteenth century, Europeans tended to fetishize the native peoples with whom they came into contact by viewing them simultaneously as monstrous forms of humanity and as quintessential objects of desire. Whence the alternative impulses to exterminate and to redeem the native peoples. But even more basic in the European consciousness of this time was the tendency to fetishize the European type of humanity as the sole possible form that humanity in general could take. This race fetishism was soon transformed, however, into another, and more virulent form: the fetishism of class, which has provided the bases of most of the social conflicts of Europe since the French Revolution" (*Tropics*, 194–95).

11. "His costume was elegant, and well adapted to his form: linen trousers, and untanned yellow leather boots, such as are made at the Western Isles; a broad-striped cotton shirt; a red Cashmere shawl around his waist as a sash; a vest embroidered in gold tissue, with a jacket of dark velvet, and pendant gold buttons, hanging over his left shoulder, after the fashion of the Mediterranean seamen; a round Turkish skull-cap, handsomely embroidered; a pair of pistols, and a long knife in his sash, completed his attire" (Marryat, 434–35).

12. "Cleveland himself was gallantly attired in a blue coat, lined with crimson silk, and laced with gold very richly, crimson damask waistcoat and breeches, a velvet cap, richly embroidered, with a white feather, white silk stockings, and red-heeled shoes, which were the extremity of finery among the gallants of the day. He had a gold chain several times folded round his neck, which sustained a whistle of the same metal, the ensign of his authority. Above all, he wore a decoration peculiar to those daring depredators, who, besides one, or perhaps two brace of pistols at their belt, had usually two additional brace, of the finest mounting and workmanship, suspended over their

shoulders in a sort of sling, or scarf of crimson ribbon" (Scott, 532–33).

13. Interestingly, Peter Fryer's description of the appearance of slave-ship captains has much in common with the pirate captain, perhaps suggesting an allegorical connection between the characterization of Mendez and the slave trading system, which would have been in full flower in 1744: "These slave-ship captains were the elite of their calling, identifiable not only by their 'privelege Negroes' but also by their gaudy laced coats with big silver or gold buttons, their cocked hats, the silver or gold buckles on their shoes. Most of them, whatever they had been like when they entered the trade, turned into brutal tyrants. But it was a trade that tended to attract sadists" (Fryer, 55).

14. See Edward Said, *Orientalism*, New York: Vintage, 1979.

15. Of course, Mendez's popularity with audiences would seem to suggest that this goal was not achieved.

## Notes to Chapter 4

1. From the statement of George Lake in the papers submitted by Governor Eyre describing the oath Paul Bogle, a central rebel leader, asked his followers to take in meetings previous to the Morant Bay riot.

2. The specifics of the rebellion are from the Royal Commission's Report and Supporting Documents; Heuman, *'The Killing Time': The Morant Bay Rebellion in Jamaica* (1994) and *Between Black and White: Race, Politics, and the Free Coloreds in Jamaica, 1792–1865* (1981); and Lorimer, *Colour, Class and the Victorians* (1978).

3. Thomas Carlyle, *Occasional Discourse on the Nigger Question*, London: Thomas Bosworth, 1853.

4. Information about the reception of accounts of the rebellion in England is from Bernard Semmel, *The Governor Eyre Controversy* (1962). Heuman also provides information about English reception of the news of the rebellion, but his source is primarily Semmel.

5. H. L. Malchow argues that "the fascination in the press with the grisly anatomical details of Jamaican mutilation resonated strongly with similar preoccupations with the dissection theater and the cannibal feast" (Malchow, 211), thus suggesting a link between the discourses surrounding both the Burke and Hare scandal and the stream of colonial uprisings in the first half of the nineteenth century.

6. "News of the rebellion reached London ahead of Governor Eyre's report of the events of Morant Bay. Jamaican newspapers as well as passengers on an earlier ship had already publicized the rebellion, and the British press had reprinted some of the stories emanating from Jamaica. When Eyre's dispatch arrived on 16 November, the reaction in the Colonial Office was one of relief that the insurrection had been suppressed. However, there was also concern about the manner in which the rebellion had been put down" (Heuman, *Killing*, 164).

7. The following is from a footnote to the *Autobiography*: "Among the most active members of the Committee were Mr. P. A. Taylor, M.P., always faithful and energetic in every assertion of the principles of liberty; Mr. Goldwin Smith, Mr. Frederic Harrison, Mr. Slack, Mr. Chamerovzow, Mr. Shaen, and Mr. Chesson, the Honorary Secretary of the Association" (Mill, 209n).

8. 7167. You saw him shot, what became of you?—I was hiding, as I was in the

house. I was compelled to hide from the soldiers.

7168. Did you see it from your house then?—Yes.

7169. From your own house you saw him shot; were you in the house?—I was in the house when he was shot.

7170. And you could see it from your house, it was so near as that?—Yes, between my gate and the treehead cut off as a post.

7171. He was taken straight from your house and was shot?—Yes.

7172. Was he tied to the tree?—Tied to the tree.

7173. Who shot him?—The soldiers. (Report, II:148)

9. In the continued testimony, the first discrepancy surfaces about whether the brother was hit with a sword:

7183. Did not you say a short time ago that you did not see that?—Yes, I did say it.

7184. Which do you say now?—I say that he received three balls.

7185. Attend; you say he had a chop over the brow?—Yes.

7186. Did you see that chop given?—Yes.

7187. Do you mean to say that?—Yes. (Report, II:148)

10. 7195. And did you say before, when you told this story to this gentleman, that you did not see that sword blow given?—The soldier gave it to him.

7196. Did you say you did not see it given; do you understand the question?—I saw the whole of them in the crowd, and the soldier struck him over the head.

7197. Only one did that you say; only one drew the sword and delivered the blow?—Yes, delivered the blow.

7198. Have you not said this morning, when you told the story before, that you did not see this done?—Understand me, sir, I was hiding myself in the house, and saw the soldiers as they came; they tied him to the post, tied him to the tree, and after that they shot him. (Report, II:148)

11. 7285. When they got to your house at 7 o'clock what did they do?—They came for Ned Bryan, and said he was a rebel. He said no, and one of the soldiers came and held Ned Bryan and James Bryan.

7286. What did they do with them?—They took them out in the road.

7287. When they got out into the road what became of them?—As they got to the road the soldiers asked for a rope, and they took the rope, and Ned Bryan said, "I am just from Kingston last night, and I am going to dead this morning. What have I done?" And a white gentleman, with a black soldier, riding a horse, was there. The whole of the black soldiers were riding, and when they carry him out in the road he said, "I am just from Kingston last night." The gentleman, who the soldier said was the doctor, had a pistol in his hand, and he took the pistol and knocked Ned Bryan on his hand, and said, "Go on; I want no chat from you." They went a little in the road and they tied the two brothers, James Bryan and Ned Bryan together, and the doctor ordered three soldiers to come off and shoot those two men. They tied him to a tree by the side of the road, and cut off the head of the tree, and three soldiers came and shot the two of them.

7288. Shot both of them?—Yes.

7289. Were they close together?—Yes; and they shot them facing each other. The three soldiers shot the two, and when they shot the two Ned Bryan was tied to the post that way, and James the other to the front, and as they shot him James dropped down, and Ned stood up, and out the soldier drew a sword out of his sheath, and chopped Ned Bryan right down. (Report, II:149)

12. 7319. (*Mr. Walcott*) Where was George Bryan when the soldiers fired?—He hid behind the patch of bush at the time.

7320. At the time the soldiers were firing at James and Edward?—Yes.

7321. Then he was not in his house at the time?—No. I begged him to hide, for the soldiers would kill him.

7322. Then he was behind the bush when the soldiers fired at James and Edward?—Yes. (Report, II:150)

13. 10,907. Is it not true that you went into the bush?—The bush was before the house, and I ran through the bush. I was in my own house.

10,908. Is it true that at the time your brother was shot you were hid in the bush?—No, I was not hid in the bush; I was in the house.

10,909. You say you went through the bush?—Yes.

10,910. Where was the bush?—On the side of the road.

10,911. At the back of your house?—No.

10,912. In front of your house?—No.

10,913. Do you say there was no bush in front of your house?—On the other side of the road.

10,914. And you were not concealed in that bush?—No.

10,915. Do you know that your sister-in-law stated that you were concealed in that bush?—No; she states I was in the bush. She don't know when I went in.

10,916. Was there anybody else shot at the same time as your brother was?—No, sir, because I did not see the other person shot, I really think.

10,917. You did not see any other person shot at the same time as your brother was?—No, I did not see the man when they were tied, but I saw the man that was on the back at the back of him.

10,918. Was there any other person shot at the same time that your brother was?—Did I see any person shot at the same time?

10,919. Yes; any other person shot at the same time your brother was shot?—No; I said that already. There was no other person shot, only farther on. (Report, II:217)

14. 10,937. Then it must have been very soon afterwards that the wife cut him down?—Soon, sir, very soon.

10,938. Did she not have to go and get a person from the town to come and take the body away?—Well, sir, it is me, the same one that took the body, and another man.

10,939. Who was the man?—Another man named Edward.

10,940. You and Edward took the body?—Yes, and buried it.

10,941. Where?—In his own yard. (Report, II:217).

15. 10,980. (*Suggested by Mr. Gorrie.*) What was the name of your brother who was shot; that you have been describing as having been shot?—What is the name of my brother?

10,981. Yes; that brother you say was shot at this time?—Ned Bryan?

10,982. Is he your brother?—My brother-in-law. Married to my sister. I call him brother.

10,983. Do you know a person of the name of James Bryan, or did you know a person named James Bryan?—A person of the name James Bryan?

10,984. Do you know a person of the name of James Bryan?—Yes.

10,985. Who is he?—Not my brother.

10,986. Any relation of yours?—No.

10,987. No relation at all?—No.

10,988. Where is James Bryan now?—I heard this one James Bryan was dead, but I don't know him.

10,989. Was he no relation of yours?—No.

10,990. None at all?—No.

10,991. You heard he was dead?—Yes.

10,992. Where did he live?—He was living down the river.

10,993. Have you any other brother?—Yes, I had one.

10,994. What name?—Name of James Bryan, too.

10,995. But I asked you whether James Bryan was your brother, and you said no?—I had one, the one that went to Kingston, of the name James Bryan.

10,996. He is your brother?—Yes.

10,997. Is he alive?—Yes.

10,998. Where is he?—At Long Bay now.

10,999. Have you any other brother?—No.

11,000. Had your brotherinlaw any brother?—Yes.

11,001. What was his name?—He had a brother named Edward Bryan.

11,002. No; he was Edward Bryan?—No, there is two of them, Ned Bryan and Edward Bryan, and he had one of the name of William Bryan that I gave to you, who was at Manchioneal, and the soldiers shot him.

11,003. Where is Edward Bryan?—At Long Bay now.

11,004 Had he any other brother?—Another in Kingston named John Bryan.

11,005. Is he alive still?—Yes. (Report, II:218)


## Notes to Chapter 5

1. In *Suggestions Towards the Future Government of India,* a work in which Martineau makes suggestions for dealing with the immediate aftermath of the 1857 Indian Rebellion, the author argues for continued rule by the East India Company rather than an assertion of control by the British government by making a comparison with what she feels is the British failure in the West Indies to deal fairly with Africans: "We have done what we could there in reparation of our misdeeds to the negro race and our favouritism to the planters; but the alternating distresses of the two races are an evidence of such serious errors in colonial government as leave us no cause for confidence that we could succeed better in ruling a greater number of races under far more difficult circumstances" (*Suggestions,* 6).

2. Jenny Sharpe suggests that events such as the "Mutiny" triggered ideas propagated in scientific writings, thus further supporting the thesis that "scientific" ideas about race had a wide cultural impact: "I want to suggest that the Indian Mutiny, along with other rebellions in the colonies, activated scientific theories of race" (Sharpe, 5).

3. Penny Tinkler argues, in her introduction to the special issue of *Women's Studies International Forum* (1998), the following: "As Catherine Hall pointed out in her WHN plenary address, it is a 'blind eye' through which we see the Empire. In other words, despite the attention that empire currently attracts, fundamental aspects of imperialism are obscured, including, importantly, the exploitative relations that underpinned it and the interconnectedness of 'home,' be it Britain or other Western nations, and empire"

(Tinker, 217). Also see Leonore Davidoff and Catherine Hall, *Family Fortunes: Men and Women of the English Middle Class, 1780–1850* (1987), for a fuller discussion of middle-class family structures and environments. However, this work has little discussion of the relation of metropolitan family arrangements and colonialism.

## Note to Conclusion

1. Robyn Wiegman argues in *American Anatomies* that Cuvier's work helped move the search for legitimizing evidence for oppressive racial distinction within the human body: "The move from the visible epidermal terrain to the articulation of the interior structure of human bodies thus extrapolated in both broader and more distinct terms the parameters of white supremacy, giving it a logic lodged fully in the body" (Wiegman, 31).

# BIBLIOGRAPHY

〜

Abrams, Yvette. "Images of Sara Bartman: Sexuality, Race, and Gender." In *Nation, Empire, Colony: Historicizing Gender and Race,* edited by Ruth Roach Pierson and Napur Chaudhuri. Bloomington: Indiana University Press, 1998.

Ackroyd, Peter. *Dickens.* New York: HarperCollins, 1991.

Altick, Richard D. *The Shows of London.* Cambridge: Belknap Press, 1978.

Anderson, Benedict. *Imagined Communities.* London: Verso, 1983.

Anonymous. "Past and Present State of Hayti." *Quarterly Review.* Vol. 21. London: John Murray, 1819.

Anonymous review of *The Hour and the Man,* by Harriet Martineau. *The Athenaeum* 5 (December 1840): 958–59.

Anonymous review of *The Hour and the Man,* by Harriet Martineau. *The Westminster Review* 35 (1841): 235–37.

Apter, Emily, and William Pietz, eds. *Fetishism as Cultural Discourse.* Ithaca: Cornell University Press, 1993.

Bachelard, Gaston. *The Poetics of Space: The Classic Look at How We Experience Intimate Places.* Trans. Maria Jolas. Boston: Beacon Press, 1964.

Barringer, Tim. "Images of Otherness and the Visual Production of Difference: Race and Labour in Illustrated Texts, 1850–1865." In *The Victorians and Race,* edited by Shearer West. Aldershot: Scolar, 1996.

Baucom, Ian. *Out of Place: Englishness, Empire, and the Locations of Identity.* Princeton: Princeton University Press, 1999.

Baudrillard, Jean. *For a Critique of the Political Economy of the Sign.* Trans. Charles Levin. New York: Telos Press, 1981.

Bayer-Berenbaum, Linda. *The Gothic Imagination: Expansion in Gothic Literature and Art.* London: Associated University Press, 1982.

Beer, Gillian. *Darwin's Plots: Evolutionary Narrative in Darwin, George Eliot and Nineteenth-Century Fiction.* London: Routledge, 1983.

Behn, Aphra. *Oroonoko and Other Writings.* 1688. Oxford: Oxford University Press, 1994.

Bernheimer, Charles. "Fetishism and Decadence: Salome's Severed Heads." In *Fetishism as Cultural Discourse,* edited by Emily Apter and William Pietz. Ithaca: Cornell University Press, 1993.

Bhabha, Homi K. "Introduction." In *Nations and Narration,* edited by Homi K. Bhabha. London: Routledge, 1990.

———. "The Other Question: Difference, Discrimination and the Discourse of Colonialism." In *Black British Cultural Studies,* edited by Houston A. Baker, Jr., Manthia Diawara, and Ruth H. Lindeborg. Chicago: University of Chicago Press, 1996.

Bindman, David. *Ape to Apollo: Aesthetics and the Idea of Race in the 18th Century.* London: Reaktion Books, 2002.

Bolt, Christine. *Victorian Attitudes to Race.* London: Routledge & Kegan Paul, 1971.

Brantlinger, Patrick. *The Spirit of Reform: British Literature and Politics, 1832–1867.* Cambridge: Harvard University Press, 1977.

———. *Rule of Darkness: British Literature and Imperialism, 1830–1914.* Ithaca: Cornell University Press, 1988.

Brooks, Peter. *Reading for the Plot.* New York: A. A. Knopf, 1984.

Burg, B. R. *Sodomy and the Pirate Tradition: English Sea Rovers in the Seventeenth Century Caribbean.* New York: New York University Press, 1995.

Burke, Edmund. *A Philosophical Enquiry into the Origin of our Ideas of the Sublime and Beautiful.* Oxford: Oxford University Press, 1990.

Carlyle, Thomas. *Occasional Discourse on the Nigger Question.* London: Thomas Bosworth, 1853.

———. *Past and Present,* edited by Richard D. Altick (first published in 1843). New York: New York University Press, 1965.

Carolan, Katherine. "A Study of Christmas in the Works of Charles Dickens, With Special Attention to the Christmas Books." Diss. The George Washington University, 1972.

Chapman, Maria Weston. "Hayti." *The Liberty Bell.* Boston: American Anti-Slavery Society, 1842.

Chase-Riboud, Barbara. *Hottentot Venus.* New York: Doubleday, 2003.

Clarkson, T. "Thoughts on the Necessity of Improving the Condition of the Slaves in the British Colonies, with a View to their Ultimate Emancipation; and on the Practibility, the Safety, and the Advantages of the Latter Measure." London: Society for the Mitigation and Gradual Abolition of Slavery Throughout the British Dominions, 1824.

Cook, Anthony E. "Beyond Critical Legal Studies: The Reconstructive Theology of Dr. Martin Luther King, Jr." In *Critical Race Theory: The Key Writings that Formed the Movement,* edited by Kimberlé Crenshaw, Neil Gotanda, Gary Peller, and Kendall Thomas. New York: The New Press, 1995.

Cordingly, David. *Under the Black Flag.* New York: Random House, 1995.

David, Dierdre. *Rule Britannia: Women, Empire, and Victorian Writing.* Ithaca: Cornell University Press, 1995.

Davidoff, Leonore, and Catherine Hall. *Family Fortunes: Men and Women of the English Middle Class, 1780–1850.* Chicago: University of Chicago Press, 1987.

Dickens, Charles. "The Noble Savage" (first published in *Household Words,* 11 June 1853). *Reprinted Pieces: The Uncommercial Traveller and Other Stories.* Bloomsbury: The Nonesuch Press, 1938.

———. *The Letters of Charles Dickens.* The Pilgrim Edition, edited by Graham Storey and Kathleen Tillotson. Oxford: Clarendon, 1995.

———. *The Christmas Stories,* edited by Ruth Glancy. London: Everyman, 1996.

Dickens, Charles, and Wilkie Collins. "The Perils of Certain English Prisoners, and their Treasure in Women, Children, Silver, and Jewels." In *The Christmas Stories,* edited by Ruth Glancy. London: Everyman, 1996.

Douglass, Frederick. *Narrative of the Life of Frederick Douglass, An American Slave.* In *The Classic Slave Narratives,* edited by Henry Louis Gates, Jr. Baltimore: Penguin, 1987.

Drescher, Seymour. *Capitalism and Antislavery: British Mobilization in Comparative Perspective.* New York: Oxford University Press, 1987.

Eagleton, Terry. *The Ideology of the Aesthetic.* Oxford: Blackwell Publishers, 1990.

Edwards, Bryan. *An Historical Survey of the French Colony in the Island of St. Domingo.* London: John Stockdale, 1797.

Edwards, Yuko. *Politics from a Black Woman's Insides.* Written, Directed, and Produced by Yuko Edwards, 1977.

Eliot, George. *Daniel Deronda.* 1876. London: Penguin, 1995.

Ellis, Kate Ferguson. *The Contested Castle: Gothic Novels and the Subversion of Domestic Ideology.* Urbana: University of Illinois Press, 1989.

"Extent of the Indian Mutinies." *Fraser's Magazine for Town and Country.* Vol. LVII (Jan. to June, 1858): 358–62.

Eze, Emmanuel Chukwudi. *Race and the Enlightenment: A Reader.* Cambridge: Blackwell, 1997.

Fabian, Johannes. *Time and the Other: How Anthropology Makes Its Object.* New York: Columbia University Press, 1983.

Fanon, Frantz. *The Wretched of the Earth.* New York: Grove Press, 1963.

———. *Black Skins, White Masks.* New York: Grove Press, 1967.

Ferguson, Moira. *Subject to Others: British Women Writers and Colonial Slavery, 1670–1834.* New York: Routledge, 1992.

Ferrus, Diana. "A Poem for Sarah Baartman." <http://www.safrica.info/ess_info/sa_glance/history/saartjie.htm>

Finn, Margot. *After Chartism: Class and Nation in English Radical Politics, 1848–1874.* Cambridge: Cambridge University Press, 1993.

Fladeland, Betty. *Abolitionists and Working-Class Problems in the Age of Industrialization.* Baton Rouge: Louisiana State University Press, 1984.

Freud, Sigmund. "Fetishism." 1927. *The Standard Edition of the Complete Psychological Works of Sigmund Freud.* Vol. XXI. Trans. James Strachey. London: Hogarth Press, 1981.

Frye, Northrop. *Anatomy of Criticism.* Princeton: Princeton University Press, 1957.

Fryer, Peter. *Staying Power: The History of Black People in Britain.* London: Pluto Press, 1984.

Gamman, Lorraine, and Merja Makinen. *Female Fetishism.* New York: New York University Press, 1994.

Gates, Henry Louis, Jr. "Editor's Introduction: Writing 'Race' and the Difference It Makes." In *"Race," Writing, and Difference.* Chicago: The University of Chicago Press, 1985.

———. "Introduction." *The Classic Slave Narratives.* Baltimore: Penguin, 1987.

———. *The Signifying Monkey.* Oxford: Oxford University Press, 1988.

Geggus, David. "British Opinion and the Emergence of Haiti, 1791–1805." In *Slavery and British Society,* edited by James Walvin. Baton Rouge: Louisiana State University Press, 1982.

Genette, Gérard. *Figures of Literary Discourse.* Trans. Alan Sheridan. New York, Columbia University Press, 1982.

Gilman, Sander L. "Black Bodies, White Bodies: Toward an Iconography of Female Sexuality in Late Nineteenth-Century Art, Medicine, and Literature." In *"Race," Writing and Difference*, edited by Henry Louis Gates, Jr. Chicago: University of Chicago Press, 1985.

Gilroy, Paul. *"There Ain't No Black in the Union Jack": The Cultural Politics of Race and Nation.* Chicago: University of Chicago Press, 1987.

Glancy, Ruth. "Introduction." *The Christmas Stories.* London: Everyman, 1996.

Gould, Stephen Jay. *The Flamingo's Smile: Reflections in Natural History.* New York: W. W. Norton, 1985.

Grant, James. *First Love & Last Love: A Tale of the Indian Mutiny.* 1868. London: Routledge, 1887.

Halberstam, Judith. *Skin Shows: Gothic Horror and the Technology of Monsters.* Durham: Duke University Press, 1995.

Hall, Catherine. *White, Male and Middle-Class.* New York: Routledge, 1988.

———. *Civilising Subjects: Metropole and Colony in the English Imagination 1830–1867.* Chicago: University of Chicago Press, 2002.

Hall, Stuart. "New Ethnicities." In *Black British Cultural Studies,* edited by Houston A. Baker, Jr., Manthia Diawara, and Ruth H. Lindeborg. Chicago: University of Chicago Press, 1996.

Hearst, David. "Colonial Shame: African Woman Going Home after 200 years." *The Guardian* 30 (April 2002): 13.

Helsinger, Elizabeth K., Robin Lauterbach Sheets, and William Veeder, eds. *The Woman Question.* 3 vols. New York: Garland, 1983.

Heuman, Gad J. *Between Black and White. Race, Politics, and the Free Coloreds in Jamaica, 1792–1865.* Westport: Greenwood, 1981.

———. *'The Killing Time': The Morant Bay Rebellion in Jamaica.* New York: Macmillan Caribbean, 1994.

Hobsbawm, Eric. *The Age of Capital, 1848–1875.* New York: Vintage, 1996.

Hobson, Janelle. "The 'Batty' Politic: Toward an Aesthetic of the Black Female Body," *Hypatia* 18:4 (Fall 2003): 87–105.

Holt, Thomas C. *The Problem of Freedom: Race, Labor, and Politics in Jamaica and Britain 1832–1938.* Baltimore: The Johns Hopkins University Press, 1992.

Iser, Wolfgang. *The Act of Reading.* Baltimore: The Johns Hopkins University Press, 1978.

James, C. L. R. *The Black Jacobins: Toussaint L'Ouverture and the San Domingo Revolution.* New York: Vintage Books, 1989.

Keenan, Thomas. "The Point Is to (Ex)Change It: Reading Capital, Rhetorically." In *Fetishism as Cultural Discourse,* edited by Emily Apter and William Pietz. Ithaca: Cornell University Press, 1993.

Kelsall, Malcolm. *The Great Good Place: The Country House and English Literature.* London: Harvester Wheatsheaf, 1993.

Kemble, Frances Anne. *Journal of a Residence on a Georgian Plantation in 1838–1839.* Athens: The University of Georgia Press, 1984.

Kingsley, Charles. "Cheap Clothes and Nasty." *Alton Locke, Tailor and Poet, An Autobiography.* London: Macmillan, 1911.

Knox, Robert. *The Races of Men: A Fragment.* London: Henry Renshaw, 1850.

———. *Great Artists and Great Anatomists; A Biographical and Philosophical Study.* Reprint of the 1852 edition. New York: AMS, 1977.

Krips, Henry. *Fetish: An Erotics of Culture.* Ithaca: Cornell University Press, 1999.

Lane, Christopher. "The Psychoanalysis of Race: An Introduction." In *The Psychoanalysis of Race,* edited by Christopher Lane. New York: Columbia University Press, 1998.

Lefebvre, Henri. *The Production of Space.* Trans. Donald Nicholson-Smith. Oxford: Blackwell, 1991.

Lewis, Matthew. *Journal of a West India Proprietor.* Oxford: Oxford University Press, 1999.

*The Life and Times of Sara Baartman, "The Hottentot Venus."* Film by Zola Maseko. First Run/Icarus Films, 1998.

Lightman, Bernard. "Introduction." In *Victorian Science in Context,* edited by Bernard Lightman. Chicago: University of Chicago Press, 1997.

Lonsdale, Henry. *A Sketch of the Life and Writings of Robert Knox the Anatomist.* London: Macmillan, 1870.

Lorimer, Douglas A. *Colour, Class and the Victorians.* Leicester: Leicester University Press, 1978.

———. "Race, Science and Culture: Historical Continuities and Discontinuities, 1850–1914." In *The Victorians and Race,* edited by. Shearer West. Aldershot: Scolar, 1996.

———. "Science and Secularization of Victorian Images of Race." In *Victorian Science in Context,* edited by Bernard Lightman. Chicago: University of Chicago Press, 1997.

Lowenthal, David. *The Past Is a Foreign Country.* Cambridge: Cambridge University Press, 1985.

Magubane, Zine. "Which Bodies Matter?: Feminism, Poststructuralism, Race, and the Curious Theoretical Odyssey of the 'Hottentot Venus.'" *Gender & Society* 15:6 (December 2001): 816–34.

Malchow, H. L. *Gothic Images of Race in Nineteenth-Century Britain.* Stanford: Stanford University Press, 1996.

Martineau, Harriet. *Suggestions Towards The Future Government of India.* London: Smith, Elder & Co., 1858.

———. *Society in America.* 1837. 3 vols. New York: AMS, 1966.

———. *The Hour and the Man.* 1841. New York: AMS, 1974.

———. *Autobiography.* Vol. 2. London: Virago, 1983.

———. *Harriet Martineau's Letters to Fanny Wedgwood,* edited by Elisabeth Sanders Arbuckle. Stanford: Stanford University Press, 1983.

Marryat, Captain Frederick. "The Pirate." 1836. *The Works of Captain Marryat with Illustrations.* Vol. 20. New York: Peter Fenelon Collier, 1900.

Marx, Karl. "The Fetishism of Commoditie." In *Karl Marx The Essential Writings,* edited by Frederic L. Bender. Boulder: Westview Press, 1986.

McCallum, E. L. *Object Lessons: How to Do Things with Fetishism.* Albany: State University of New York Press, 1999.

McClintock, Anne. *Imperial Leather: Race, Gender, and Sexuality in the Colonial Contest.* New York: Routledge, 1995.

McLaughlin, Thomas. "Figurative Language." In *Critical Terms for Literary Study,* 2nd ed., edited by Frank Lentricchia and Thomas McLaughlin. Chicago and London: University of Chicago Press, 1995.

Memmi, Albert. *The Colonizer and the Colonized.* New York: The Orion Press, 1965.

Metz, Christian. *The Imaginary Signifier: Psychoanalysis and the Cinema.* Trans. Celia Britton, Annwyl William, Ben Brewster, and Alfred Guzzetti. Bloomington: Indian University Press, 1982.

Midgley, Clare. *Women Against Slavery: The British Campaigns, 1780–1870.* London: Routledge, 1992.

Mill, John Stuart. *Autobiography of John Stuart Mill.* New York: Columbia University, 1924.

Minh-ha, Trinh T. *Woman Native Other: Writing Postcoloniality and Feminism.* Bloomington: Indiana University Press, 1989.

Mitchell, Sally. *Daily Life in Victorian England.* Westport and London: Greenwood, 1996.

Morrison, Toni. *Playing in the Dark: Whiteness and the Literary Imagination.* Cambridge: Harvard University Press, 1992.

Mukherjee, Rudrangshu. "'Satan Let Loose Upon the Earth': The Kanpur Massacres in India in the Revolt of 1857." *Past and Present* 128 (August 1990): 92–116.

Mulvey, Laura. *Fetishism and Curiosity.* Bloomington: Indiana University Press, 1996.

Nayder, Lillian. "Class Consciousness and the Indian Mutiny in Dickens's 'The Perils of Certain English Prisoners.'" *Studies in English Literature* 32 (4) (Autumn 1992): 689–705.

Oddie, William. "Dickens and the Indian Mutiny." *The Dickensian* 68 (January 1972): 3–15.

Ott, Thomas O. *The Haitian Revolution 1789–1804.* Knoxville: University of Tennessee Press, 1973.

Patterson, Lee. "Literary History." In *Critical Terms for Literary Study,* 2nd ed., edited by Frank Lentricchia and Thomas McLaughlin. Chicago: The University of Chicago Press, 1995.

Paxton Nancy L. "Mobilizing Chivalry: Rape in Flora Annie Steel's *On the Face of the Waters* (1896) and Other British Novels about the Indian Uprising of 1857." In *The New Nineteenth Century: Feminist Readings of Underread Victorian Fiction,* edited by Barbara Leah Hannan and Susan Meyer. New York: Garland, 1996.

Peters, Catherine. The *King of Inventors.* Princeton: Princeton University Press, 1991.

Pietz, William. "The Problem of the Fetish, 1." *Res* 9 (Spring 1985): 5–17.

———. "The Problem of the Fetish, 11: The Origin of the Fetish." *Res* (Spring 1987): 23–45.

———. "The Problem of the Fetish, 111a: Bosman's Guinea and the Enlightenment Theory of Fetishism." *Res* (Autumn 1988): 105–23.

Poovey, Mary. *Uneven Developments: The Ideological Work of Gender in Mid-Victorian England.* Chicago: University of Chicago Press, 1988.

———. *Making a Social Body: British Cultural Formation 1830–1864.* Chicago: University of Chicago Press, 1995.

Pratt, Mary Louise. *Imperial Eyes: Travel Writing and Transculturation.* New York: Routledge, 1992.

"Prospects of the Indian Empire." *The Edinburgh Review.* No. CCXVII (January 1858): 1–50.

Rae, Isobel. *Knox the Anatomist.* Springfield, MA.: Charles C Thomas, 1964.

Rediker, Marcus. *Between the Devil and the Deep Blue Sea.* Cambridge: Cambridge University Press, 1987.

"Report of the Jamaica Royal Commission 1866. Part I. Report." *House of Commons Par-*

*liamentary Papers.* Vol. XXX. 1866. 1–41 [Chadwyck-Healey Microfiche 72.232].

"Report of the Jamaica Royal Commission 1866. Part II. Minutes of Evidence and Appendix." *House of Commons Parliamentary Papers.* Vol. XXXI, 1866. 1–1172. [Chadwyck-Healey Microfiche 72.233–72.245].

Reports from Commissioners Regarding the Jamaica Disturbance. "Papers Laid Before the Royal Commission of Inquiry by Governor Eyre." *House of Commons Parliamentary Papers.* Vol. XXX, 1866. 1–484. [Chadwyck-Healey Microfiche 72.227–72.232].

*The Return of Sara Baartman.* Film by Zola Maseko. First Run/Icaraus Films, 2003.

Richards, Evelleen. "Huxley and Woman's Place in Science: The 'Woman Question' and the Control of Victorian Anthropology." In *History, Humanity and Evolution: Essays for John C. Greene,* edited by James R. Moore. Cambridge: Cambridge University Press, 1989.

———. "The 'Moral Anatomy' of Robert Knox: The Interplay between Biological and Social Thought in Victorian Scientific Naturalism." *Journal of History and Biology* 22:3 (Fall 1989): 373–436.

Richards, Thomas. *The Imperial Archive: Knowledge and the Fantasy of Empire.* London: Verso, 1993.

Ritchie, Robert C. *Pirates: Myths and Realities.* The James Ford Bell Lectures, Number 23. University of Minnesota: The Associates of the James Ford Bell Library, 1986.

Roberts, Diane. *The Myth of Aunt Jemima.* New York: Routledge, 1994.

Robinson, Jane. *Angels of Albion: Women of the Indian Mutiny.* London: Viking, 1996.

Roper, Michael, and John Tosh. "Introduction." In *Manful Assertions: Masculinities in Britain since 1800,* edited by Michael Roper and John Tosh. London: Routledge, 1991.

Said, Edward. *Orientalism.* New York: Vintage, 1979.

———. *Culture and Imperialism.* New York: Vintage, 1993.

Sanders, Prince. *Haytian Papers. A Collection of the Very Interesting Proclamations, and other Official documents; Together with Some Account of the Rise, Progress, and Present State of The Kingdom of Hayti.* 1816. Westport: Negro University Press, 1969.

Sartre, Jean-Paul. "Introduction." In *The Colonizer and the Colonized,* by Albert Memmi. New York: The Orion Press, 1965.

Schwarz, Daniel R. "Performative Saying and the Ethics of Reading: Adam Zachary Newton's *Narrative Ethics.*" *Narrative* 5.2 (1997): 188–206.

Scott, Sir Walter. *The Pirate.* 1821. *Waverly Novels.* Volume XIII. London: Macmillan, 1900.

Semmel, Bernard. *The Governor Eyre Controversy.* London: MacGibbon and Kee, 1962.

Sharpe, Jenny. *Allegories of Empire: The Figure of Woman in the Colonial Text.* Minneapolis: University of Minnesota Press, 1993.

Sharpley-Whiting, T. Denean. *Black Venus: Sexualized Savages, Primal Fears, and Primitive Narratives in French.* Durham: Duke University Press, 1999.

Shepherdson, Charles. "Human Diversity and the Sexual Relation." In *The Psychoanalysis of Race,* edited by Christopher Lane. New York: Columbia University Press, 1998.

Society for the Mitigation and Gradual Abolition of Slavery throughout the British Dominions. "Substance of the Debate in the House of Commons on the 15th May, 1823, on a Motion for the Mitigation and Gradual Abolition of Slavery Throughout the British Dominions." London: Ellerton and Henderson, 1823.

Spivak, Gayatri. *The Spivak Reader: Selected Works of Gayatri Chakravorty Spivak,* edited by Donna Landry and Gerald Maclean. New York: Routledge, 1996.

Spurr, David. *The Rhetoric of Empire.* Durham: Duke University Press, 1993.

Stepan, Nancy. *The Idea of Race in Science: Great Britain 1800–1960.* Hamden: Archon Books, 1982.

Stocking, George W., Jr. "'What's in a Name?' The Origins of the Royal Anthropological Institute." *Man* 6 (1971): 369–90.

———. *Victorian Anthropology.* New York: Free Press, 1987.

Thomas, Gillian. *Harriet Martineau.* Boston: Twayne, 1985.

Tinkler, Penny. "Introduction to Special Issue: Women, Imperialism, and Identity." *Women's Studies International Forum* 21.3 (1998): 217–22.

Trollope, Frances. *The Life and Adventures of Jonathan Jefferson Whitlaw; or Scenes on the Mississippi.* 3 vols. London: Richard Bentley, 1836.

Turley, Hans. *Rum, Sodomy, and the Lash: Piracy, Sexuality, and Masculine Identity.* New York: New York University Press, 1999.

Tuson, Penelope. "Mutiny Narratives and the Imperial Feminine: European Women's Accounts of the Rebellion in India in 1857." *Women's Studies International Forum* 21:3 (1998): 291–303.

Underhill, Edward Bean. *The West Indies: Their Social and Religious Condition.* 1862. Westport: Negro University Press, 1970.

Viswanthan, Gauri. "Currying Favor: The Politics of British Educational and Cultural Policy in India, 1813–1854." *Social Text* 19–20 (1988): 85–104.

———. *Masks of Conquest: Literary Study and British Rule in India.* Oxford: Oxford University Press, 1998.

Webb, R. K. *Harriet Martineau: A Radical Victorian.* London: Heinemann, 1960.

Wetzel, David. *The Crimean War: A Diplomatic History.* New York: Columbia University Press, 1985.

White, Hayden. *Metahistory: The Historical Imagination in Nineteenth-Century Europe.* Baltimore: Johns Hopkins University Press, 1975.

———. *Tropics of Discourse: Essays in Cultural Criticism.* Baltimore: Johns Hopkins University Press, 1985.

Wiegman, Robyn. *American Anatomies: Theorizing Race and Gender.* Durham: Duke University Press, 1995.

Wilberforce, William. "An Appeal to the Religion, Justice, and Humanity of the Inhabitants of the British Empire, in Behalf of the Negro Slaves in the West Indies." London: J. Hatchard and Son, 1823.

Williams, Eric. *Capitalism and Slavery.* New York: Capricorn Books, 1944.

Williams, Raymond. *Keywords.* New York: Oxford University Press, 1985.

Wiss, Rosemary. "Lipreading: Remembering Saartjie Baartman." *The Australian Journal of Anthropology* 5.1–2 (1994): 11–40.

Woodward, Christopher. *In Ruins.* New York, Pantheon Books, 2001.

Young, Robert J. C. *Colonial Desire.* New York: Routledge, 1995.

# INDEX

⌐

Aborigines Protection Society. *See* race: and anthropological exploration

Abrams, Yvette, 147–49, 156

Ackroyd, Peter, 78

aesthetic. *See* race: aesthetics and

Africans, 7, 10, 15, 17, 24, 35, 39, 41, 52–54, 64, 69, 150; physiognomy of, 29, 30

African American literature: Signifyin(g) practices of, 22; and the Signifyin(g) Monkey figure, 42

*After Colonialism* (ed. Prakash). *See* Prakash, Gyan

Altick, Richard, 146–47

American slavery, 15

Anthropological Society of London, 57–58, 72–73, 103, 163n10; and the exclusion of women, 57; and racial attitudes of British public, 58

*Athenaeum, The,* 27, 28–29

Ba(a)rtman(n), Sara(h), 12, 45–46, 141, 142–57; and the ethic of care, 142, 155, 156; and *Politics from a Black Woman's Insides* (Edwards), 146

Barringer, Tim, 57

Beer, Gillian, 49, 159n1, 165n19

Beyer-Berenbaum, Linda, 136

Bhabha, Homi K., 11, 88

Bindman, David, 46; and George Mosse, 46

Bolt, Christine, 46, 105

Brantlinger, Patrick, 6, 12, 16, 81, 102; and the "Imperial Gothic," 135–36, 144,

145, 146

Burg, B. R., 91

Buxton, Thomas Fowell, 24

Caliban, 7–8, 17

Carlyle, Thomas, 99, 102–3, 137, 159n2

Carolan, Katherine, 78–79

Cohn, Bernard, 18

Collins, Wilkie, 75, 76–77, 90, 94. *See also* "The Perils of Certain English Prisoners" (Dickens and Collins)

community, 19

Cook, Anthony E., 19

Cordingly, David, 91

Critical Race Theory, 17

Cultural Studies, British, 16

*Daniel Deronda* (Eliot). *See* Eliot, George

David, Deirdre, 163n11

Davis, David Brion, 30

deconstruction, 19, 30

Dickens, Charles, 11, 92, 102–3; and the Christmas tale, 77–80; and the Indian Rebellion, 80–81. *See also* "The Perils of Certain English Prisoners" (Dickens and Collins)

Douglass, Frederick, 33

Drescher, Seymour, 23

Eagleton, Terry, 5–6, 143

Eliot, George, 7–8, 11, 13, 14, 16, 17, 159n1; and Jewish identity in *Daniel Deronda,* 17

181

14, 16, 20, 27; and biology, 7, 9, 52, 57, 60, 100, 111, 152, 162n6; and ethical issues, 16–17; and European revolutions of 1848, 62, 163n15; and Governor Eyre's justification of violence, 108–9; and hero figure, 21, 28–29; and history, 51–52, 66–67; and humanitarianism, 7, 23, 55–56, 150; and irrationality, 9, 17, 19; and nationalism, 61–62 ; and figure of the "Negro," 8–9, 16, 53–54, 57; and the "other," 12, 123, 138, 141, 143, 145–46 ; and scientific racism, 14, 44, 55–56, 58; and skin color, 30–32; as a signifier, 10, 13, 20; and the status of gentleman, 59; strategies of reading and interpretation of, 20, 21, 35, 40–42; tropism and tropes of, 6–7, 9, 11, 13, 14, 15, 16–19, 44, 149

*Races of Men, The* (Knox). *See* Knox, Robert

Rae, Isobel. *See* Knox, Robert: Isobel Rae, biographer of

reading strategies. *See* race: strategies of reading and interpretation of

"Report of the Jamaica Royal Commission 1866," 11–12, 95, 96, 105–19, 120, 141, 147, 156; racial differences articulated by, 114

Richards, Evelleen, 54

Richards, Thomas, 106–7, 118, 119

Roberts, Diane, 159n3

Robinson, Jane, 124–25, 126

Roper, Michael, 93

Royal Commission (Jamaica). *See* "Report of the Jamaica Royal Commission 1866"

ruins (architectural) and ruin sites, 12, 121; in *First Love and Last Love* (Grant), 122–23, 128, 130–41, 146; in *The Hour and the Man* (Martineau), 35–37, 130, 133, 134; in "Perils of Certain English Prisoners," 86, 130–31, 133

Sahib, Nana. *See* Indian Rebellion (1857), Nana Sahib and

Said, Edward, 14, 160n9

Sartre, Jean-Paul, 111

scapegoat, 77, 84, 87–89, 94

Schwarz, Daniel R., 16

Scott, Sir Walter, 89, 90, 92

Sharpe, Jenny, 12, 77, 93, 123, 170n2

Sharpley-Whiting, T. Denean, 151–52

Society for the Mitigation and Gradual Abolition of Slavery Throughout the British Dominions, 24–25

Spivak, Gayatri, 19

St. Domingo Revolution (1790), 10, 15, 21, 22, 29, 31; British involvement in, 25–26; and the French National Assembly, 26; and Napoleon Bonaparte, 26, 39–40

Stepan, Nancy, 6, 49

Stocking, George, 47, 48, 55–56, 103, 162n8, 162n9, 163n10, 163n13

Suleri, Sara, 12

taxonomy: empirical, 97, 106, 117, 119, 120, 152; racial, 46, 152, 156

Tinkler, Betty, 170–71n3

Tosh, John, 93

Trollope, Frances, 160n7

trope. *See* race: tropes and tropism

"truth" and truth-telling, 97, 106, 119; data collection and "facts" as a measure of, 106–7, 114, 119; Victorian belief in, 11, 107; and Royal Commission, 11, 116;

Turley, Hans, 91

Tuson, Penelope, 124

Underhill, Edward. *See* Morant Bay Rebellion (Jamaica, 1865), and Edward Underhill

Victorian racial tropism. *See* race: tropes and tropism

violence, 12, 113, 145–46, 155–56; in colonial India, 126; in *First Love and Last Love* (Grant), 125; in *The Hour and the Man* (Martineau), 28; and the Morant Bay Rebellion (Jamaica, 1865), 112, 115, 122

Viswanathan, Gauri, 160n9

West Indies, 7, 15, 23, 26, 96–99, 113
*Westminster Review, The,* 29, 42–43
Wetzel, David, 62, 163n15
White, Hayden, 6, 13–14, 88, 166n10
Wiegman, Robyn, 171n1

Wilberforce, William, 25
Williams, Eric, 30, 160n8
Wiss, Rosemary, 151
Woodward, Christopher, 36

Young, Robert J. C., 61, 103

CPSIA information can be obtained
at www.ICGtesting.com
Printed in the USA
BVHW032211100721
611610BV00015B/88